A Foretaste of Proust

Marcel Proust
1er Août 91 Cabourg

J E Blanche

A Foretaste of Proust

A Study of Proust and his precursors

Margaret Mein,
M.A., Oxon., B.A., Ph.D., London
Lecturer in French at Westfield College, London University.

SAXON  HOUSE

SAXON HOUSE D. C. Heath Ltd.
Westmead, Farnborough, Hants, England

ISBN 0 347 05001 8
Library of Congress Catalog Card Number 74-3907
Printed in Great Britain by Robert MacLehose & Co Ltd, The University Press, Glasgow

TO EUGÈNE VINAVER

' "*Regardez vous-même si vous voyez mieux avec ce verre-ci, avec celui-là, avec cet autre*" '.

(*RTP*, III, 911)

'*Ces coïncidences (dans le sens géométrique et non point hasardeux), ces superpositions ou anticipations de pensée m'émeuvent infiniment.*'
CG, I, p. 220 (*Lettres à Robert de Montesquiou, 1839–1921*)

Contents

Abbreviations

Abbreviated titles by which Proust's and his precursors' works are indicated in the text:

Proust

RTP	*A la recherche du temps perdu*, Pléiade, Paris 1954, 3 vols.
JS	*Jean Santeuil* précédé de *Les Plaisirs et les jours*, Pléiade, Paris 1971
CSB	*Contre Sainte-Beuve* précédé de *Pastiches et mélanges*, Pléiade, Paris 1971
CSB (FALL)	*Contre Sainte-Beuve*, ed. R. de Fallois, Gallimard, Paris 1954
CHRON. (GALL)	*Chroniques*, Gallimard, Paris 1949 (Both *CSB* (FALL) and *CHRON.* (GALL) are used only in instances where they contain versions of texts not incorporated in the Pléiade editions.)
CG	*Correspondance générale*, Plon, Paris 1930–36, 6 vols.
LAURIS	Marcel Proust: *A un Ami: Correspondance inédite; 1903–22 (1920) Préface de Georges de Lauris*, Amiot-Dumont, Paris 1948
LR	*Lettres retrouvées*, ed. P. Kolb and L. Price, Plon, Paris 1966
Textes retrouvés	Marcel Proust: *Textes retrouvés*, ed. P. Kolb and L. Price, University of Illinois Press, Urbana 1968

Pascal

BR	*Pensées*, ed. L. Brunschvicg, Hachette, Paris 1904

Chateaubriand

MOT	*Mémoires d'Outre-Tombe*, Pléiade, Paris 1951, 2 vols.

Nerval

NER *Œuvres*, Pléiade, Paris 1960, 2 vols.

Baudelaire

BAU *Œuvres complètes*, Pléiade, Paris 1961

Novalis

NOV *Schriften*, ed. P. Kluckhohn and R. Samuel, Meyer's Klassiker Ausgaben, Leipzig 1928, 4 vols.

NF *Werke und Briefe* inclusive of *Neue Fragmente*, herausg. von A. Kelletat, Winkler-Verlag, Munich 1962

Balzac

LANGEAIS *La Duchesse de Langeais*, ed. P.–G. Castex and P. Citron: *La Comédie humaine*, Editions du Seuil, Paris 1966, Vol. 4, *Scènes de la vie parisienne*

SARR *Sarrasine*, edition as above

LYS *Le Lys dans la vallée*, edition as above, Vol. 6, *Scènes de la vie de campagne*

Eliot

Scenes *Scenes of Clerical Life*, Blackwood Cabinet (no date)

Adam *Adam Bede*, Everyman, Dent, London 1972

The Mill *The Mill on the Floss*, edition as above, 1972

Silas *Silas Marner*, edition as above, 1972

M *Middlemarch*, edition as above, 1969, 2 vols.

CORR. HAI. *The George Eliot Letters*, ed. G. S. Haight, Oxford University Press, 1954–56, 7 vols.

Fromentin

D *Dominique*, ed. Barbara Wright, Blackwell, Oxford 1965

E *Un été dans le Sahara*, Plon, Paris 1912

A *Une année dans le Sahel*, Plon, Paris 1934

M d'A *Les Maîtres d'autrefois*, Manz, Vienna (no date)

LJ *Lettres de Jeunesse*, Biographie et notes par Pierre Bianchon, Plon, Paris 1909

Flaubert

FLAU	*Œuvres*, Pléiade, Paris 1952, 2 vols.
NV	*Madame Bovary*, Nouvelle version précédée des scénarios inédits. Texte établi par J. Pommier et G. Leleu, Corti, Paris 1949
Corr. (Conard)	*Correspondance*, L. Conard, Paris 1926–33, 9 vols.
BMP	*Bulletin de la Société des Amis de Marcel Proust et de Combray*
RDM	*Revue des Deux Mondes*
RHLF	*Revue d'Histoire Littéraire de la France*

(The italics are everywhere my own unless otherwise stated.)

Acknowledgements

The following journals have kindly authorised me to reproduce here, in revised form, material first published under their auspices: *L'Esprit Créateur* (Pascal), *French Review* (Chateaubriand), *Romanic Review* (Nerval), *Australian Journal of French Studies* (Baudelaire and Balzac); *Comparative Literature* (Novalis), *Forum for Modern Language Studies* (Fromentin), *French Studies* (Flaubert).

Frontispiece portrait reproduced by kind permission of the Bibliothèque Nationale and S.P.A.D.E.M. Paris.

Prologue

The wide range of Proust's reading had already become a legend in his life-time. Not only did he have an extraordinary power to absorb whatever excited his interest, transform it into his own substance and re-create it with the imprint of originality in his work, he seems to have been equally capable of communicating his enthusiasm to others. Lucien Daudet, Gabriel de la Rochefoucauld and Georges de Lauris testify that he influenced their literary development; R. Dreyfus, Jacques-Emile Blanche and Henry Bordeaux record that he gave them the benefit of constructive criticism, and Proust's loyal friend, Fernand Gregh, seems to speak for all when he recognises a certain 'génie de l'intelligence' in Proust's exercise of the critical faculty.[1] Georges de Lauris's assertion that 'Marcel excellait à vous donner ces appétits soudains de Saint-Simon, de Chateaubriand, de Balzac' invites us to imagine for a moment Proust in the rôle of university lecturer.[2] It is not surprising to learn that Proust and his mother had once actually envisaged for him an academic career: '. . . je n'aurais pu faire dans la vie qu'une chose mais que nous placions tous deux si haut que c'était beaucoup dire, c'est un excellent professeur'.[3] Albertine's response to the narrator's informal dis-quisitions on literature would have delighted any self-appointed tutor and may reflect an unfulfilled but sublimated ambition, on Proust's part, as much as a criticism of the teaching methods which he had seen in action: ' ". . . comme vous voyez la littérature d'une façon plus intéressante qu'on ne nous la faisait étudier" ' (*RTP*, III, 381).

In Proust, more than in any other writer, an obsession with loss intensifies and is, in turn, intensified by an urge to use to the full global powers of perception and an exceptional diversity of gifts. In all Proust's multiplicity, the duality of artist and critic predominates and is reflected in the extent to which an analysis of aesthetics and, in particular, literary criticism form an integral part of his novel. Perhaps never before or since have pastiche and a complex system of literary quotations, as well as wider artistic terms of reference, been so intricately woven into the fabric of an original work of art, and para-doxically generated that originality. It is probable that, with Proust as with his narrator, the discovery of affinities between himself and other writers

1

triggered off the act of artistic creation, for the making of *rapprochements* rings an exciting change on the practice of metaphor and involves imposing a new set of relationships on elements of art as opposed to nature. For an artist of Proust's temperament, pastiche and literary criticism are so closely related to self-discovery and artistic creation that he finds it natural to mirror the characters of his novel in their artistic tastes. Perhaps most interestingly of all we see the narrator reflect the evolution of aesthetics in the nineteenth century and right into the twentieth. Despite his refusal to be identified with the narrator, Proust undoubtedly reveals, in Marcel's aesthetic development, a pattern of progression resembling his own. Proust's utterances as literary critic outside the framework of the novel, in his essays, pastiches and correspondence, provide us with a touchstone by means of which we can measure the proportion of the autobiographical element projected in the artistic tastes (and involuntary pastiches) of his characters, notably his narrator.

By use of the term 'precursor' we suggest in the first instance that there is an affinity between an author under study and one of his predecessors, but without implying the necessity for recognition by the former of any such resemblance; much less do we assume any possibility of influence. Inevitably, however, a study of precursors raises both these issues: Did Proust explicitly or implicitly recognise an affinity between any given artist and himself? If, on his part, neither kind of recognition is to hand, might he still have concurred with the present findings? Sometimes, even in the absence of exact details concerning Proust's reading (for instance, we do not know with any degree of certainty whether he read Novalis), we may find ourselves trying to imagine how he would have reacted to the works of certain authors and – more intriguing – what he personally would have dubbed 'Proustian' *avant la lettre*. In cases where we have grounds for believing that Proust had read the works under discussion, we may be tempted to go further and ask whether there is any possibility of influence, conscious or unconscious. Obviously any critic is obliged to limit the field of his own inquiry since the scope for speculation is infinite. Many lay people or artists have undergone and recorded experiences of involuntary memory; that domain is not Proust's monopoly, they may justifiably claim. The fact remains that Proust made such experience as well as certain attitudes towards time and their mode of expression so unmistakably his own that they have come to be known as Proustian for general purposes of reference. The overtones of the term 'Proustian' have increased in quantity, quality and sheer subtlety to such an extent that it is sometimes difficult to define, but this I have attempted to do in the following pages.

Next must come the question of selection. Why these precursors and not others? Here, apart from the inevitable necessity of choice dictated by reasons of space, there is the need to take, as far as possible, a representative cross-

2

section of precursors although it is impossible to avoid a certain degree of subjectivity in any such choice.

While J. Porel informs us that, 'Proust knew by heart entire passages from a wide range of authors, including Montaigne',[4] we cannot be other than baffled that he made no critical study of French literature before the seventeenth century (with reservations for the Medieval French period which plays an important part in his novel as opposed to his essays). Proust belongs to the great tradition of *moralistes* extending from Montaigne to the present day. While it is generally recognised that he seems to have concentrated his literary preferences within the seventeenth and nineteenth centuries, it might well be asked why I have chosen to analyse his affinity with Pascal rather than with Montaigne (see Ch. I, p. 22). Since Pascal has assimilated and transformed so much of Montaigne's thought, it would be extremely difficult to gauge Proust's indebtedness to Montaigne directly, on the one hand, indirectly through the reading of Pascal on the other. As I have stated (ibid., p. 22), some readers might feel that a number of features relate Proust more closely to Montaigne than to Pascal: both Montaigne and Proust seem to share in the first place a lack of religious conviction, a keen sense of flux and relativity: 'Je ne peints pas l'estre. Je peints le passage: non un passage d'aage en autre, ou, comme dict le peuple, de sept en sept ans, mais de jour en jour, de minute en minute';[5] in the second place, a cult of the oblique and a natural tendency to develop their thought 'de biais', by a series of digressions. In anticipation of Proust, Montaigne is intent upon discovering and conveying to his readers, however paradoxically, in the same breath, his own irreducible individuality and 'la forme entière de l'humaine condition.' Montaigne and Pascal might well have seemed to Proust to embody the two extremes of his own philosophical gamut: on the one hand, dilettantism born of an overwhelming conviction that man and the reality external to him are both alike subjected to flux and disintegration; on the other, a desire to replace such immanence by transcendence and to opt for commitment. In both Pascal and Proust, a powerful mystic element seems to outweigh Pyrrhonism; the difference is that the latter author seeks to satisfy in terms of art as opposed to religious faith 'l'instinct que nous ne pouvons réprimer, qui nous élève.' In their respective editions of Pascal, E. Havet and L. Brunschvicg quote parallel passages from Montaigne. We know how much delight Proust derived from appreciating one author in terms of another, and such annotation may have encouraged him in an instinctive tendency to apply the process of metaphor to literary criticism. Proust may characteristically have appreciated Pascal and Montaigne in terms of each other. There are even fewer references to Montaigne than to Pascal in the correspondence and none at all to the former in the novel. While the themes could have come from Montaigne rather than from Pascal, it seems to me likely that Proust, for the reasons already mentioned, would

3

draw them from the later *moraliste*; moreover, for Proust, Pascal would have the advantage of containing and transcending Montaigne, if it came to a choice between the two writers.

Foremost among Proust's favourite authors of the seventeenth century are Mme de Sévigné, Racine and Saint-Simon. While Proust skilfully uses the works of all three as mirror-compositions within his novel, he openly recognises his affinities with Mme de Sévigné and Saint-Simon, especially the latter. Mme de Sévigné anticipates Elstir's practice of recording impressions before these have been subjected to analysis by the intellect (*RTP*, I, 653–4). This procedure, a reliance on 'l'illusion du premier regard', is at the root of Elstir's conception and practice of metaphor, and Proust transposes it into literature, thereby enriching his style (where the order of perceptions prevails) and his method of character-portrayal, in so far as he uses the observer's illusions about others as the starting-point in an indefatigable search for truth. Both Saint-Simon and Dostoïevsky may be said to have anticipated Proust's application of such a technique to character-portrayal (Ch. I, p. 23), and the narrator makes no attempt to disguise his own fascination with the very approach which Proust perfects, 'le côté Dostoïevsky de Mme de Sévigné'. The narrator's elucidation of this flurry of metaphor contains more than a hint of Proust's intense interest in self-contradiction as the key to human complexity:

'Il est arrivé que Mme de Sévigné, comme Elstir, comme Dostoïevsky, au lieu de présenter les choses dans l'ordre logique, c'est-à-dire en commençant par la cause, nous montre d'abord l'effet, l'illusion qui nous frappe. C'est ainsi que Dostoïevsky présente ses personnages. Leurs actions nous apparaissent aussi trompeuses que ces effets d'Elstir où la mer a l'air d'être dans le ciel. Nous sommes tout étonnés après d'apprendre que cet homme sournois est au fond excellent, ou le contraire.'

(*RTP*, III, 378–9; cf., ibid., III, 983)

In addition, the introduction of Mme de Sévigné's *Lettres* within the novel admirably serves in itself the cause of character-portrayal since, in its capacity as *livre de chevet* of Marcel's mother and grandmother, this choice of book illuminates our understanding of the relationship between the two women and, in turn, between them and the narrator. So vividly does Proust see Mme de Sévigné's affection for her daughter as a metaphor of the love between Marcel's grandmother and mother, in his own novel, that it is difficult to say with certainty where the stress falls at a given moment; when Mme de Villeparisis disparages Mme de Sévigné, she is at the same time deprecating the grandmother, who takes the remark personally: ' "Est-ce que vous ne trouvez pas que c'est un peu exagéré, ce souci constant de sa fille, elle en parle trop pour que ce soit bien sincère. Elle manque de naturel." Ma grand'mère trouva la discussion inutile et, pour éviter d'avoir à parler des choses qu'elle aimait devant quelqu'un qui ne pouvait les comprendre, elle cacha, en posant

4

sos nac sur eux, les *Mémoires de Madame de Beausergent*' (*RTP*, I, 697). In significant contrast to Mme de Villeparisis, Charlus sees in Mme de Sévigné's excess of maternal affection affinities with his own abnormality.

With Saint-Simon, Proust had a particularly deep sense of kinship and he cherished the aim of succeeding him as memorialist of his own time (*RTP*, III, 1044). Within his function as writer of memoirs, Saint-Simon must have further endeared himself to Proust by his preoccupation with the theme of homosexuality. The *Mémoires* serve as a mirror-composition in Proust's novel, in a dual capacity. They are significantly the favourite reading of Swann and Charlus, but their implications are even more far-reaching: inspired by his genius for pastiche and governed by a strong sense of determinism, Proust boldly suggests in the Guermantes a repetition of figures and events portrayed by his predecessor at the court of Louis XIV. This conception of a recurrent pattern imposed by a spirit of history, which seeks re-incarnation in successive generations, resembles the Nietzschean theory of 'l'éternel retour' and such a belief in the cyclic is sharply opposed to traditional French currents of thought on the subject. Proust's style and method of characterisation, notably his Dostoievskyan preoccupation with the self-contradiction inherent in human nature, bring him very close indeed to Saint-Simon. A. Thibaudet recognised this affinity, admittedly somewhat obliquely, when he acclaimed Saint-Simon as the most Balzacian of French writers before Balzac 'comme Proust sera le plus balzacien après Balzac' (see Ch. VI, p. 111). After studying Proust's stylistic affinities with Saint-Simon, L. Spitzer has found them so striking that he wonders whether Proust, in his pastiche, adopted Saint-Simon's style or whether he adapted his style to that of Saint-Simon, and he reaches a compromise without prejudice to the strength of this particular parallel: 'The correct formulation seems to be that Proust has amalgamated Saint-Simon's style and his own'.[6] For a detailed study of Saint-Simon's affinities with Proust, I would refer the reader to Herbert de Ley: *Marcel Proust et le Duc de Saint-Simon*.[7]

Saint-Simon's life-span (1675–1755) entitles him to rank as an eighteenth-century author but, apart from a strong predilection for this writer, Proust seems to have displayed little interest in the literature of the eighteenth century. A reference in one of Mme Proust's letters strengthens the impression that his interests lay elsewhere.[8] Unlike his teacher, M. Traves, Jean Santeuil rejected eighteenth-century literature 'puisqu'elle n'était nullement à sa manière, comme la littérature du XIXe siècle, l'exposé des vérités mystérieuses qui étaient pour lui la seule vérité' (*JS*, 480). However, Rousseau may have escaped Proust's reservations. He would be of interest to Proust, if only because he figures in the lineage of French literary introspectives extending from Montaigne to Gide. Further, he may well have served as a bridge to Proust's nineteenth-century interests.

One cannot help wondering whether Proust noted and admired Rousseau's masterly analysis of incidents of involuntary memory in the *Confessions*.[9] Certainly he could hardly have failed to appreciate the affinity between Rousseau and George Sand. The grandmother had originally chosen, as birthday presents for the narrator, Musset's poetry, a volume of Rousseau and *Indiana* (*RTP*, I, 39), but her husband's disapproval and her own desire to avoid giving her grandson 'quelque chose de mal écrit' caused her to decide finally on *La Mare au diable, François le Champi, La Petite Fadette* and *Les Maîtres-Sonneurs*. Although George Sand ranks as one of Marcel's favourite authors during his childhood, Proust implies that it is an enthusiasm which the narrator outgrows. While Marcel failed to share his mother's and grandmother's admiration for George Sand's 'bonté' and 'distinction morale' (*RTP*, I, 42; cf., ibid. III, 14) and found her prose 'si commune' (*RTP*, I, 43), no doubt Proust continued to identify with the grandmother in approving both George Sand's love of nature and her preservation of the past by the literary use of dialect. In a letter to his friend Georges de Lauris, during the composition of *A la recherche*, Proust clearly distinguishes between his early liking for George Sand and his reactions on reaching maturity: 'Ne croyez que j'aime George Sand. Ce n'est pas un morceau de critique. C'est comme cela à cette date-là. Le reste du livre corrigera'.[10]

Any claim to list George Sand as an important precursor of Proust must therefore be subject to reservations. However, her novel *François le Champi* is of cardinal importance as a mirror-composition within *A la recherche*. The narrator's mother read to him from its pages after the 'drame du coucher' and it therefore comes to symbolise capitulation to the child's wishes and acceptance of his weakness. More important still, George Sand relates how the affection between François and his adoptive mother, Madeleine, grows into a love between husband and wife. The kiss which the heroine, Madeleine, gives to François thus marks the sublimation of the mother-son relationship, an outcome poignantly denied to Marcel in all his love-affairs. At the same time, defeat is transformed into victory when the book associated with his childhood love of George Sand and with his abdication of will-power becomes the pivot of an experience of involuntary memory, proving to be the very novel which the narrator finds in the library of the Guermantes as a prelude to the discovery of his vocation.

Like George Sand, with whom in many respects she affords a parallel (Ch. VII, pp. 122 ff.), not least as counterweight to French Naturalism, George Eliot is a novelist of childhood, but, in contrast to George Sand, her affinity with Proust is more than a passing resemblance and her influence on his development may be considered profound. Of all the English writers whom Proust most admired, and their number includes Dickens, Ruskin, Emerson and Hardy, she seems to me to rank with Ruskin as a major influence and it is for this reason that I have chosen her to represent Proust's English precursors. To her Proust owed much of his impetus and inspiration to develop a theory of memory and to attempt a transposition in the French novel of a sense of duration which he found brilliantly exemplified by English novelists in general (Ch. VII, p. 121).

Proust openly recognises Chateaubriand, Nerval and Baudelaire as his precursors primarily because they derived from involuntary memory a technique of transition from one time-level to another; and his indebtedness in this respect is discussed in detail in the relevant chapters. In addition, all three acknowledged precursors take their place with Amiel in the nineteenth-century phase of the line of literary introspectives mentioned above. All the writers concerned are intensely preoccupied with the relationship between the self and external reality, with what is so often a shadowy line of demarcation between the inner and outer worlds. Nerval intrigues Proust by the extent to which he stresses the qualitative difference of each individual's reaction to the outer world as opposed to the generality of experience, accounted authentic and, for the most part, uncritically accepted as such. Is not Proust's narrator set upon analysing the difference between the dream and reality, 'noms de pays' and 'le pays'? *A la recherche du temps perdu* could be seen as an artist's courageously sustained attempt now to confront the dream with reality, now, however paradoxically, to analyse his 'état de rêve' with his conscious mind, without destroying 'une réalité que la seule lumière de l'intelligence suffirait à détruire, semble-t-il' (*CSB*, 641; see Ch. III, pp. 50 and 60, n. 4).

Nerval's constant desire to probe the connection between inner and outer worlds relates him intimately to exponents – particularly in the Romantic movement – of the German literature which he admired and, within that range, perhaps most closely to Novalis, a poet who was intent upon discovering 'wo sich Innen- und Aussenwelt berühren' (see Ch. III, p. 50 and Ch. V, pp. 86–7). I have investigated the possibility that Proust may have read Novalis in translation. Certainly Gide was deeply interested in him: 'Il faudra traduire *Heinrich von Ofterdingen* sans plus attendre'.[11] Proust, for his part, mentions Novalis in his correspondence and, in my opinion, independently of the moot question of influence, a deep affinity exists between the minds of the two writers. Equally intriguing is the question whether Nerval read Novalis (see p. 63). At times, he seems to echo him in variations on the theme: 'Der Traum, ein Leben' and, in the process, reproduces the very texture of Novalis's thought. Compare with: 'Die Welt wird Traum und der Traum wird Welt' (Ch. V, p. 87), 'l'épanchement du songe dans la vie réelle'; and 'la veille est encore plus remplie de rêves que le sommeil' (*NER*, II, 392). (See also *NER*, I, 365 and in the present book Ch. III, pp. 50–1.) I have drawn attention to L. Cellier's conjecture that Nerval may have undergone Novalis's influence through the intermediary of Heine (Ch. III, Notes for further

7

reading, p. 63). Thus, it would not seem beyond the realms of possibility that Proust may have absorbed something of Novalis's thought, if not directly, then through his own reading of Nerval. It is just possible that he learnt of Gide's or Du Bos's interest in Novalis. I have chosen Novalis to represent German authors with whom Proust reveals affinities and by whom he may have been influenced directly or indirectly through the medium of the Symbolists and such writers as Nerval.

W. A. Strauss describes a certain category of nineteenth-century writers as 'embarked upon a journey to discover the bonds between inner and outer worlds',[12] and he groups them according to whether they adopt, for the most part, an external or a more subtle psychological approach in an attempt to fulfil their quest. It is significant that, while W. A. Strauss recognises Proust's dichotomy of intellect and intuition, his dualism of Realist and Romantic (or Symbolist), he sees the stress as falling ultimately on the second quality in each instance, and attaches supreme importance to Proust's Symbolist vein. He considers that Proust consistently favours an oblique approach as opposed to a frontal attack upon whatever seems to defy analysis by its obscurity, notably the subconscious:

> What Balzac and Wagner tried to achieve largely by external means, Nerval, Proust and Baudelaire and certain other writers tried to accomplish by an inner alchemy, particularly by the transforming or transcendental power of memory, reaching out towards a 'vita nuova'.[13]

It would seem perfectly justifiable to include Chateaubriand in the company of 'certain other writers' who had recourse to 'the transforming or transcendental power of memory'. In all three of the precursors whom Proust openly acknowledges in *Le Temps retrouvé* (*RTP*, III, 919–20), the action of involuntary memory is characterised by 'une sensation transposée'; nor is it a pure coincidence that two of the writers with whom Proust recognises such a close affinity are generally regarded as Symbolists *avant la lettre*. A particularly strong affinity exists between Proust and Baudelaire. For both men, the transposition of sensation is at once fundamental to the functioning of involuntary memory (*RTP*, III, 920), and integral to so much of their imagery.

Perhaps W. A. Strauss would associate Flaubert and Fromentin with Balzac and Wagner in the sense that all concerned adopted largely 'external means' in their investigation of the bonds between the outer and inner worlds? However that may be, how can one best define Proust's literary relationship to Balzac, Flaubert and Fromentin? To Balzac, Proust probably owed the supreme impetus to pass beyond pastiche to the creative act. As I observe in Chapter VI, in relation to no author so much as Balzac did Proust feel the imperative need to resort to both pastiche and parody (within and outside the novel) as a means of exorcising what might have threatened to become, in his

8

own case, an obsessive presence. Perhaps the danger lay in the fact that, for Proust, Balzac represents 'une force de la nature', stands midway between nature and art and embodies both the challenge to the artist to move beyond the rough-hewn, and equally the temptation to linger in a buffer-state, a kind of 'no-man's land' or limbo, ominously looking out on both the paradise of artistic creation and the inferno of artistic sterility. Probably in this ambivalence lies the vital key to the fascination which Balzac never ceased to exert upon Proust. Whatever reasons dictated Proust's choice of Balzac to stand with Nerval and Baudelaire in the *Contre Sainte-Beuve*, their passion for analysis of the irrational and of the creative process must have been crucial in strengthening his sense of affinity with them and in determining him to champion their cause.

Merely by his consistent exaltation of art above life, Flaubert would seem to afford a sharp contrast to Balzac and, in this respect, to draw correspondingly closer to Proust. According to the latter, Flaubert is undoubtedly Balzac's superior in his power to convey the flow of time (Ch. IX, p. 162). It is primarily Flaubert's consummate mastery of style and, more specifically, his use of tenses to reflect time, which absorb Proust and command his admiration. The rhythmic dance of tenses when a scent overwhelms Emma, causing her to confuse past and present (*FLAU*, I, 425), dramatically reveals a strongly Proustian aspect of Flaubert which repays closer analysis and seems to me fully to justify a study of Flaubert as precursor of Proust (Ch. IX, pp. 162 and 169).

About Fromentin, Proust's statements are non-committal and even on occasion contemptuous. It remains a matter for interesting speculation why Proust should have decided to associate a part of Mme Verdurin's past with Fromentin by disclosing that she was once the 'Madeleine' in the latter's novel (Ch. VIII, p. 144). Skilfully Proust sets the disclosure within the pseudo-Goncourt diary (*RTP*, III, 709, 710, 712–18, 720). Nowhere does Proust make a direct allusion to *Dominique* (1863), so aptly termed 'roman du souvenir' and a favourite book of his contemporaries, notably Gide[14] and Mauriac.[15] This novel is likely to have been of supreme interest to Proust in particular, for a variety of reasons: firstly, it plays an absorbing set of variations on the interwoven themes of time and memory; secondly, it reflects an outlook divided between the claims of Classicism and Romanticism and seems finally to opt for the former. Independently of the question of any possible influence exerted by Fromentin on Proust, the evidence of affinities between the two writers makes a comparative study particularly rewarding in this instance.

I have set Chateaubriand, Nerval and Baudelaire in a category apart from the other precursors because Proust has openly recognised their crucial rôle in bringing about the narrator's discovery of his vocation. Otherwise I have observed a chronological order in the arrangement of the chapters.

9

The Proustian manifesto concerning the rôle of metaphor in artistic creation (*RTP*, III, 889) seems to await application to literary criticism. Further, Proust himself encourages us in this direction, since the detection of analogies lies equally at the root of his critical and creative processes. Indeed, he draws no rigid line of demarcation between literary creation and literary criticism. Pastiche, conceived as a re-creation of the original, occupies a position somewhere midway between literary criticism and artistic creation proper. With parody, whether it be voluntary or involuntary (*CSB*, 594) Proust associates spontaneity; in literary criticism, however, he discerns a conscious intervention of the analytical faculty. Accordingly he sees a switch of function as responsible for his producing now a pastiche of Flaubert, 'de la critique littéraire "en action" ' (*CG*, IV, 227, 18 March 1908), now a critical essay on the same author, 'un travail inverse' in fact (*CSB*, 595). It would then appear that, for Proust, creative activity stems from an endless interaction between conscious and unconscious impulses, literary criticism generating literary pastiche and vice versa (*CSB*, 595). Proust may have envisaged as supreme function of his novel the power to release in successive generations of readers the faculty of criticism and authorship, indissolubly one.

As I have stated towards the end of Chapter IV, p. 78, the latest examinations of manuscripts have led critics to believe that it was Proust's original intention to graft on his novel what we have come to know as *Contre Sainte-Beuve* but that he renounced any such plan at the end of 1909. However, by a kind of Gidean *composition en abyme*, anticipating that of *Les Faux-Monnayeurs*, the narrator's attempts to fulfil his vocation seem to echo and sometimes parody Proust's situation and attitudes as he writes his novel. Moreover, the narrator's power to observe himself in the act of memory and artistic creation (*RTP*, I, 44 ff., 172 ff., 180–2, 717 ff.; III, 13, 261 etc.) testifies to a capacity for 'auto-contemplation' such as he justifiably or otherwise attributes to Balzac (see Ch. VI, p. 103) while, for many readers, it already brilliantly foreshadows Valéry.

As I have suggested above, the characters of *A la recherche* are given the chance to become literary critics. Further, Proust at once extends the function of literary criticism in the novel and indulges his fondness for parody when he contrives that the Guermantes should unconsciously re-enact Balzac in the 'red slippers scene' (see Ch. VI, p. 103); that Mme de Villeparisis should provide us with a pastiche of Sainte-Beuve (*RTP*, I, 722; see p. 103 and p. 116, note 7) and the narrator discover a pastiche of the *Journal des Goncourt*. Proust's characters not only reveal facets of their personalities but give an extra dimension and depth to the narrative when they use the binoculars of other novelists to review incidents: as for instance, when the marriage of the young Cambremer with Mlle d'Oloron is seen from the viewpoint of Marcel's mother as 'la récompense de la vertu . . . un mariage à la fin d'un roman de

10

Mme Sand', but from that of the narrator, in whom the reaction significantly remains an unvoiced thought: '... le prix du vice ... un mariage à la fin d'un roman de Balzac' (*RTP*, III, 658); again, most significantly, when Saint-Loup, who is primarily a Balzacian, attempts to assess M. de Norpois in terms of Stendhal's Count Mosca and, more daringly still, appraises the narrator himself in relation to Stendhal and Balzac (*RTP*, II, 106).

As a critic, Proust found himself drawn by his 'bonhomme de l'analogie' – the narrator's and his own 'personnage intermittent' – to make literary *rapprochements*, to discern 'entre deux œuvres une partie commune' and, in addition, to discover his own precursors, 'ramiers fraternels' as he styles them. There is no doubt that he revelled in the paradox of such 'réminiscences anticipées', in the new reversal of time-laws and in the movement of retrospection which the detection of affinities involves:

> ... certains artistes d'une autre époque ont, dans un simple morceau, réalisé quelque chose qui ressemble à ce que le maître peu à peu s'est rendu compte que lui-même avait voulu faire. Alors il voit en cet ancien comme un précurseur; il aime chez lui sous une tout autre forme, un effort momentanément, partiellement fraternel. Il y a des morceaux de Turner dans l'œuvre de Poussin, une phrase de Flaubert dans Montesquieu.
>
> (*RTP*, II, 816)

Within literary criticism proper, Proust regularly applies a process of extended metaphor, seeming to appreciate one writer fully only in terms of another; the whole experience is an exact replica of his need to savour one particular sensation within the halo of another or several others and thereby reach the general, extra-temporal essence (*RTP*, III, 889). Thus, even in the genre of literary criticism, Proust expresses his own conception of artistic creation: the renewal of the world by a change of perspective:

> Et voici que le monde (qui n'a pas été créé une fois, mais aussi souvent qu'un artiste original est survenu) nous apparaît entièrement différent de l'ancien, mais parfaitement clair ... Tel est l'univers nouveau et périssable qui vient d'être créé. Il durera jusqu'à la prochaine catastrophe géologique que déchaîneront un nouveau peintre ou un nouvel écrivain originaux.
>
> (*RTP*, II, 327)

It is mainly as a result of establishing an analogy between two particular sensations, between two particular authors that he will glean 'des impressions vraiment esthétiques', glimpse 'l'essence commune' and be inspired to create in turn. Only after the narrator has reassured himself that 'une sensation transposée' lies at the root of the creative impulse in Chateaubriand, Nerval and Baudelaire, does he feel encouraged to found his own work on the transposition in time which is involuntary memory (*RTP*, III, 918). Quite independently, however, of the moot question of literary influence, no one more than Proust can have relished the discovery of a precursor (*RTP*, II,

11

420), attracted as he always was by the study of affinities, regarded as a variation on the theme of analogies. In the field of literary criticism, Proust has already, by personal example, prepared the way for the study of one writer in terms of another. As stated above, he applies the process of metaphor to his act of literary criticism, incapable as he is of fully appreciating author or experience except indirectly in terms of other authors, other experiences. The analogy between the *Cantiques* of Racine and lines of a poem by Valéry, 'Palme', awakens his mind to a whole series of literary affinities, one subtly contained within another, 'et dans cet univers, un autre plus interne encore':

> Ne trouvez-vous pas que là Racine ressemble un peu à Paul Valéry, lequel a retrouvé Malherbe en traversant Mallarmé?[16]

By a coincidence no less curious than those which Proust mentions in his letter to Montesquiou (quoted p. v of this book), it is possible that the study of affinities between the novelist and some of his suggested precursors may lead us to a deeper understanding of 'ce qu'a senti le maître', making us 'les lecteurs de lui-même'; an extension, this, to Proustian literary criticism, of the master's own practice of transposition.

I have singled out in the work of writers acknowledged by Proust as his precursors as well as in that of 'd'autres encore', not yet treated on an equal footing with Chateaubriand, Nerval and Baudelaire, features which seem to me to be Proustian *avant la lettre*. It has been my aim to appreciate the selected writers in terms of Proust and vice versa. I have been prompted throughout by the hope that such an exercise will act as 'une sorte de ces verres grossissants' (*RTP*, III, 1033), and serve to sharpen our vision of Proust himself.

Notes

[1] Fernand Gregh: *Mon Amitié avec Marcel Proust*, Grasset, Paris 1958, p. 76

[2] *LAURIS*, p. 15

[3] M. Proust: *Lettres à Mme Catusse*, Paris 1947, p. 205

[4] J. Porel: *Fils de Réjane*, Plon, Paris 1951, I, p. 328

[5] Montaigne: *Œuvres complètes*, Pléiade, Gallimard, Paris 1962, *Essais Livre III*, ch. 2, 'Du Repentir', p. 782

[6] L. Spitzer: *Stilstudien* II, M. Hueber, Munich 1928, p. 485

[7] *Illinois Studies in Language & Literature* 57, University of Illinois Press, Urbana 1966

[8] M. Proust: *Correspondance avec sa mère*, 1887–1905 Plon, Paris 1953, p.11

[9] Rousseau: *Œuvres complètes* I, Pléiade, Gallimard, Paris 1959, p. 226; see also ibid., n. 5 p. 1344

[10] *LAURIS*, p. 178 in a letter dated by P. Kolb end of November/December 1909

[11] A. Gide: *Journal* 1889–1939 Pléiade, Gallimard, Paris 1951, p. 39; see also ibid., p. 51

[12] W. A. Strauss: *Proust and Literature: the Novelist as Critic*, Harvard University Press, 1957, p. 128

[13] Ibid.

[14] A. Gide: 'Les Dix romans français que . . .' *Incidences*, Gallimard, Paris 1924, p. 154

[15] F. Mauriac: *D'autres et moi*, Grasset, Paris 1966, p. 147

[16] Marcel Proust: *LR*, p. 144

Chapter I

Pascal

Pascal a connu exactement ce que Proust a appelé 'les intermittences du cœur', comme en témoignent ces lignes étonnantes: 'L'attachement à une même pensée fatigue et ruine l'esprit de l'homme. C'est pourquoi pour la solidité du plaisir de l'amour, il faut quelquefois ne pas savoir que l'on aime et ce n'est pas commettre une infidélité parce qu'on n'en aime pas d'autre; c'est reprendre des forces pour mieux aimer.'
(Mauriac: *Rencontre avec Pascal*, Paris 1926, pp. 17–18)

. . . la perpétuelle nouveauté que nous trouvons à cette présence qui est 'une cessation d'inquiétudes' – (trois cents pages de Proust tiennent dans ces deux mots) . . .
(ibid., p. 19)

While one cannot fail to detect in Mauriac's thought a strongly Pascalian element springing partly from natural affinity, partly from influence, one is much less prepared to expect *rapprochements* between Pascal and Proust. Mauriac speaks for many critics when he describes *A la recherche du temps perdu* as 'une œuvre d'où Dieu est terriblement absent.'[1] Yet just as Pascal's work portrays 'la Misère de l'homme sans Dieu', before complementing this picture by that of 'la Félicité de l'homme avec Dieu', Proust's novel might appear to reflect 'Misère et Félicité' in its own newly invented terms, with an attempted substitution of art and memory for God and grace: a *Paradise lost* and a *Paradise regained* outside time.[2] Proust seems to draw extensively upon

15

Pascal, especially upon the latter's fund of psychological analysis, while reserving the right to substitute artistic for religious terms of reference. Many Catholic writers draw parallels between Pascal and Proust. Chief amongst such critics, Henri Massis conceives of both men as salvaging the vestiges of their respective epochs and worlds in the manner of superhuman memorialists. However, the markedly original sense in which M. Massis is accused of having 'pascalisé' Proust, raises further important and fundamental issues and provides the antithesis to Mauriac's approach:

> ... si par rencontre, j'ai nommé Pascal à propos de Proust, c'était pour définir l'ordre de problèmes où, sans qu'il y prétende, Marcel Proust nous incline quand nous voulons donner un sens moral, c'est-à-dire *humain*, à sa propre aventure. En l'humanisant – car on le déshumanise par l'éviction de tout élément moral – peut-être l'ai-je du même coup 'christianisé' et cela dans la mesure où le christianisme assume le péché. C'est ainsi que je l'ai 'pascalisé'.[3]

The lack of a moral sense on the part of Charlus, Morel and their kind is perhaps chiefly responsible for giving Mauriac the impression that 'God is absent from the work.'[4] Proust himself, however – and in turn the reader – is never long free from a conviction of sin and retribution such as one encounters in the Old Testament (*RTP*, II, 614–15). God is far from absent when, through the narrator's frenzied search for evidence of perversion in all around him, the author projects his own belief that this sin is the greatest tare and poisons all relationships. It is almost as though, at a remove, Proust had assumed the function of 'la conscience humaine,' of a deity ministering retributive justice or an avenging angel.

By his desire to clarify, notably in the form of *maximes*, the rich complexity of human experience, Proust continues the tradition of the seventeenth-century French *moralistes*: Pascal, La Rochefoucauld and La Bruyère. While in spirit and style Proust's novel often reflects a deep indebtedness to such writers, his correspondence is scattered with interesting allusions to the first and the last named. We find him comparing with discernment the reflections of La Bruyère and Pascal on the theme of friendship.[5] Particularly worthy of attention in relation to the subject of the present inquiry is the fact that Proust notes with apparent approval Georges de Lauris's 'parallèle entre Montaigne-Renan Pascal-Barrès.'[6] Proust believes that he detects in Princesse Bibesco's book, *Les Huit Paradis*, 'des phrases à la Barrès,' or are they, on second thoughts, 'à la Pascal? (*CG*, V, 138).

Proust could not have failed to notice the Pascalian current in the philosophy of Bergson; the parallel between Pascal and Bergson was noted by such critics as M. Le Roy, Georges Sorel, Wilfred Monod, Henri Franck and Edouard Berth, and it was finally sanctioned by Bergson himself in 1915. In an article entitled 'La Philosophie', published in the *Revue de Paris* of 1915, the philosopher contrasted with Cartesian rationalism 'un courant qu'on pourrait appeler sentimental, à condition de prendre le mot: "sentiment" dans l'acceptation que lui donnait le XVIIe siècle et d'y comprendre toute connaissance immédiate et intuitive.' Bergson clearly associates Pascal's 'esprit de finesse' with his own 'intuition', when he describes the seventeenth-century 'moraliste' as having introduced into philosophy a certain 'mode of thought which is not pure reason, since by the *esprit de finesse* it corrects what is geometrical in reasoning and is not either mystical contemplation, since it attains results which every one can verify and control.' He concludes that, 'à Pascal se rattachent les doctrines modernes qui font passer en première ligne la connaissance immédiate, l'intuition, la vie intérieure, l'inquiétude spirituelle.'[7]

While Proust is not known to have discussed any possible affinity between his own thought and that of Pascal, many critics have drawn *rapprochements* between Proust and Bergson. In light of such affinities, whether acknowledged or merely mooted, it is all the more interesting that first and foremost among the features which relate Proust to Pascal is precisely the conception of the rôles to be assigned to reason and intuition respectively. While it is impossible to prove influence in this connection, Proust often seems to be alluding directly or indirectly to Pascal, when not consciously parodying Descartes.[8] Is not the *Pensée; '*Le cœur a ses raisons que la raison ne connaît point' re-echoed and renewed in Proust's repeated confession to a failure on the part of the intellect?

> ... j'avais cru bien connaître le fond de mon cœur. Mais notre intelligence, si lucide soit-elle, ne peut apercevoir les éléments qui le composent . . . cette connaissance que ne m'auraient pas donnée les plus fines perceptions de l'esprit, venait de m'être apportée . . . par la brusque réaction de la douleur.
> (*RTP*, III, 420; cf. ibid., III, 423)

So great is the tension between reason and intuition in Proust's work and so delicate the balance which he has established and sustained between these two poles of human behaviour that critics sharply disagree about which of the two extremes predominates. A. Boase asserts that, in contrast to Gide, Proust's 'primary impulse is a desire to rise above the multitudinous waters of experience, to see the world as vision' and that he 'aspires to the Apollinian ecstasy, Gide to the Dionysian.'[9] V.–L. Saulnier, however, takes the opposite view:

> Contre l'intellectualisme, Proust affirme le primat de l'impression, seul 'critérium de vérité', gage de 'perfection' et de pure 'joie'. Il a le tort d'ériger ce principe en système: 'L'impression est pour l'écrivain ce qu'est l'expérimentation pour le savant.'
> (*RTP*, III, 880)[10]

This wide divergence of views merely reflects the intensity of Proust's inner state of division between the orders of 'la raison' and 'le cœur', and the extent to which he is preoccupied by a desire to reconcile the two poles of his nature and thus resolve an 'inner contradiction' as great, in his own case, as

17

any between 'l'ange' and 'la bête' in the mind and work of Mauriac (see *RTP*, I, 569–70 and III, 866). By his own confession, Proust's novel is, in fact, his deliberate attempt to resolve the antinomy of *le cœur* and *la raison*. Will he not draw the substance of his work from the 'truths' apprehended by both these faculties and, as a result, endow his writing with 'le velours' and 'la force' respectively, with mystery and clarity, however paradoxical such a combination may seem? While implying that his preference goes to 'ces vérités mystérieuses', Proust insists on the reconciliation of intuition and intellect:

> Je sentais pourtant que ces vérités que l'intelligence dégage directement de la réalité ne sont pas à dédaigner entièrement, car elles pourraient enchâsser d'une matière moins pure, mais encore pénétrée d'esprit, ces impressions que nous apporte hors du temps l'essence commune aux sensations du passé et du présent, mais qui, plus précieuses, sont aussi trop rares pour que l'œuvre d'art puisse être composée seulement avec elles.
>
> (*RTP*, III, 898)

It is possibly because, in Proust's case, the gulf is so great between feeling and thought, the projection of imagination and absolute beauty, impression and idea, and the transition so studied from the particular to the general, that he is given to syncopation, registering the impact of impressions and ideas either before or after their advent in time, in their absence, rarely if ever in their presence, and never the two categories simultaneously (*RTP*, III, 932). Analogy between two sensations – one in the past and the other in the present – seems to be Proust's surest means of bridging the gap between the particular and the general and thereby attaining the 'essence commune' or the spiritual, his 'céleste nourriture' and his desired element.

In the main, Proust seems to be united with Pascal in following the order of 'l'écrivain' as opposed to that of 'le savant', since he places 'l'impression' first and 'le travail de l'intelligence' second (*RTP*, III, 880); however, it is ironically in the sphere of love that he parts company with his precursor and goes the scientist's way. The narrator recognises that it is anything but reason which enlightens him about 'les premiers principes' and Albertine's connection with Mlle Vinteuil. This realisation does not prevent him from still looking to reason to take the initiative, to reconnoitre and clear the ground; in fact, he accepts trial and error as a necessary preliminary to the inevitable compromise which will consist for him, as for Pascal, in the recognition by reason of the heart's sovereignty within its respective order and of the ultimate superiority of intuition as an instrument of knowledge:

> Mais – et la suite le montrera davantage, comme bien des épisodes ont pu déjà l'indiquer – de ce que l'intelligence n'est pas l'instrument le plus subtil, le plus puissant, le plus approprié pour saisir le vrai, ce n'est qu'une raison de plus pour commencer par l'intelligence et non par un intuitivisme de l'inconscient, par une foi aux pressentiments toute faite. C'est la vie qui, peu à peu, cas par cas, nous permet de

18

remarquer que ce qui est le plus important pour notre cœur, ou pour notre esprit, ne nous est pas appris par le raisonnement, mais par des puissances autres. Et alors, c'est l'intelligence elle-même qui, se rendant compte de leur supériorité, abdique, par raisonnement, devant elles, et accepte de devenir leur collaboratrice et leur servante. Foi expérimentale.

(RTP, III, 423)

The last part of this quotation closely resembles Pascal's bold affirmation of the supremacy of the 'heart' which, by a poignant irony of paradox, reason alone can fully appreciate. Here, too, Proust joins Pascal in conceiving of intuition, or 'des puissances autres', as the faculty that understands general, first principles. In the conception and execution of a new kind of *roman d'aventure*, which is to bear an affinity to the *roman d'analyse* by its very quality of introspection, Proust seeks to establish a balance between reason and intuition. He is immediately involved in a veritable *tour de force*, or 'un travail de sauvetage' as he calls it. Inevitably he is confronted both with 'ce problème intellectuel peut-être le plus grand de tous pour un artiste': the inadequacy of reason to reach the truth unaided, and with the paradoxical interdependence of the two spheres of experience. It is precisely to the Pascalian distinction between the orders of the 'heart' and the mind, to the ironical dependence of the one upon the other for the very recognition of its supremacy, that Proust will return repeatedly and triumphantly but without his predecessor's 'pensée de derrière la tête' of Christian apologetics:

> Et cette infériorité de l'intelligence, c'est tout de même à l'intelligence qu'il faut demander de l'établir. Car si l'intelligence ne mérite pas la couronne suprême, c'est elle seule qui est capable de la décerner. Et si elle n'a dans la hiérarchie des vertus que la seconde place, il n'y a qu'elle qui soit capable de proclamer que l'instinct doit occuper la première.

('Projets de Préface' CSB, 216)

By his attempt to analyse feeling, to 'penser . . . ce qu'il avait senti', Proust goes beyond Pascal and, indeed, defies the mutual impenetrability of the two worlds of emotion and thought. For Pascal, the two orders are in the last resort mutually exclusive:

> . . . il est aussi inutile et aussi ridicule que la raison demande au cœur des preuves de ses premiers principes, pour vouloir y consentir, qu'il serait ridicule que le cœur demandât à la raison un sentiment de toutes les propositions qu'elle démontre, pour vouloir les recevoir.

(Pensée 282)

and it is fully conscious of his own temerity that Proust attempts to square the circle:

> C'est un peu le même genre d'effort prudent, docile, hardi, nécessaire à quelqu'un qui dormant encore, voudrait examiner son sommeil avec l'intelligence, sans que cette intervention amenât le réveil. Il y faut des précautions mais bien qu'enfermant en apparence une contradiction, ce travail n'est pas impossible.

(LR, 158; cf., RTP, I, 45)

While Proust's criterion of authentic experience is 'la transformation de sa volupté en connaissance',[11] and his aim is to 'rendre les impressions claires jusque dans leurs profondeurs' (*RTP*, III, 877 and 880), and to 'ne s'attacher qu'à ce qui lui semble déceler quelques lois générales', he never denies the difficulty of his self-imposed task of 'déchiffrage': 'On distingue et avec quelle peine la figure de ce qu'on a senti' (ibid., III, 896). To the gulf between *sentir* and *penser*, corresponds another which separates the particular from the general: man feels the particular, he knows the general,[12] or, as Pascal asserts: 'Le cœur a son ordre, l'esprit a le sien qui est par principe et démonstration' (*Pensée BR*, 283). For Proust, as for Valéry, to live and to feel are not in themselves sufficient: 'Il faut savoir ce qu'on sent et savoir qu'on vit.'

It is precisely this cleavage between thought and feeling which gives rise to 'un moment de vide', to the 'intermittences du cœur' in the sphere of aesthetics no less than in the realm of human reactions generally:

> Nous sentons dans un monde, nous pensons, nous nommons dans un autre, nous pouvons entre les deux établir une concordance mais non combler l'intervalle.
>
> (*RTP*, II, 50)

In common with Pascal, Proust sees 'l'intermittence' as 'une loi de l'âme' but, whereas his predecessor had stressed its operation in relationships between human beings, even more between man and God ('Tu ne me chercherais pas, si tu ne m'avais trouvé'), Proust detects it in memory: 'aux troubles de la mémoire sont liées les intermittences du cœur' (*RTP* II, 756); jealousy and love (ibid., III, 29 and 106); grief (ibid., II, 96); self-knowledge (ibid., I, 771); personality (ibid., II, 1035); and heredity (ibid., III, 353).[13] He outstrips his precursor by analysing the operation of this phenomenon in the sphere of aesthetic appreciation: the narrator attributes to the 'intervalle' or 'faille' (ibid., II, 50) between feeling and thought his own difficulty in discerning in La Berma's performance an approximation to absolute beauty, in correlating impression and idea; whereas he should have moved from the former to the latter, the Pascalian and the Proustian order par excellence,[14] he did the reverse: '... comme si mes applaudissements ... naissaient non pas de mes impressions même, mais comme si je les rattachais à mes idées préalables ...' (ibid.). While Proust stresses perhaps more than Pascal the difficulties of interchange between the two orders, between impression and idea, both men conceive of intuition as taking the place of the intellect in the understanding of general, first principles and, at the same time, both imply the impossibility of reason superseding the 'heart' in any respect. Thus, in the example just quoted, Proust extends and applies to aesthetics Pascal's theory of the orders, and proves conclusively that, in this sphere also, 'ce qui est le plus important pour notre cœur ou pour notre esprit ne nous est pas appris par le raisonnement mais par des puissances autres' (*RTP*, III, 423):

20

... notre esprit attentif a devant lui l'insistance d'une forme dont il ne possède pas d'équivalent intellectuel, dont il lui faut dégager l'inconnu ... Il se demande: 'Est-ce beau? ce que j'éprouve, est-ce de l'admiration? ...' Et ce qui lui répond ... c'est l'impression despotique causée par un être qu'on ne connaît pas, toute matérielle, et dans laquelle aucun espace vide n'est laissé pour la 'largeur de l'interprétation.'

(ibid., II, 49)

Et la différence qu'il y a entre une personne, une œuvre fortement individuelle et l'idée de beauté existe aussi grande entre ce qu'elles nous font ressentir et les idées d'amour, d'admiration.

(ibid., II, 50)

It might be argued that, in love and aesthetic enjoyment equally, the very lack of correlation between thought and feeling is nature's means of disarming a potentially destructive intellect. Ironically, and paradoxically, the lover and the artist may derive their greatest inspiration from the mediocre in humanity and art. Proust admits that 'des morceaux insipides' of Wagner's music had triggered off his own response and creative impulse more readily than passages of undisputed greatness. Feeling must here have prevailed to the virtual exclusion of the intellect. Yet Proust joins Pascal in disparaging the use of reason divorced from intuition in aesthetics. He echoes Pascal: 'La raison ... ne peut mettre le prix aux choses' in the following statement from *Le Temps retrouvé*:

Mais dès que l'intelligence raisonneuse veut se mettre à juger des œuvres d'art, il n'y a plus rien de fixe, de certain; on peut démontrer tout ce qu'on veut.

(*RTP*, III, 893)

The narrator's failure to feel and think other than successively during La Berma's performance is heralded and partly paralleled by Proust's absence of response to the masterly interpretation of Saint-Saëns at the Conservatoire concert (*CSB* (FALL), 328). Here, Proust attributes the human failure to respond to absolute beauty to the disservice rendered by the imagination in anticipating what for once lies outside its province. In this case, there is a dichotomy of imagination and intellect rather than of feeling and thought, to account for the moment of blankness when the listeners are confronted with the absolute:

La vraie beauté est en effet la seule chose qui ne puisse répondre à l'attente d'une imagination romanesque. Toutes les autres choses ne sont pas inférieures à l'idée qu'elle s'en faisait: l'habileté l'émerveille, la vulgarité la flatte ... Mais la beauté ... n'a point à sa disposition tous ces charmes.

(*CSB* (FALL), 328; cf., *RTP*, III, 932, fn)

It is, however, primarily in the sphere of love that Pascal's interpretation of 'les intermittences du cœur' anticipates Proust.[15] To the succession of selves within the personality corresponds, for Pascal and Proust, the multiple nature of one individual's love. On the human inability to 's'attacher à une même

21

pensée', Pascal bases his theory of the *divertissement*: 'Notre nature est dans le mouvement; le repos entier est la mort' (*Pensée* 129). This stress on mobility as the essence of the human condition undoubtedly has strong overtones of Montaigne: 'Notre vie n'est que mouvement' (Montaigne: *Essais* III, 13) and L. Brunschvicg makes the *rapprochement* in the notes of his edition. A fascinating 'lineage' (Montaigne: Pascal: Proust) materialises in relation to the theme of the *ondoyant* alone and its far-reaching implications:

> Car ce que nous croyons notre amour, notre jalousie, n'est pas une même passion continue, indivisible. Ils se composent d'une infinité d'amours successifs, de jalousies différentes et qui sont éphémères, mais par leur multitude ininterrompue donnent l'impression de la continuité, l'illusion de l'unité.
>
> (*RTP*, I, 372)

Some readers might feel Proust is closer to Montaigne than to Pascal, notably in his lack of religious conviction, his keen sense of time, flux and relativity, and in his tendency to develop thought by a process of digression. On the other hand, Proust may have been attracted to Pascal more strongly, principally because Pascal preferred commitment to dilettantism.

While Pascal implies fragmentation and multiplicity within one love, it is another *moraliste* of his century, La Rochefoucauld, who actually elaborates this notion to the point at which it is Proustian *avant la lettre*, for he conceives of the lover's restless movement from one quality to another of the person loved as a long 'inconstance' in the midst of constancy itself, a compromise accommodating the two poles of human desire:

> La constance en amour est une inconstance perpétuelle, qui fait que notre cœur s'attache successivement à toutes les qualités de la personne que nous aimons, donnant tantôt la préférence à l'une, tantôt à l'autre; de sorte que cette constance n'est qu'une inconstance arrêtée et renfermée dans un même sujet.
>
> (*Maxime* 175; see *BR*, p. 130)

Not only does Proust concede the possibility that the *intermittences*, these blanks of emotion, operate within love for one person (that of Swann for Odette, of the narrator for his grandmother or for Albertine), he goes further than Pascal by applying this law to a series of love-affairs within the experience of one individual (*RTP*, III, 908). In addition, he consistently sees the processes of love and artistic creation as indivisible; to the change of model in the world of art corresponds our transfer of affection from one person to another in our private lives as individuals. He applies equally to both spheres the claim that 'constancy' exists, however paradoxically, in the midst of 'inconstancy'.

Proust's belief that events can be either apprehended on the intellectual level or grasped intuitively on the emotional plane, in all their complex integrality, is really an extension of the Pascalian theory of the orders of 'l'esprit' and 'le cœur' (*Pensées* 282 and 283). Proust seems to conceive of the 'mode of thought' which, as already mentioned, Bergson associates with Pascal. He implies the existence of a faculty of intuition which has the power both to grasp the particular and understand general first principles, thus surpassing reason, which has no such ambivalence.[16] Proust and Pascal appear to be united here. Even as Proust wished that his novel could be composed entirely of oblique truths grasped intuitively, so Pascal had expressed the desire 'que nous n'eussions jamais besoin de la raison et que nous connussions toutes choses par instinct et par sentiment' (*Pensée* 282). The narrator experiences his grandmother's death first as an abstraction through the channel of reasoning alone; the latter faculty proves as inadequate to convey the essence of his loss as voluntary memory or 'la mémoire de l'intelligence' to restore the essence of the past. Proust explains the fact that 'par le menu la mort nous pille' by assuming our dependence on the memory of the emotions as opposed to the memory of the intellect for realisation of this and other abstractions. He seems to say '*La mort* sensible au cœur et non à la raison', just as he will echo Pascal when he so arrestingly defines love as 'l'espace et le temps rendus sensibles au cœur' (*RTP*, III, 385; cf., *Pensée* 278):

> ... nous croyons ne plus aimer les morts, mais, c'est parce que nous ne nous les rappelons pas; revoyons-nous tout d'un coup un vieux gant et nous fondons en larmes, par une grâce, un pédoncule de réminiscences ....[17]

Acting in his capacity as novelist, Proust will render time tangible by confronting us with its materialisation rather than by any attempt to convey it in abstract terms:

> Et maintenant je comprenais ce que c'était que la vieillesse – la vieillesse qui de toutes les réalités est peut-être celle dont nous gardons le plus longtemps dans la vie une notion purement abstraite ... sans comprendre ... ce que cela signifie, jusqu'au jour où nous apercevons une silhouette inconnue, comme celle de M. d'Argencourt, laquelle nous apprend que nous vivons dans un nouveau monde; ... je comprenais ce que signifiaient la mort, l'amour, les joies de l'esprit, l'utilité de la douleur, la vocation, etc.
>
> (*RTP*, III, 932, fn)

Proust applies arrestingly to his novelist's technique of narration and description the tenet that impressions take precedence over ideas. The portrayal of sensations in the order of their occurrence, their testimony as yet uncorrected by the intervention of the intellect – this is an integral feature of Proust's literary style. It is as though he built a whole aesthetic and ultimately ethic on Pascal's thesis of the fallibility of the senses:

> ... encore faudrait-il peindre la guerre comme Elstir peignait la mer, par l'autre sens, et partir des illusions, des croyances qu'on rectifie peu à peu, comme Dostoïevsky raconterait une vie.
>
> (*RTP*, III, 983)

A particularly notable example of Proust's power to enlist errors of sense perception in the cause of art and to integrate sensory illusions in the very form and substance of literary style is afforded by his depiction, in a single sentence, of a carriage-ride from Douville into the heart of the transplanted Verdurin salon. Throughout this short episode, Proust records without modification the narrator's errors of sense perception, stressing always that part of the impression 'engainée dans l'esprit', and consistently presenting objects 'dans l'ordre de nos perceptions au lieu de les expliquer d'abord par leur cause' (*RTP*, I, 653). From that point he moves outwards, bearing the reader with him in a virtual process of trial and error, and finally, by a masterly stroke, he encloses the whole of the Verdurin dinner-party between the coach-journey to La Raspelière and the return (ibid., II, 1095–6).

On such issues as the tyranny exercised by the imagination ('cette partie dominante de l'homme'), the proportion of error introduced into human vision by our inescapable failing of subjectivity, and the faulty recording of external reality occasioned now by the senses, now by the mind (ibid., III, 140), now by a combination of the two media, there is complete unanimity between Pascal and Proust. Both writers give absorbing commentaries on the stages by which they progress to the final discovery: '. . . je me disais combien il est difficile de savoir la vérité dans la vie' (ibid., III, 620). Proust's novel will reflect the author's sincere desire to approximate as closely as possible to the truth by multiplying viewpoints to infinity, by indulging his Argus complex, his passion to 'voir l'univers avec les yeux d'un autre, de cent autres . . .' Such is his response to the challenge offered to every artist by the irreducible individuality of each person's vision:

> L'univers est vrai pour nous tous et dissemblable pour chacun . . . Oui, j'ai été forcé d'amincir la chose et d'être mensonger, mais ce n'est pas un univers, c'est des millions, presque autant qu'il existe de prunelles et d'intelligences humaines, qui s'éveillent tous les matins.
>
> (ibid., III, 191)

Imagination, like the senses and in co-operation with the latter, is the accomplice of subjectivity. For Pascal, this faculty is comparable to the senses in its power to favour illusion (*Pensée* 82). Proust develops interestingly the theory that, combined with the anxiety of love, it sets in motion the 'modèle chéri', faults our photographic equipment and 'nous empêche d'obtenir de l'être aimé une image bien nette' (*RTP*, I, 489). It is the snapshots as yet untouched by the intellect or emotion which are authentic. A dramatic moment occurs when Marcel suddenly sees his grandmother with a detached, mechanical part of himself; for once she appears to him outside 'le système animé, le mouvement perpétuel de [son] incessante tendresse' (*RTP*, II, 140). The substitution for 'l'œil' of 'une plaque photographique' affords a Pascalian deflation of 'un académicien qui veut appeler un fiacre' (ibid., II, 141).

Concerning the gulf between reality on one hand and the impression recorded by the imagination and the senses on the other, Proust is in complete agreement with Pascal:

> ... le monde visible ... n'est pas le monde vrai, nos sens ne possédant pas beaucoup plus le don de la ressemblance que l'imagination, si bien que les dessins enfin approximatifs qu'on peut obtenir de la réalité sont au moins aussi différents du monde vu que celui-ci l'était du monde imaginé.
>
> (ibid., I, 548)

Whatever differences exist between the Pascalian and the Proustian 'qualities of vision,' it is from the same acceptance of the fallibility of the senses that Pascal argues man's dependence on the supernatural for salvation, and Proust sanctions an artistic re-creation of the world. When sensory illusions momentarily overpower if not suspend reason or 'l'intelligence', Proust sees art as the result, Pascal the corruption of human nature before Divine intervention:

> L'homme n'est qu'un sujet plein d'erreur, naturelle et ineffaçable sans la grâce. Rien ne lui montre la vérité. Tout l'abuse; ces deux principes de vérités, la raison et les sens, outre qu'ils manquent chacun de sincérité, s'abusent réciproquement l'un l'autre. Les sens abusent la raison par de fausses apparences; et cette même piperie qu'ils apportent à la raison, ils la reçoivent d'elle à leur tour; elle s'en revanche. Les passions de l'âme troublent les sens, et leur font des impressions fausses. Ils mentent et se trompent à l'envi.
>
> (*Pensée* 83)

The narrator is capable of extending from the material to the mental plane the reversal of laws formulated by reason. A notable example occurs when Marcel, hearing distinctly the waves break below the cliff at La Raspelière, deduces that, given purity of atmosphere, sound can traverse more easily vertical than horizontal distances. He realises the proximity of what only appears to be remote, and the whole incident prefigures, in relation to external space, the ease with which involuntary memory transcends the laws of time in 'l'espace intérieur', thanks to the purity of oblivion. It is not in order to convey 'la misère de l'homme sans Dieu' that Proust here glories in the 'renversement de nos impressions habituelles' but, rather, in the style of Montaigne, to 'rudoyer la raison' and demonstrate the fallibility of the senses (*RTP*, II, 898; cf., ibid., III, 406).

Proust must have been fascinated by the presence of 'une dernière illusion à détruire', for his novel abounds in illustrations of the manner in which errors of sense perception 'nous faussent l'aspect réel de ce monde': '... les sons n'ont pas de lieu' (ibid., II, 75); '... la perte d'un sens ajoute autant de beauté au monde que ne fait son acquisition' (ibid., II, 77); final location of sound leads to synaesthesia (ibid., III, 406). After analysing 'une erreur d'acoustique', Proust reaffirms his belief that 'il est très difficile de situer un son dont la place ne nous est pas connue...' (ibid., II, 97-8). A 'mirage optique' precedes a striking auditive illusion (ibid., II, 391) and both are eclipsed by Marcel's impression of music from the Pilgrims' Chorus, as the landing door closes on the draughts from the staircase (ibid.). Before destroying the illusion, however, Proust will exploit to the full the poetry of analogy (ibid., III, 1045 and 736). Even as illusions of the senses are capable of re-creating the world in a moment wrested from the sway of reason, so a break in what is for Pascal no less than for Proust 'l'habitude abêtissante' (ibid., III, 544) can renew our vision of life (ibid., III, 918).

In another vein, Proust draws from the interplay between the senses and the reason striking comic effects. His point of departure for an analysis of the verbal blunders committed by Françoise is a generalisation worthy of Pascal: 'Le témoignage des sens est lui aussi une opération de l'esprit où la conviction crée l'évidence' (ibid., III, 190). It will be recalled that Françoise includes amongst her foibles the inability to give the correct time! (ibid., III, 156). More amusing still – and Proust leaves us to speculate whether heredity might be the cause of yet another of 'ces défauts particuliers, permanents, inguérissables que nous appelons maladies' – Françoise shares with the 'maître d'hôtel' the inability to correct faults of pronunciation. Here, for good measure, Proust gives us the male and female French counterparts of Mrs Malaprop. Comedy runs riot when the hotel-keeper disastrously confuses the word *pissotière* with *pistière* (ibid., III, 190). Proust adds a virtual anti-Pascalian comment on the ineradicable nature of the manager's faulty comprehension: 'Mais l'erreur est plus entêtée que la foi et n'examine pas ses croyances' (ibid.).

Pascal had cited as further proof of human fallibility the ease with which one person can condition another's judgement. The author of 'l'art de persuader' and writer of Christian apologetics no doubt realised how powerful a rhetorical weapon he wielded, both creatively and destructively in the *Pensées* and in the *Provinciales* respectively, and could therefore write from the heart: 'Qu'il est difficile de proposer une chose au jugement d'un autre sans corrompre son jugement par la manière de la lui proposer!' (*Pensée* 105) On a lesser scale, Proust here again elaborates Pascal's thought. As proof that subjectivity not only falsifies the vision of the original witness but continues its effect by a chain-reaction from one person to another, he describes the power of the *concierge* of a restaurant to reverse the potentially favourable reactions of others to beauty. With their judgement thus corrupted, the *chasseurs* see in the youthful niece of Mme de Guermantes 'les quatre-vingts ans que, par plaisanterie ou non, avait donnés le concierge à la "vieille rombière"' (*RTP*, III, 191). In this instance, the classical reaction to 'La belle Hélène' swings into reverse and the chance element of sexual desire, mysteriously left out of play as far as the 'jeune beauté' is concerned (but possibly operative when the *chasseurs* find beauty in 'l'une des deux caissières de l'hôtel, rongée d'eczéma, ridicule de grosseur'), assumes much the same importance as for Pascal 'ce je ne sais quoi', the length of Cleopatra's nose! (Cf., J. Mouton, *Proust* pp. 74–6.)

Pascal's generalisations on the subjectivity of love, on the manner in which, incapable of detached observation, every person unconsciously brings external reality into conformity with 'l'original de sa beauté', all these reflections are virtually interchangeable with the Proustian variations. Mauriac's comment on Pascal could be applied with equal force to Proust:

> Pascal a pressenti que c'est nous-mêmes qui nous cherchons dans les autres et que nous créons de notre propre substance l'objet de notre passion . . . il n'ignorait pas que nous ne nous éprenons pas de la beauté, mais d'une certaine beauté à notre mesure . . .[18]
> *(Rencontre avec Pascal, p. 17)*

Proust seems to me to be particularly Pascalian when he sees merely as an extension of the fallibility of the senses the subjectivity of vision in love no less than in art, the former so often for him the prefiguration of the latter:

> Je pourrais, bien que l'erreur soit plus grave, continuer, comme on fait, à mettre des traits dans le visage d'une passante, alors qu'à la place du nez, des joues, et du menton, il ne devrait y avoir qu'un espace vide sur lequel jouerait tout au plus le reflet de nos désirs.
> *(RTP III, 1045; cf., Pensée 124)*

Love affairs no less than human relationships in general – as portrayed in Proust's novel – seem to provide one long commentary on subjectivity, on the cult of 'une certaine beauté à notre mesure', from Swann's love for Odette, and Marcel's successive ventures, through the liaison of Charlus with Morel, Saint-Loup with Rachel and 'Charlie' to the passion of the Duc de Guermantes for 'la dame en rose'.

Equally Proust re-applies, in the context of love, Pascal's thesis of 'La Justice et la Raison des Effets', when he shrewdly discerns the necessity for 'qualités empruntées' such as trappings, insignia and uniform to suggest to the observer that the persons concerned partake of 'une vie inconnue', infinitely attractive to the imagination. Here, Proust seems to continue and annotate Pascal (*Pensée* 82) by switching from government and public life to the course of love itself the sphere in which he analyses the rôle of the imagination. Proust points the contrast between two suitors, one a commoner – and therefore perpetually at a disadvantage, all the more so if he lacks handsome features! – the other a king whose supreme advantages of heredity and 'la force' already form 'une vie spéciale' in their own right and amply compensate for any physical defect, perhaps without the lover's recourse to special attire. While conceding to kings 'une vie spéciale' which is founded in heredity and accrues from their appeal to the popular imagination down the ages,

Proust carries his predecessor's thought a stage further in masterly fashion: '... l'uniforme rend les femmes moins difficiles pour le visage; elles croient baiser sous la cuirasse un cœur différent, aventureux et doux ...' (*RTP*, I, 100).[19]

Yet again Proust re-applies a Pascalian *Pensée* in the sphere of love. For the original: 'Nous ne cherchons jamais les choses mais la recherche des choses' (*Pensée* 135), he substitutes his own version: 'Nous ne cherchons jamais les *femmes* mais la recherche des *femmes*' (*RTP*, III, 413, fn). More generally, whatever the focus of desire for Proust, enjoyment hinges upon the challenge of a quest: 'une dernière recherche à entreprendre', upon the uncertainty if not impossibility of possession: 'une dernière illusion à détruire', since 'Plus le désir avance, plus la possession véritable s'éloigne' (*RTP*, III, 450). 'La recherche des choses' rather than 'les choses' might well be termed Proust's supreme *divertissement*, heightened in his own case, no doubt, by the prospect of imminent death, which always makes the as yet unrealised virtuality infinitely desirable by setting it effectively beyond all possibility of attainment. In a different context, Saint-Loup's death seems to the narrator all the more difficult to bear because it leaves tragically unfulfilled so much potential happiness of friendship (*RTP*, III, 847–8).

Pascal anticipates Proust by the extent to which he is preoccupied by the enigma of human identity, the mystery of personality. Does the individual consist of a baffling number of apparently unrelated facets, a series of autonomous *moi* – the 'images' of Swann, Odette, Cottard, Vinteuil, Elstir, etc., vary according to the eye-witness – or is there some mysterious unity, 'la constance' in the midst of 'l'inconstance', which ultimately defies analysis? Proust seems to share Pascal's despairing conclusion about this issue:

> Où est donc ce *moi*? s'il n'est ni dans le corps, ni dans l'âme? et comment aimer le corps ou l'âme, sinon pour ces qualités, qui ne sont point ce qui fait le moi, puisqu'elles sont périssables? car aimerait-on la substance de l'âme d'une personne abstraitement, et quelques qualités qui y fussent? Cela ne se peut, et serait injuste. On n'aime donc jamais personne, mais seulement des qualités.
>
> (*Pensée* 323)

Again, when he inveighed against the law of flux: 'C'est une chose horrible de sentir s'écouler tout ce qu'on possède' (*Pensée* 212), Pascal had foreshadowed Proust, but, while the former used the revelation of relativity, succession, and transience to strengthen the case for the *pari*, the latter writer has no such religious conviction or apologist's urge to sustain him. With the difference of a deep, almost pagan 'regret des choses qui s'en vont', only intensified by his lack of belief in immortality, Proust remains at what is for Pascal merely a stage on his religious journey: 'Rien ne s'arrête pour nous' (*Pensée* 72).

28

To the transience of external nature and society corresponds the constant flux within human nature itself, a microcosm of both the former: '... j'ai connu que notre nature n'était qu'un continuel changement...'(*Pensée* 375). Pascal gives a veritable point of departure for one of Proust's central themes: that a single human personality should contain a succession of selves is a necessary condition of man's subjection to time: 'Je n'étais pas un seul homme mais le défilé d'une armée composite...' (*RTP*, III, 489). Before Proust, Pascal had stated that one person contains or even transcends an epoch. Like Proust (ibid., III, 913 and 771), he constantly compares the individual to the nation and draws identical conclusions (*Pensée* 122).

In these circumstances, the law of syncopation between desire and its fulfilment appears ineluctable: 'Tout ce qui fut un désir devient un fait mais quand on ne le désire plus.' Pascal virtually annotates Proust:

> ... nos désirs nous figurent un état heureux, parce qu'ils joignent à l'état où nous sommes, les plaisirs de l'état où nous ne sommes pas; et, quand nous arriverions à ces plaisirs, nous ne serions pas heureux pour cela, parce que nous aurions d'autres désirs conformes à ce nouvel état.
>
> (*Pensée* 109)

From the observation of flux within one personality and the consequent syncopation between desire and fulfilment, it is a short step to the discovery that the desires and affections of two persons are far less likely to synchronise:

> Il n'aime plus cette personne qu'il aimait il y a dix ans. Je crois bien: elle n'est plus la même, ni lui non plus. Il était jeune et elle aussi; elle est tout autre. Il l'aimerait peut-être encore, telle qu'elle était alors.
>
> (*Pensée* 123)

The last statement particularly invites comparison with Proust: 'Car la femme qu'on revoit quand on ne l'aime plus, si elle vous dit tout, c'est qu'en effet ce n'est plus elle, ou que ce n'est plus vous: l'être qui aimait n'existe plus' (*RTP*, III, 602-3). The narrator finds himself seized with the longing to possess women seen and desired in the past. Then, abruptly he realises that he has been deceived by memory into thinking of the past as the present and that time's passing makes an anachronism of his love (ibid., III, 628).

If Mauriac had been asked to select the *Pensée* of Pascal which comes closest to formulating the tragedy of the human condition, would it not have been: '... tout le malheur des hommes vient d'une seule chose, qui est de ne savoir pas demeurer en repos, dans une chambre' (*Pensée* 139)? The same reflection would seem to have made its impact on Proust also, if we substitute the preoccupation of aesthetics for that of religion. For the cause of art, almost 'ad maiorem *artis* gloriam', Proust felt impelled to immure himself within a cork-lined room and to re-create reality at a remove from 'l'usage délicieux et criminel du monde', which seemed to him to interpose between the artist and his work the same barrier as between the saint and his God. Proust evolved a cult of solitude. Ironically he continued to draw upon his recollections of society for the very substance of his work but illness eased the necessity of withdrawal in order to create; here again, once granted the difference of religion, the affinity of thought with Pascal is very strong indeed (compare *Pensée* 82 and *RTP*, I, 570. See also Pascal's 'Prière pour le bon usage des maladies'). In both men, illness seemed to engender and enhance a sense of spirituality: 'Les malades se sentent plus près de leur âme'.

Independently of the Christian points of reference which underlie Pascal's contention that sickness brings man closer to God, Proust sees in suffering 'un serviteur obscur', indispensable to the deepening of self-knowledge and the creation of art. The power of thought to generalise human experience releases Proust's narrator from the mesh of the particular by allowing him to sublimate personal suffering in the form of art: 'Les idées sont des succédanés des chagrins' (ibid., III, 906). The fact that he uses a cult of spirituality to temper his 'regret des choses qui s'en vont' reflects, on Proust's part, a love of the ephemeral because it is ephemeral, a pure gratuitousness reminiscent of one of his favourite poets, Vigny, and incompatible with any religious belief in immortality. Sufficient for Proust the precarious and limited survival, in human memory, of such mortal things as the Montalivet Salon, long since extinct (*RTP*, III, 284–5). However differently they may be seen to conceive of man's ultimate destiny, both writers are united in believing that 'Pensée fait la grandeur de l'homme'; for Proust, absolutely and finally; for Pascal, only in the interval before discovery of the paradox that the quest and the *intermittences du cœur* prove man's possession of the infinite.

Notes

[1] 'Du seul point de vue littéraire, c'est la faiblesse de cette œuvre et sa limite: la conscience humaine en est absente . . . Ce n'est point ici le chrétien qui juge: le défaut de perspective morale appauvrit l'humanité créée par Proust, rétrécit son univers.' F. Mauriac: *Du côté de chez Proust*, Table Ronde, Paris 1947, p. 67. Despite the latter date, in 1938 Mauriac had occasion to revise this view which had been published originally in an article entitled 'Sur la tombe de Marcel Proust,' *Revue hebdomadaire* 2 décembre 1922, pp. 5–9. 'On a parfois fait état d'un jugement que je portai au lendemain de sa mort sur ce trou béant laissé dans l'œuvre de Proust par l'absence de Dieu. J'en mesure aujourd'hui l'injustice.' See *D'autres et moi*, Grasset,

Paris 1966, p. 157: review of Bruno Gay-Lussac's 'Les Enfants aveugles'. Camus conceives of Proust as taking the part of the creature against the Creator and initiating 'une révolte créatrice contre les puissances de la mort et de l'oubli.' On the 'absence of God' from Proust's work, he writes: 'Si cela est vrai, ce n'est point parce qu'on n'y parle jamais de Dieu, mais parce que ce monde a l'ambition d'être une perfection close et de donner à l'éternité le visage de l'homme'. *L'Homme révolté*, IV, 'Révolte et art' *Essais*, Pléiade, Paris 1965, pp. 670–1. For a review of this question, see J. Mouton: *Proust*, 'Ecrivains devant Dieu' Desclée de Brouwer 1968, pp. 20–23: see also ibid., pp. 54–60, where the important theme of profanation in Proust's work is discussed.

[2] G. Poulet: *Etudes sur le temps humain*, Plon, Paris 1950, p. 173. 'Dans la pensée proustienne, la mémoire joue le même rôle surnaturel que la grâce dans la religion chrétienne.'

[3] *Pascal et Port-Royal*, Arthème Fayard, Paris 1962: 'Pascal et Proust' pp. 48–50. There undoubtedly lies beneath the surface of *A la recherche du temps perdu* a whole set of references to Christianity: see A. King: *Proust*, Oliver & Boyd, London 1968, pp. 82–91. Marcel's spiritual journey reflects Calvary (*RTP*, III, 1018). See the Notes for further reading for mention of other studies of parallels between Proust and Pascal as opposed to attempts to prove influence. The present chapter likewise is concerned primarily with resemblances between the two authors.

[4] F. Mauriac: *Du côté de chez Proust*, p. 66. Proust's world here contrasts sharply with that of Mauriac; Du Bos believed that he had found in the power of Mauriac's characters to know themselves and to recognise 'la boue', proof that the novelist could portray evil without 'connivence'.

[5] See Proust's letter to Antoine Bibesco (1901), *Les Cahiers Marcel Proust*, no. 4, *Au Bal avec M. Proust* Gallimard, Paris 1928, pp. 16–18.

[6] *LAURIS*, Lettre V (1904).

[7] H. Bergson: *Ecrits et Paroles*, Presses Universitaires de France, Paris 1957–59. See 'La Philosophie' pp. 413–36; p. 415.

[8] [L'intuition est] 'la chose du monde la plus répandue' (*RTP*, III, 345). Saint-Loup parodies Pascal when Marcel, after asking his friend to intervene on his behalf with Mme de Guermantes, can barely summon courage to ask for a photograph of the latter and nervously requests permission to *tutoyer* Robert, no doubt thinking that this step will create a favourable atmosphere! '. . . cela vous ennuierait-il que nous nous tutoyions? – Comment m'ennuyer, mais voyons! *joie! pleurs de joie! félicité inconnue!*' (ibid., II, 102). (Here, the italics are Proust's.) This veiled reference to Pascal is omitted from the index of the Pléiade edition but mentioned by J. Mouton, *Proust*, p. 76. See also, *RTP*, III, 792.

[9] R. L. Graeme Ritchie: *France: a Companion to French Studies*, Methuen

31

London 1949, ch. X: A. Boase, 'French Literature in the Twentieth Century,' pp. 358–9.

[10] V.-L. Saulnier: *La Littérature française du siècle romantique*, Presses Universitaires de France, Paris 1966, p. 117.

[11] The narrator's interest is confined to works 'où il y a un mystère à pénétrer.' He strives to 'dissiper le mystère . . .' by applying 'la lumière croissante mais hélas! dénaturante et étrangère de [son] intelligence' (*RTP*, III, 371–2).

[12] '. . . il fallait tâcher d'interpréter les sensations comme les signes d'autant de lois et d'idées, en essayant de penser, c'est-à-dire de faire sortir de la pénombre ce que j'avais senti, de le convertir en un équivalent spirituel' (*RTP*, III, 878–9). For a more intensive treatment of this whole question of the general and the particular, see the present author's article: 'Le général et le particulier dans l'œuvre de Proust' (*BMP*, 1970).

[13] Proust parts company with Pascal, however, when he considers moral failings to be 'comme une maladie intermittente de l'esprit' (*RTP*, II, 1090).

[14] Cf., *RTP*, III, 423. Proust's anxiety to interchange impression and idea may well be an extension of his preoccupation with the Symbolist *correspondances*.

[15] *Discours sur les passions de l'amour*, *BR*, p. 130. The editor attributes this treatise to Pascal and the authenticity of the *Discours* has been extensively debated since. What is of chief interest here, however, is whether, like Mauriac, Proust read it as Pascal's. It was readily accessible in both the Havet and the Brunschvicg edition and the editors concerned were willing to vouch for its authenticity.

[16] It is interesting that, on occasion, Proust seems to conceive the particular in terms of the general, perhaps reflecting his own state of division between Platonism and a belief in the artist's irreducible individuality; the term, 'l'essence', usually associated with the general and the exercise of the intellect, is applied to the particular and to the realm of feeling, in the description of the human desire for the unique: '. . . nous en voulons à l'eau de la gemme et aux mots du langage de n'être pas faits uniquement de l'essence d'une liaison passagère et d'un être particulier' (*RTP*, I, 219).

[17] Léon Pierre-Quint: *Proust et la Stratégie Littéraire* avec des lettres de Marcel Proust à René Blum, Bernard Grasset et Louis Brun, Corrêa, Paris 1954, p. 61. Cf., Ch. III, p. 61, n. 16.

[18] Compare *Discours sur l'Amour*, *BR*, p. 127 and *RTP*, III, 502 and II, 370.

[19] Art, or, more specifically, Odette's resemblance to Botticelli's Zipporah, gives Swann the illusion that he is penetrating 'une vie spéciale', 'inconnue' and correspondingly enhances his love, giving it an aesthetic dimension (*RTP*, I, 224–5).

Notes for further reading

F. Mauriac draws frequent comparisons between Proust and Pascal notably in *Rencontre avec Pascal*, Edition des Cahiers libres, Paris 1926. Henri Massis studies this *rapprochement* in 'Pascal et Proust' *Pascal et Port-Royal*, Arthème Fayard, Paris 1962, pp. 48–50. Other studies of parallels between Proust and Pascal, as opposed to attempts to prove influence, include:

H. Bonnet   *Le Progrès spirituel dans l'œuvre de Proust*, Paris 1949.

G. Poulet   *Les Métamorphoses du cercle*, Plon, Paris 1961. Chapter on Pascal, pp. 49–72.

J. Mouton   *Proust*, 'Ecrivains devant Dieu' Desclée de Brouwer 1968 pp. 19, 74–6 and 100.

A. Barnes   'Proust et Pascal' *Proust, Europe*, Paris August-September 1970, pp. 193–204. A. Barnes debates but finally leaves open the question of Pascal's possible influence on Proust, before proceeding to analyse parallels and affinities.

Chapter II

Chateaubriand

Le cercle de mes jours, qui se ferme, me ramène au point de départ. Sur la route que j'ai jadis parcourue, conscrit insouciant, je vais cheminer vétéran expérimenté, cartouche de congé dans mon shako, chevrons du temps sur le bras, havresac rempli d'années sur le dos. Qui sait? peut-être retrouverai-je d'étape en étape les rêveries de ma jeunesse?

(*MOT*, II, 488; 1830)

Encore si l'homme ne faisait que changer de lieux! mais ses jours et son cœur changent.

(ibid., I, 43; 1812)

It may be to his capacity as outstanding writer of *Mémoires* in his own century – which he serves in this respect as loyally as ever did Saint-Simon the seventeenth and eighteenth – that Chateaubriand owes the power of his initial impact on Proust.[1] By a mirror-technique integral to his novel, Proust discloses the characters' *livres de chevet* and, under this dispensation, Chateaubriand receives a fair measure of interest from the protagonists. The narrator, who here speaks for the author, ranks Chateaubriand beside Baudelaire and Nerval as one of his acknowledged precursors. While Proust is understandably more guarded and detached, in his self-appointed rôle of literary critic, than the characters of his novel, his artistic preferences are no less revealing (*RTP*, III, 918–19). For the characters, the narrator, and – Proust hopes – for the readers, literary criticism will act as an aid towards

35

self-discovery, towards that ultimate ideal of 'lecture d'eux-mêmes' which inspired him to write his novel (*RTP*, III, 1033).

'Idolâtrie esthétique' is a besetting sin of at least three readers of Chateaubriand in Proust's work, and each reveals this failing in relation to his literary preferences. Swann would buy a drawing, if Chateaubriand had described it (*RTP*, I, 521); prompted by a similar artistic *snobisme*, Charlus admires a grey dress on the score of Balzacian associations and Marcel will favour Albertine because she has the tresses of Laura Dianti, of Eléonore de Guyenne and of 'sa descendante si aimée de Chateaubriand' (*RTP*, I, 920).

When it comes to style, Bergotte finds *Atala* 'plus doux' than *La Vie de Rancé*. By admitting that 'il est vrai qu'il y avait dans le style de Bergotte une sorte d'harmonie . . .' the narrator seems to imply the inevitable subjectivity of any writer's literary judgements. Indeed, he adds humorously that Bergotte 'disait ce mot-là comme un médecin à qui un malade assure que le lait lui fait mal à l'estomac et qui répond: "C'est pourant bien doux" ' (*RTP*, I, 556).

In the important matter of preserving the aroma of the past in style and vocabulary, Chateaubriand ranks high in Proust's opinion as a result of seeming, in certain stories of the *Mémoires d'Outre-Tombe*, to effect the same kind of compromise as George Sand between 'ce qui eût semblé trop involontairement provincial, ou au contraire artificiellement lettré' (*RTP*, III, 35).[2] The closeness of this situation to parody may have been its chief attraction in Proust's eyes; he makes the following significant comment on the distinctive spoken styles of Mlle Marie Gineste and Mme Céleste Albaret:

> Je n'ai jamais connu de personnes aussi volontairement ignorantes, qui n'avaient absolument rien appris à l'école, et dont le langage eût pourtant quelque chose de si littéraire que, sans le naturel presque sauvage de leur ton, on aurait cru leurs paroles affectées.
>
> (*RTP*, II, 846)

Does not Proust's own description of the telephonists as *Danaïdes* (*RTP*, II, 133) fuse the literary affectation and provincial *sauvagerie* in much the same way as Céleste's reproaches to the narrator (and to Proust?) (*RTP*, II, 848)? To Gaston Gallimard of the *N.R.F.* had Proust not written of a part of his book where 'Deux "courrières" me parlent un peu à la façon des jeunes Indiennes de Chateaubriand'?[3]

Proust parodies Chateaubriand's oratorical style more directly both in the pastiche of *L'Affaire Lemoine*[4] and in the passage where M. de Guermantes finds fault with the narrator's article. Proust is possibly criticising, here, his own early addiction to Chateaubriand's style. One detects his rare propensity for self-criticism (*RTP*, III, 589). There is also in the novel a brilliant parody of the Romantics' fondness for moonlit scenes.[5] Self-consciously the narrator quotes to Mme de Villeparisis a phrase from Chateaubriand, Vigny or Hugo, at the same time pointing to the moon in the sky. In truly Proustian style, the fact that Marcel is quoting from memory causes him to ring an interesting change on the original: 'Elle répandait ce vieux secret de mélancolie.'[6]

First, by disparaging Chateaubriand's private life and then, more cogently, by relating her father's parody of the former's predilection for moonlight, Mme de Villeparisis attempts to destroy the aura with which the boy had invested the Romantic writer. It was apparently common practice at her home, on a moonlit night, for any new guest to be persuaded to take Chateaubriand for a walk round the castle . . . The ulterior motive on her father's part was obvious to those already familiar with the rite (*RTP*, I, 722). Here, as in the pastiches proper, Proust's instinctive recourse to parody combines with his extreme self-awareness to save him from blind literary infatuation (*CSB*, 594–5).

Proust believes that he has in common with his three acknowledged precursors, only to a more pronounced degree, an acute susceptibility to the power of two like sensations both to restore the past in essence and – contrary to all scientific principles – to reflect this reversal of the laws of time in an actual shift of scene (*RTP*, III, 918–19). As illustration of this trait in Chateaubriand, Proust cites two incidents in the *Mémoires d'Outre-Tombe*, one of involuntary memory proper (*MOT*, I, 76), the other of a special character and consequently in a class of its own (ibid., I, 211).

The thrush's song at Montboissier transports the hearer into the forgotten realm of childhood, 'le domaine paternel' of Combourg, and in the process quite surprisingly causes the major events of the intervening period to recede. It further compels the memorialist to shift his attention from momentous historical events to the intimacy of an inner life only temporarily displaced. There is interplay between the two spheres, and the thrush's song induces one of the *rêveries* which Chateaubriand enlists Montaigne's authority to describe as all-powerful: 'elles régentent notre âme' (*MOT*, I, 76). The 'jours perdus' anticipates Proust's 'temps perdu' and it requires only the later writer's aesthetic for a moment to be enjoyed outside time, as a result of the chance encounter between analogous past and present sensations; the symmetry between the two elements of time anticipated and time recalled is already Proustian (*MOT*, I, 76).

The second incident transcends the order of an experience of involuntary memory to become a symbol of the evocative, of that experience at a remove, which alone was destined to remain valid for Proust always, in the oblique vision of 'une chose vue à travers une autre'. The heliotrope, discovered far from its native shore and itself 'la plante exilée', reflected originally in the *Mémoires d'Outre-Tombe* the state of Chateaubriand, the *émigré*, briefly casting anchor in Newfoundland, and literally an artist in exile. How much more subtly for Proust, whose creative powers operated under the impact of memory, never of immediate sensation – 'trop en son pouvoir' – does this plant seem to symbolise the artist's condition, his power to create only in the absence of direct stimulus, and his consequent withdrawal into 'la solitude des espaces intérieurs'. The flower effectively embodies the essence of nostalgia, since it concentrates memory within its scent, and there is already the Proustian 'regret des choses qui s'en vont' in 'toutes les mélancolies des regrets, de l'absence et de la jeunesse' (*MOT*, I, 211).

What Proust describes as 'une des deux ou trois plus belles phrases des *Mémoires d'Outre-Tombe*' (*MOT*, I, 211 and *RTP*, III, 919) expresses a cult of the unrealised, of virtuality and of absence to the point of resembling a rarefication of his own ideas on the subject. By the mere fact of being borne on the wind of an alien shore, the scent of heliotrope seems to symbolise the gratuity of memory, the precariousness of the artist's condition and reception, as well as to evoke regrets for lost youth and the sadness which accompanies exile and unfulfilled potentiality (*RTP*, III, 847–8).

As a memorialist alone, Chateaubriand must have seemed to Proust to rank as his precursor and even to invest this rôle with a certain ambivalence. He sees his predecessor as the recorder not only of great historical events but of the apparently trivial, minute details of experience which impart meaning to a man's inner life, and form perhaps the private diary (*RTP* III, 728 and 919). Did Proust here attempt to vindicate the duality of his own rôle as memorialist, his own personal sense of loyalties divided between the general and the particular? Certainly, within his own work, he is conscious of a similar ambivalence in his dual rôle as writer of *Mémoires* in the tradition of Saint-Simon and Chateaubriand, and as recorder of what normally lies on the fringe of historical and social events, his central subject of study. Proust is keenly aware of what he would readily have termed *une vie en marge*, a natural landscape framing and intensifying his intellectual life proper. He extends the term 'memoirs' to apply to a recording of the natural setting associated with intellectual discoveries and historical events (*RTP*, I, 183–4).

Chateaubriand's preoccupation with the *minutiae* of plant life seems to offset and ease his self-appointed task to focus his attention on the wider horizons of historical events. Proust does not hesitate to sanction the memoir-writer's displacement of attention, after all a Proustian trait, and he places at the top of an imaginary hierarchy the people whose inner life supersedes major political events (*RTP*, III, 728). When Chateaubriand's personal interests seem to syncopate with, if not actually displace his function as recorder of history, he ranks correspondingly high in Proust's opinion. He anticipates the latter's sense of syncopation: 'Les mêmes heures ne sonnent pas pour tous'; but with the difference that his own power to detect a lack of synchronisation between the particular and the general is closely associated with his 'double vision' of naturalist and historian (*MOT*, I, 259). There is evident, here, on

Chateaubriand's part, a sense of guilt that his naturalist's interest should even momentarily displace major issues. At Zurich, September 1832, he confesses that he was interested only in 'le souvenir de Lavater, et de Gessner, les arbres d'une esplanade qui domine les lacs, le cours de la Limath, un vieux corbeau et un vieil orme' (*MOT*, II, 596), and he adds half humorously, as proof of his own awareness that rival interests strive within him for the ascendancy: '. . . j'aime mieux cela que tout le passé historique de Zurich, n'en déplaise même à la bataille de Zurich' (*MOT*, II, 596). His penchant towards reverie determines his preference for the minute detail of plant or animal life, for the intimate as opposed to the obvious grand-scale panorama afforded by history: 'La transition du monde ne vaut pas le passage de ces flots et, quant aux rois, j'aime mieux ma fourmi' (*MOT*, II, 504-5).[7]

Similarly Proust will associate the child's contemplation of nature with the memoir-writer's study of a king and conceive of himself as 'mémorialiste de la nature' (*RTP*, I, 184). Already, 'du côté de Méséglise' and 'du côté de Guermantes', Marcel had related intellectual discoveries and emotional experiences to the particular setting in which they occurred, and now the author can proudly say: '. . . mon exaltation les a portés [ce parfum d'aubépine, un bruit de pas, une bulle etc.,] et a réussi à leur faire traverser tant d'années successives . . .' (*RTP*, I, 184).

Chateaubriand reverts constantly to the fascination of 'les particularités les plus éphémères' and seeks to justify his preference for the peripheral on the grounds that such minor stimuli, precisely by falling wide of our habitual focus of attention – 'les intérêts émoussés refroidis par leur répétition et leur multitude' (*MOT*, I, 485) – command a complete spontaneity of response. Proust will develop this line of argument and analyse the power of a break of habit to renew our vision of the world. Between Montpellier and Narbonne, an expanse of digitalis ('cette mer de tiges empourprées') plunges Chateaubriand into a state of reverie, marking 'un retour à [son] naturel', 'une attaque de [ses] songeries', whose intensity he discovers to be in direct relation to the insignificance of the scene before him – to its remoteness both from the play of intellect ('Ne vaut-il pas mieux s'attendrir sans savoir pourquoi . . . ?') – and from deadening repetition: 'Tout est usé aujourd'hui, même le malheur' (*MOT*, I, 485). Chateaubriand seems to anticipate here Proust's cult of the peripheral, apparently trivial sensations, as likely to yield, both in the present and later, far more than the central and often grandiose objects which normally focus attention (*MOT*, I, 484–5).

In Chateaubriand's case, the memorialist of history has as counterpart the memorialist of the natural world, especially in so far as the latter sphere is inextricably and, at times, inexplicably interwoven, on an emotive level, with the artist's most intimate personal experiences (cf., Fromentin, Ch. VIII, pp. 148 ff.). From what appears to be detached observation, as when using all the powers of perception at his command Chateaubriand describes minutely the movements of the swallows (*MOT*, I, 97), to a more intimate sphere, where emotions and observations interweave – in fact, to the 'passionate memory' of George Eliot and Proust it is only a short distance. Rapidly and almost imperceptibly the fine detail and the apparently trivial become important because of personal associations. The moonbeam glimpsed between the leaves of 'un berceau de tilleuls' came to form an integral part of the garden where Chateaubriand waited for Madame Récamier (*MOT*, II, 215–16).

While for Proust art alone enables man to convey the irreducibly individual quality of vision, destined otherwise to 'rester le secret éternel de chacun', Chateaubriand just falls short of fusing memory and art (*MOT*, I, 43). At the crucial moment he halts; after describing Combourg in terms of his affective memory, he despairs of conveying to others the true essence of his childhood (*MOT*, I, 46). For Chateaubriand as for Proust, the lover is a potential artist. Associations infuse poetry into the apparently most trivial scene:

> ... le paysage est sur la palette de Claude le Lorrain, non sur le Campo-Vaccino.[8] Faites-moi aimer, et vous verrez qu'un pommier isolé, battu du vent, jeté de travers au milieu des froments de la Beauce; une fleur de sagette dans un marais ... une chauve-souris même remplaçant l'hirondelle autour d'un clocher champêtre, tremblotant sur ses ailes de gaze dans les dernières lueurs du crépuscule; toutes ces petites choses, rattachées à quelques souvenirs, s'enchanteront des mystères de mon bonheur ou de la tristesse de mes regrets.
>
> (*MOT*, II, 593)

Memories orchestrate with the past Chateaubriand's reactions to such an autumnal flower as the *colchique*, even as they will later Proust's response to the hawthorn; this is nothing less than the 'passionate memory' mentioned earlier when the autumn crocus becomes the medium for the rebirth of past associations (*MOT*, II, 596). Chateaubriand will again associate autumn indelibly with these flowers almost in the style of a painter[9] but no doubt under the spell of recollected emotion still as he surveys the scarred towers of Salzburg, 'vieux champions du temps ... restés seuls debout sur le champ de bataille des siècles' (*MOT*, II, 844).

Proust's narrator wonders why three trees on the road to Hudimesnil arouse within him 'un bonheur profond' (*RTP*, I, 717 ff.) and the mystery long remains unsolved. Without taking the process of analysis to such lengths, Chateaubriand already lights on analogy as partly responsible for his otherwise inexplicable reaction to a poplar-lined road, imbued with that quality of movement ('l'avenue tournoyante'), which is so often an indispensable prelude to involuntary memory in Proust's experience. Emotions on the personal and historical level here intermingle characteristically and the ultimate mood is one of nostalgic regret for 'ce qui ne se retrouve jamais' (*MOT*, II, 729).

As further proof of Chateaubriand's sensitiveness to analogy between past and present, one might mention an incident which occurred at Hohlfeld. In the course of a short halt there, while supper was being prepared, the author climbed a rock overlooking part of the village; again he seeks, like Proust, within himself, the original of a scene whose arresting *décor* is matched by a pattern of movement and sound (*MOT*, II, 731). It is characteristic of Chateaubriand that, on his second visit to Hohlfeld, he looks for a repetition of the earlier experience and then realises the 'idéalisation forcée' imposed by memory and already prefiguring artistic creation (*MOT*, II, 859).

As a memorialist, Chateaubriand inevitably finds himself impelled to examine and analyse the nature of memory and of time itself: '. . . les heures ne suspendent point leur fuite; ce n'est pas l'homme qui arrête le temps, c'est le temps qui arrête l'homme' (*MOT*, I, 108). From early childhood he had occasion to be grateful for the particular kind of memory with which he personally was endowed. The fact that it was of a markedly auditive variety enabled him to extricate himself from at least one difficult situation, as for instance when he was able to repeat word for word the reading just delivered by the Principal of his college. He often has reason to muse upon 'sa mémoire extraordinaire', 'sa mémoire tyrannique' which responds primarily to numbers and words. Although he admits that the 'mémoire des mots' did not survive for him in its entirety but gave place to 'une autre plus singulière dont il aura peut-être l'occasion de parler',[10] its strongly auditive character seems to be responsible for at least one further, fully realised, and another potential episode of involuntary memory left unmentioned by Proust.

Near Linz, in September 1833, Chateaubriand was making his way through the woods when the sound of crows, indelibly associated with his childhood, released deep within him a flood of memories in which Combourg was preserved intact. There is no trace here of the analysis which he had applied to the thrush's song but he is just as authentically transported into the past as before. Once again he owes the experience to a sound so often heard in the setting of his own childhood, perhaps on the periphery of a central experience. The consequent reversal of time-laws, making him 'contemporain d'un autre temps de sa vie', contributes powerfully to the familiar pattern of this book where the author's past is forever rising to the surface of the present and surprising him by its immediacy, and its power to remain intact (*MOT*, II, 847).

Proust singled out 'le chant de la chouette' as Chateaubriand's characteristic note: 'son cri à lui' (*CSB*, 651; cf., *MOT*, II, 604). At the same time we know from the *Mémoires* that their author prized as one of his 'joies de l'automne' 'le rassemblement des corneilles dans la prairie de l'étang, et leur perchée à l'entrée de la nuit sur les plus hauts chênes du grand Mail' (*MOT*, I, 96). Undoubtedly the fact that Chateaubriand had gleaned from natural life and stored within himself a wealth of impressions, auditive, visual and olfactory, unrivalled in subtlety and exactitude of detail, enabled him to command a range of sensory experience on which chance analogies of the present could make their impact at close intervals throughout his course as a memorialist.

Although the analogy responsible for evoking the past may sometimes elude him, the memory released loses nothing of its vividness for all that; however great his bafflement, Chateaubriand obviously relished such an experience of the *déjà vu*. There is a notable example of his failure to account for an incident of involuntary memory when an accident occurred to the coach in which he was travelling, and necessitated a halt at Woknabrück, about 23 or 24 September 1833. The reader is free to search for the analogy apparently lost, at least momentarily, to Chateaubriand himself; here as elsewhere in the *Mémoires*, wide open spaces are for the author particularly evocative (*MOT*, II, 845).

Chateaubriand's reflections on the strata formation of memory frequently have a Proustian character, especially his impression that memories live at various depths in geometrical, almost geological formation. At Verona, he recalls how great a number of his contemporaries had died since 1822, remarking that, while no one recalls the conversation round Metternich's table, a lark's song near Verona will almost infallibly remind the hearer of Shakespeare. Here the importance which Chateaubriand attributes to the individual's literary memory anticipates Proust's theory that the arts, and music in particular, may involve a deeper level of the personality than experience of life at first hand, affecting only the *moi social* (*MOT*, II, 768). What follows is even more strikingly Proustian since the writer has been so effectively transported from the present into the past that he has to make a conscious readjustment to his inner sense of time before he can conform again to external reality. The rebirth of the past under the impact of identical surroundings is of course Romantic rather than strictly Proustian but the conscious effort, on Chateaubriand's part, to readjust the inner time rhythm is markedly Proustian: 'En sortant de Vérone, je fus obligé de changer de mesure pour supputer le temps passé; je rétrogradais de vingt-sept années, car je n'avais pas fait la route de Vérone à Venise depuis 1806'[11] (*MOT*, II, 768).

The very function of memoir-writer was calculated to intensify Chateaubriand's already instinctive preoccupation with time. He records events mostly at a considerable interval after their occurrence. Hence a lack of synchronisation between writer and event, which sets the *Mémoires* apart from the *journal* in the sense of day-to-day notations and brings them a degree closer to the novel, to the re-creation of reality by a *moi* writing of 'absent things as if they were present', and even syncopating with events. Here the

42

phenomenon of *intermittences du cœur*, at least in its negative aspect, conditions Chateaubriand's art. The perspective inevitably shifts, as the personality of the memorialist undergoes the laws of flux and he no longer responds to places with the same reactions as before. There is often a Proustian sense of disintegration accompanying this anticipation of a Proustian theme: '. . . les maisons, les routes, les avenues, sont fugitives, hélas! comme les années'[12] (*RTP*, I, 427), as in the following: '. . . Dieppe est vide de moi-même; c'était un autre *moi*, un *moi* des premiers jours finis, qui jadis habita ces lieux, et ce *moi* a succombé, car nos jours meurent avant nous' (*MOT*, I, 435). (Cf., Nerval, Ch. III, p. 58).

The writer concludes that it is impossible to preserve inner unity in face of the laws of flux, dramatically so when he is engaged in writing memoirs, for his mind and emotions have outpaced the events he now narrates: 'Du reste, c'est un supplice de conserver intact son être intellectuel, emprisonné dans une enveloppe matérielle usée . . . Ne suis-je pas moi-même quasi-mort? Mes opinions ne sont-elles pas changées? Vois-je les objets du même point de vue?' (*MOT*, I, 435–6).

In the *Avant-Propos*, Chateaubriand disowns any obligation for the writer of memoirs to record his observations on historical events in their immediate shadow. History and the memorialist are both in such a constant state of flux the one in relation to the other, that Chateaubriand despairs of ever distinguishing between the time-levels of his own personality reflected in his narration.[13] Monsieur J.-A. Bédé has already commented on the Proustian nature of the passage concerned, without, however, stressing the 'unité indéfinissable' as perhaps the most Proustian feature of all. I refer to Proust's belief that from the very confusion of layers of time there springs in art, as opposed to life, the unity of style which we recognise as the hallmark of a particular author, his unique 'quality of vision': '. . . les rayons de mon soleil, depuis son aurore jusqu'à son couchant, se croisant et se confondant, ont produit dans mes récits une sorte de confusion, ou, si l'on veut, une sorte d'unité indéfinissable; mon berceau a de ma tombe, ma tombe a de mon berceau; mes souffrances deviennent des plaisirs, mes plaisirs des douleurs, et je ne sais plus, en achevant de lire ces *Mémoires*, s'ils sont d'une tête brune ou chenue' (*MOT*, I, 2). The whole passage is a striking commentary on Proust's theory that man is 'cet être sans âge fixe'.

Further, as a result of having – to quote his own words – 'hypothéqué sa tombe', the writer of the *Mémoires* was obliged to renounce the original plan for their publication fifty years after his death. Threatened as he was with their imminent appearance in part, *en feuilleton*, and therefore compelled to revise their content for publication of a section during his lifetime, and the rest immediately after his death, he became engaged in an acute struggle against time. It was his practice to mark chapters with the word *revu* and the date of the revision but, in spite of all his care, he eliminated some sections to which occasional references still remained in the part of the work allowed to stand.

Quite apart from his rôle of memoir-writer, Chateaubriand is the first to confess to a predilection for the past (*MOT*, I, 2 and I, 938). The latter seems to be as natural an element for him as for Proust. We are even reminded of Proust when persons absent are paradoxically more vividly present before Chateaubriand than those still within his reach in reality; here we have the positive aspect of the *intermittences du cœur* as applied to the art of the memoir-writer. Accordingly, the shores of Ostend from which he had embarked for Jersey in 1792 revive in 1815 Chateaubriand's memory of persons associated with his first exile [14] (*MOT*, I, 938).

From recording what might well be termed 'conventional' involuntary memory, however, Chateaubriand proceeds to analyse more deeply his own tendency to react more powerfully to things and persons in their absence than in their presence. This characteristic and the cult of memory serve his function as historian. In contrast, Proust will explore the psychological implications of the *intermittences* in the sphere of individual and artistic experience. Chateaubriand anticipates the Proustian tendency to react to persons most strongly in their physical absence, notably after their death, but he relates this propensity closely to his rôle as writer of memoirs. The following seems to be Chateaubriand's version of the *intermittences*: 'Des personnes mêmes dont je ne me suis jamais occupé, si elles meurent, envahissent ma mémoire: on dirait que nul ne peut devenir mon compagnon s'il n'a passé à travers la tombe . . .' (*MOT*, I, 938).

Chateaubriand and Proust are united in the belief that after a friend's death the lack of physical presence makes the individual concerned all the more vividly present in the imagination as well as in the reaches of memory. It is perhaps a complement of this 'presence after death' that, by a kind of premonition, or anticipation of the future, Chateaubriand should feel the loss of his friends more acutely just before their death than subsequently (*MOT*, I, 343). However, Chateaubriand's anticipation of personal loss in the death of friends is ultimately more than counterbalanced and compensated by his powers of memory and imagination.

In respect of his intense preoccupation with the past, Chateaubriand yet again aligns himself with Proust. In seeking out with greatest interest not only the lost years of his own childhood but also the time spent by Mme Récamier or other friends far from his ken, in striving to recover all, in fact, that would seem to be lost beyond recall, he is making his personal effort to offset the tendency for everyone to become through the passage of time 'un monde isolé', admittedly charged with a fund of experience, yet so individual as to constitute an effective barrier to communication and shared experience.

44

Chateaubriand suffers most acutely from this sense of separation when Mme Récamier, paying her homage to the departed Mme de Staël, becomes temporarily lost to the author, engulfed as she is by a flood of personal recollections: 'Deux mondes divers, mais liés par une secrète sympathie, nous occupaient, Madame Récamier et moi. Hélas! ces mondes isolés,[15] chacun de nous les porte en soi; car où sont les personnes qui ont vécu assez longtemps les unes près des autres pour n'avoir pas des souvenirs séparés?' (*MOT*, II, 605–6).

This sense that each person is a world within himself, cut off from others by the exigencies of separation in time, is heightened for Chateaubriand when he falls in love with a person so much younger than himself, namely Charlotte. It is then that he writes the famous *Amour et Vieillesse* in capitulation to time's ascendancy, and freely recognises the impossibility of union between youth and age, in themselves the supreme syncopation: '. . . le jour viendrait où le regard d'un jeune homme [t'arracherait] à ta fatale erreur, car même les changements et les dégoûts arrivent entre les amants du même âge. Alors [de] quel œil me verrais-tu? quand je viendrais à t'apparaître dans ma forme naturelle'[16] (*MOT*, II, 1134–5).

In view of his acute sensitiveness to time, it is natural that Chateaubriand should analyse and illuminate a whole range of human relationships, especially in so far as, subjected to flux, they cause an observer to doubt any alleged unity of personality. This is a problem which will preoccupy Proust, forever absorbed by the spectacle of relationships constantly changing perspective in proportion as they are subject to the laws of time and space. Swann, Vinteuil, Elstir present aspects of their personality varying chameleon-like according to the circle in which these figures move, the person with whom they may chance to find themselves at any given moment, and the composition of the observer's memories of the same period. Chateaubriand cannot be surprised that the friends who knew only isolated facets of his personality in childhood and whose knowledge of him remains artificially halted at that point, should have difficulty in recognising him after a considerable lapse of time. Of the Trémaudan family, unable to reconcile their memory of the child with what they now hear of the mature man, the writer of memoirs, Chateaubriand states that they merely reveal a fundamental human incapacity to correlate past and present.[17] Here in the personal key to which the *genre* of memoirs lends itself – prefigured in essence – is the theme of recognition which Proust will moot so often in the course of his novel, before solving fully, in the Salon de Guermantes, at the supreme moment of confrontation with Time's marionettes, this haunting enigma of shifting perspectives:

Ils ont douté longtemps que l'homme dont ils entendaient parler fût le *petit chevalier*. Le recteur ou curé de Combourg, l'abbé Sévin, celui-là même dont j'écoutais le prône a montré la même incrédulité; il ne se pouvait persuader que le polisson, camarade des paysans, fût le défenseur de la religion; il a fini par le croire, et il me cite dans ses sermons, après m'avoir tenu sur ses genoux. Ces dignes gens, qui ne mêlent à mon image aucune idée étrangère, qui me voient tel que j'étais dans mon enfance et dans ma jeunesse, me reconnaîtraient-ils aujourd'hui sous les travestissements du temps?[18] Je serais obligé de leur dire mon nom, avant qu'ils me voulussent presser dans leurs bras.

(MOT, I, 52)

Notes

[1] *LAURIS*, Lettre XLI (1908)

[2] In many of the stories which he relates in his *Mémoires*, Chateaubriand passes abruptly from the most vivid concrete detail to a mythological plane and thus creates a mock heroic effect by sheer contrast. By this suddenness of transition, he virtually anticipates parody (*MOT*, I, 265).

[3] See *Les Cahiers Marcel Proust*, no. 6, N.R.F. Gallimard, Paris (1932) 177, letter to Gaston [Gallimard], XI. 21 (cf., Ch. VIII, p. 147)

[4] *Textes retrouvés*, pp. 42–3 cf., *CSB*, 598

[5] Did Proust ever light upon a passage from the *Mémoires* where Chateaubriand for once describes the moon both lyrically and humorously? (*MOT*, I, 589) The whole paragraph in question covers an amazingly wide range of tones including parody, sheer comedy and finally a note of melancholy, as Chateaubriand recalls absent friends. However, it is above all by the delicately ironical description of the moon that Chateaubriand seems to sketch his own pastiche in advance.

[6] *RTP*, I, 721. The quotation from *Atala* reads in the original; '. . . ce *grand* secret de mélancolie qu'elle aime à raconter aux *vieux* chênes'.

[7] Cf., *MOT*, I, 485. One is vividly reminded, here as elsewhere, of Proust's version of 'le cadastre des fortunes' (*RTP*, III, 1019); cf., also *MOT*, I, 24.

[8] Cf., Proust: *CSB*, 177–8.

[9] Chateaubriand anticipates Elstir's vision of the sea in terms of the land and vice versa (*MOT*, I, 201). See also ibid., I, 200. Chateaubriand's choice of a site for his tomb reflects his fondness for a fusion of land and sea (ibid., I, 21–2). See ibid., I, 41–2, for what is perhaps Chateaubriand's most poetic anticipation of Elstir's metaphor.

[10] Perhaps Chateaubriand refers here to the strong propensity of his memory to work by a process of analogy on every possible occasion, threatening his need to move forward and resist the mesmerism of the past (*MOT*, II, 585).

[11] By what is virtually a process of *intermittences du cœur*, but applied to a personal sense of injury, Chateaubriand requires an interval of time before he can react to the wrong inflicted upon him (*MOT*, I, 157). Compare Nerval:

46

Depuis trois ans, par le temps prenant force,
Ainsi qu'un nom gravé dans une écorce,
Son souvenir se creuse plus avant!

('La Grand'mère) (NER, I, 19) (See Ch. III, p. 55)

¹² Chateaubriand anticipates Proust's 'maisons fugitives', *MOT*, II, 595. Compare ibid., I, 43; quoted as one of the epigraphs at the head of this chapter; also ibid., II, 488 and II, 625.

¹³ Compare with this deeper and inner *intermittence* the earlier syncopation between emotions recorded and those contemporary of the narration (*MOT*, I, 2).

¹⁴ As so often happens, places release memories and, in this respect, Chateaubriand aligns himself with the Romantic school: Lamartine ('Le Lac'); Hugo ('Tristesse d'Olympio'); Wordsworth ('Tintern Abbey'); rather than with Proust, for whom not so much places as apparent *trivia* of sensations, tangential features are capable of reviving the past. However, Chateaubriand is equally given to the more distinctly Proustian type of *reviviscence*, as we have seen in such incidents of involuntary memory as the thrush's song, the sight and sound of the *corneilles*, the symmetry of a line of poplars, where the random analogy between past and present suffices to release the former.

¹⁵ Cf., *MOT*, I, 43

¹⁶ See also ibid., 1135–8. Compare Proust's fear that only disaster can result from an aging man's love of youth (*RTP*, II, 884).

¹⁷ Cf., *RTP*, III, 931

¹⁸ Cf., *RTP*, III, 920 ff., and III, 933 (The italics, *'petit chevalier'*, in the passage quoted are Chateaubriand's own).

Notes for further reading

For a study of the affinities between Proust and Chateaubriand, see

J.-A. Bédé	'Chateaubriand et Marcel Proust' *Modern Language Notes*, XLIX (June 1934) pp. 353–60
Pierre Jaquillard	'Chateaubriand, Proust et nous,' *BMP*, No. 5, 1955, pp. 63–77
W. A. Strauss	*Proust and Literature*, Harvard University Press 1957 pp. 123–5, 128 and 159
P.-L. Larcher	'Proust et Chateaubriand,' *BMP*, No. 19, 1969, pp. 897–914
L. Védrines	'Proust et Chateaubriand,' ibid., pp. 914–16

Chapter III

NERVAL

... ces mystérieuses lois de la pensée que j'ai souvent souhaité d'exprimer et que je trouve exprimées dans Sylvie *– j'en pourrais compter, je le crois, jusqu'à cinq et six ...*

('Gérard de Nerval', *CSB*, 239)

Les souvenirs d'enfance se ravivent quand on a atteint la moitié de la vie. C'est comme un manuscrit palimpseste dont on fait reparaître les lignes par des procédés chimiques.

('Angélique', *NER*, I, 191)

Proust had considered giving to *A la recherche du temps perdu* 'un titre tout nervalien: *La Vie rêvée*'[1], and, conversely, he had suggested as appropriate for almost all of Nerval's work a title which had served to designate a part only of his own: 'Les Intermittences du cœur' ('A propos du "style" de Flaubert' *CSB*, 599). It is probable that Proust compounded the version: 'La Vie rêvée' from Nerval's early and accepted title for *Aurélia*: 'Le Rêve et la Vie', already charged with Spanish and Austrian overtones; Grillparzer's *Der Traum ein Leben* (1834) was based on Calderón's *La vida es sueño*. One might be tempted to take the synthesis a stage further and claim that both Nerval and Proust are primarily concerned with 'les intermittences de la vie rêvée', namely with the alternation of life and the dream: '. . . il vaut mieux rêver sa vie que la vivre, encore que la vivre ce soit encore la rêver, mais moins mystérieusement et moins clairement à la fois, d'un rêve obscur et lourd, semblable au rêve épars dans la faible conscience des bêtes qui ruminent'

(*JS*, 111). In the work of both writers, the dreamer constantly alternates with the analyst and there emerges a dual personality. Between extreme subjectivity and madness, Proust sees only a difference of degree, not of kind, and he may have sensed the same threat to his own attempt to express the qualitative difference of the individual reaction: 'cette essence . . . en partie subjective et incommunicable' (*RTP*, III, 885; cf., *CSB*, 234).

For Proust and Nerval, extreme subjectivity ultimately involves the artist in the necessity to admit the existence of what defies expression and to resort to evocation as the supreme means of enlisting the reader's own creative urge (*CSB*, 242).[2] In Nerval's case, by a poignant irony, and as a consequence of his particular form of madness, the gap between the ideal and its realisation occurs constantly within the dream itself, since his double is forever usurping the poet's rightful place: Hakem is forestalled by Yousouf in 'Les Deux Califes' of *Druses et Maronites*.[3]

Probably the first of the mysterious laws of thought which Proust found expressed in *Sylvie* and in Nerval's work generally is the close connection between art and dreams. Indeed, he sees folly serve Nerval's art of creation in proportion as sleep, dreams, oblivion or the involuntary may be said to underlie every artist's creative power in general. In the manner of a dream, the culmination of one work becomes for Nerval the point of departure of the next. For Nerval, Proust and the artist in general, the aim remains constant: to analyse the dream without destroying it and, although the subject's analysis of his dreams while he is still asleep seems to be a paradox, Proust would have us believe that such a process of salvage is not impossible.[4] Proust leaves us to conjecture how thin is the division between the dream dominated still by the subject's power to analyse on one hand, and complete absorption, engulfment in the subjective to the point of no return, on the other. In fact, he draws an analogy between the notation of illusions already on the way to madness, and the recording of 'les états de conscience qui conduisent de la vie au sommeil, jusqu'au moment où le sommeil rend le dédoublement impossible' (*CSB*, 234). So great is the tension between the subconscious and the intellect in Proust's case, however, that he is fully prepared to undertake the challenge presented by experience which ultimately defies analysis.[5]

Nerval went as far as he could in almost superhuman efforts to 'diriger [son] rêve éternel au lieu de le subir' (*NER*, I, 429; cf., *Aurélia NER*, I, 412); in the process, he stretched the act of self-division beyond all hitherto known limits. Under the influence of hashish and in apparent defiance of Pascal's experience of life as 'un songe un peu moins inconstant', Nerval contends that '[la] veille est encore plus remplie de rêves que [le] sommeil' (*NER*, II, 392). By a fascinating variation on the theme of 'les intermittences', 'Das Leben wird Traum und der Traum wird Leben' as for Novalis.[6] Proust records precisely the same experience of an interchange between dreams and waking life: 'L'existence n'a guère d'intérêt que dans les journées où la poussière des réalités est mêlée de sable magique. Tout un promontoire du monde inaccessible surgit alors de l'éclairage du songe, et entre dans notre vie . . .' (*RTP*, I, 865).

The account of 'une insomnie' or 'une demi-somnolence' in which the writer of *Sylvie* sees pass before him, within a short space of time, 'les tableaux les plus saillants d'une longue période de la vie'[7] (*NER*, I, 244), may well have given Proust the first impetus to set his opening chapter in an atmosphere of half-sleeping, half-waking. The Proustian narrator's dreamy awareness of rooms in which he has slept is simultaneously an act of memory and anticipation and introduces the reader to the places where the action of the novel will unfold. Proust would seem to require no further justification for the setting of his first chapter but, as he implies later, he is here reflecting symbolically, in the structure of his novel, the close relationship of sleep and dreams to the very substance of human life: '. . . car on ne peut bien décrire la vie des hommes si on ne la fait baigner dans le sommeil où elle plonge et qui, nuit après nuit, la contourne comme une presqu'île est cernée par la mer' (*RTP*, II, 85). Like his precursor, Proust will reveal, in 'un souvenir à demi rêvé', the essence of his narrative. His originality is that he reflects in 'ces évocations tournoyantes' the narrator's uncertainty about where he is on awakening. One 'tournoiement de rêve' so dramatically reverses time-laws as to justify a reference to Gilberte Swann as Mme de Saint-Loup, and Proust's 'Chambres' thus form an unsurpassed mirror-composition of an entire novel: '. . . généralement je ne cherchais pas à me rendormir tout de suite; je passais la plus grande partie de la nuit à me rappeler notre vie d'autrefois à Combray chez ma grand'tante, à Balbec, à Paris, à Doncières, à Venise, ailleurs encore, à me rappeler les lieux, les personnes que j'y avais connues, ce que j'avais vu d'elles, ce qu'on m'en avait raconté' (*RTP*, I, 9).

The chapter of *Sylvie* in which Nerval, 'plongé dans une demi-somnolence', sees 'toute sa jeunesse repasser en ses souvenirs', is entitled 'Adrienne' and, indeed, serves to reveal the latter character as still supreme in the narrator's mind, while Sylvie is as yet nothing more than a figure in the background; further, it discloses that the love which the writer experienced for an actress, Aurélie, as recounted in the opening chapter, takes its origin in a previous affair with Adrienne: 'Tout m'était expliqué par ce souvenir à demi rêvé' (*Sylvie*, Ch. III, *NER*, I, 246). Nerval's process of interweaving one experience with another, in fact of loving one person in terms of another, is at once Proustian and an integral part of his narrative technique, colouring his style and imagery: 'La ressemblance d'une figure oubliée depuis des années se dessinait désormais avec une netteté singulière; c'était un crayon estompé par le temps qui se faisait peinture, comme ces vieux croquis de maîtres admirés dans un musée, dont on retrouve ailleurs l'original éblouissant' (*NER*, I, 247).

By a closely related process, Proust's narrator considers that the pink hawthorns, seen in the present, are to the white, seen in the past, as a painting to a sketch, the memory of the past preparing and enhancing the enjoyment of the present (*RTP*, I, 139). By an identical process of analogy, Swann enjoys art and particularly Botticelli's *Zipporah* in the person of Odette; in a passage closely resembling the one from *Sylvie* just quoted above, Proust discovers to his great delight that the particular and the general are made available for Swann's enjoyment together as in an experience of involuntary memory: 'Peut-être . . . avait-il gardé suffisamment une nature d'artiste pour que ces caractéristiques individuelles lui causassent un plaisir en prenant une signification plus générale, dès qu'il les apercevait, déracinées, délivrées, dans la ressemblance d'un portrait plus ancien avec un original qu'il ne représentait pas' (*RTP*, I, 223).

While Nerval flinches at the prospect of an extension of metaphor to the sphere of human relationships: 'Aimer une religieuse sous la forme d'une actrice! . . . et si c'était la même! Il y a de quoi devenir fou! . . .', Proust, for his part, frequently pauses to comment on the mutual affinities which associate and unify any person's successive love-affairs (*RTP*, I, 832; III, 1015, 1020). In fact, by the process of 'entrecroisement' and 'superposition' which he instinctively favours, Proust extends such analogies between the successive love-affairs of any one individual to include also the relationships of other protagonists: '. . . si mon amour pour Albertine avait répété avec de grandes variations, l'amour de Swann pour Odette, l'amour de M. de Guermantes rappelait celui que j'avais eu pour Albertine' (*RTP*, III, 1015). Not only does Swann's love for Odette prefigure that of Marcel, his *alter ego*, for Gilberte, but both relationships contain in essence the narrator's love for Albertine. Here as elsewhere, however, Proust fulfils his aim to go beyond Nerval[8]: he discerns in the successive expressions of love an underlying unity and subjectivity of vision anticipating the irreducible individuality of art itself (ibid., III, 252 and 263).

Nerval's cult of analogy was fostered by his belief that the human soul migrates from the body of one person to that of another. Before his crisis of 1840–41, he accounted for resemblances by conjecturing the existence of a universal type, belonging to the world of essences and of which appearances alone give the impressions of individuals. One might here compare Proust's belief in a universal intelligence (cf., *RTP*, I, 568). However, Nerval's theory that souls go from one body to another in an eternal present, merges indistinguishably with his madness, and, as a result, forms become for him fluid to the point of the Protean. Fitfully one appearance melts into another and, in *Sylvie*, the heroine of that name, Adrienne and Aurélie become at times inextricably interfused. Nerval's narrator loves one in the form of another, and, in the process, demonstrates the most baffling psychological

52

complexity of which the *intermittences* are capable: 'l'histoire d'un cœur épris de deux amours simultanés' (*NER*, I, 269) – a Dostoievskian development. By virtue of the fact already mentioned – that love for Aurélie 'avait son germe dans le souvenir d'Adrienne' (*NER*, I, 246), now a nun – the past finds unexpected renewal and rich orchestration in the context of the present: 'Ermenonville!... tu as perdu ta seule étoile, qui chatoyait pour moi d'un double éclat. Tour à tour bleue et rose comme l'astre trompeur d'Aldébaran, c'était Adrienne ou Sylvie, – c'étaient les deux moitiés d'un seul amour. L'une était l'idéal sublime, l'autre la douce réalité' (*NER*, I, 272).

There seems to be a constant tension throughout Nerval's work between unity of personality, the lost and virtually irrecoverable ideal on the one hand, and diversity, flux and disloyalty to the past on the other.[9] Proust is haunted by his discovery that destruction is a necessary condition of creation and that love and friendship bear irrefutable traces of man's perpetual inconstancy: 'Certes, ces amitiés nouvelles pour des lieux et des gens ont pour trame l'oubli des anciennes '(*RTP*, I, 670–1).[10] Similarly torn between the rival claims of unity and diversity, Nerval's narrator compromises between past and present for he sets out deliberately to give to one love the setting previously associated with another. By this 'profanation de [ses] souvenirs' (*NER*, I, 360), he prefigures within love the kind of metamorphosis favoured by artistic creation: according to Proust, a series of models offer their 'instants de pose' (*RTP*, III, 900 and 905), in both contexts. 'Alors j'eus le malheur de raconter l'apparition de Châalis, restée dans mes souvenirs. Je menai Sylvie dans la salle même du château où j'avais entendu chanter Adrienne' (*NER*, I, 265); 'J'avais projeté de conduire Aurélie au château, près d'Orry, sur la même place verte où pour la première fois j'avais vu Adrienne' (ibid., 271).

In Proust's aesthetic and practice, art and love are closely allied. Nerval equally implies a deep analogy between the two spheres. It is often difficult to distinguish at what point the search by Nerval's narrator for an ideal in the transitory appearance of love passes over into an aesthetic, there to give rise to a certain hesitancy about form. Proust discerns, here, a failure of creative power, and proof that Nerval, like Baudelaire in this respect, falls short of the ideal of classicism: '. . . selon moi, il n'y [a] qu'une seule manière de peindre une chose . . .' (*CSB*, 638); whereas, of Nerval: 'on peut même dire . . . que ses vers et ses nouvelles ne sont (comme les *Petits Poèmes en prose* de Baudelaire et *Les Fleurs du Mal*, par exemple) que des tentatives différentes pour exprimer la même chose' (*CSB*, 234). Proust further attributes such uncertainty of expression to a lack of will-power, to an inability to 'créer sa forme d'art en même temps que sa pensée' (ibid., 234), to a tendency to hang unduly upon the intervention of the intellect (ibid., 240), and thereby destroy any initial unity. In Nerval, Proust cites as examples of *correspondances* the poet's variations on the theme of 'le pampre' and 'la rose': to 'la treille où le pampre à la rose s'allie,' he compares 'la fenêtre de Sylvie . . . où le pampre s'enlace aux rosiers' (ibid., 235). This literary detection already sets Proust well on the way to recognising Nerval's cult of the leitmotif [11]: 'Et d'ailleurs c'est ensuite à chaque maison dans *Sylvie* que nous voyons les roses s'unir aux vignes' (*CSB*, 235). The conflict between Proust's 'intellectualism' and his 'irrational transcendentalism'[12] remains, and when, as here, he stresses the fundamental unity of an artist's work, discerning the same imprint in all the successive forms of expression,[13] he once again aligns himself with the Symbolists as also in his practice of synaesthesia.

It seems inevitable that one so preoccupied with analogy as Nerval should himself cultivate the *correspondances*, which relate sensations to each other and reflect a spiritual unity. In the preamble to his *Voyage en Orient*, he recalls a passage in Rousseau's *Confessions* and meditates upon the delights afforded by combining sense-media, noting the desire of the Austrians, particularly of the Viennese, to satisfy several senses at once: 'Faut-il croire que plusieurs impressions réunies se détruisent ou fatiguent les sens? Mais ne serait-il pas vrai plutôt qu'il résulte de leur choix une sorte d'harmonie, précieuse aux esprits d'une activité étendue?' (*NER*, II, 44, n.2, 1280–1).

Professor Marie-Jeanne Durry claims[14] that the attraction of one sensation by another in Nerval's work is to be distinguished from the Symbolist *correspondances* proper, since there is, in the former case, dependence on the element of chance rather than any deep spiritual unity. I would agree that, in the following example and elsewhere in Nerval's work, there is an interplay of sensations rather than the transposition proper so consistently admired and exemplified by Proust himself. In the example cited by Professor Durry, Nerval records in highly evocative terms a moment of emotion, on the part of Balkis, in the presence of Soliman: 'Chargée du parfum des lis, des tubéreuses, des glycines et des mandragores, la brise nocturne chantait dans les rameaux touffus des myrtes; l'encens des fleurs avait pris une voix: le vent avait l'haleine embaumée . . .' (*NER*, II, 538).

The 'intermittences du cœur' must have been central amongst the laws which Proust detected in Nerval. The term implies a syncopation between emotions and the events which provoke them, and Proust uses the title to designate an entire section of *Sodome et Gomorrhe* (*RTP*, II, 751–81)[15] concerned with the narrator's delayed reaction to his grandmother's death. This particular section may well have stood in the same relation to the rest of the novel as the poem, 'La Grand'mère', to the aesthetic and achievement of Nerval. The essence of the Proustian narrator's preoccupation with the law of *intermittence* seems to stem from the incident of the grandmother's death and to distil from this event into the rest of *A la recherche du temps perdu*. Proust openly declares intermission to be one of the 'lois de l'âme' (*RTP*, I, 591), governing oblivion, 'cette grande force intermittente' (ibid., II, 756 and

III, 447); love and suffering (ibid., I, 585); jealousy, 'une maladie inter-mittente' (ibid., III, 29); personality (ibid., II, 1035) and moral failings, 'une maladie intermittente de l'esprit' (ibid., II, 1090).

Nerval's poem, 'La Grand'mère', is a perfect variation of its kind on the Proustian theme: 'Les mêmes heures ne sonnent pas pour tous'. In the four successive stanzas two syncopations are reflected. First, others lament the grandmother's death, while the poet experiences a blank and is reproached for lack of feeling:

> Moi seul, j'errais dans la maison, surpris
> Plus que chagrin . . .

Then the others forget and move into a phase of indifference at the very moment when the death, long since past, becomes to Nerval for the first time a present reality. The poet's second syncopation is the more dramatic and Proustian[16] for reflecting a poignant dependence on memory:

> Douleur bruyante est bien vite passée:
> Depuis trois ans, d'autres émotions,
> Des biens, des maux, – des révolutions, –
> Ont dans les cœurs sa mémoire effacée.

> Moi seul j'y songe et la pleure souvent;
> Depuis trois ans, par le temps prenant force,
> Ainsi qu'un nom gravé dans une écorce,
> Son souvenir se creuse plus avant!

$$(NER, I, 19)$$

The 'intermittences du cœur' and a desire to implement by art the creative urge latent within the act of memory[17], these characteristically Nervalian reactions, combined with a love of music, particularly of Wagner, would seem to lead naturally to a technique of leitmotif within literature itself. Nerval readily acknowledges his affinity of outlook with Wagner: 'Mes idées que je n'expose pas souvent, se rapportent assez à celles de Wagner'.[18] The technique of *rappels* whereby details, apparently unimportant on their first appearance, assume significance retrospectively, is an art perfected by Proust and it develops the process of involuntary memory in terms of structure. It is already present, in essence, in the short story which Proust admired most: *Sylvie*. One such detail, repeated as a leitmotif, is the theme of archery. First it appears in the notice which releases the crucial episode of involuntary memory at the opening of the story: 'Demain, les archers de Senlis doivent rendre le bouquet à ceux de Loisy' (*NER*, I, 244).

Immediately the narrator sees himself as a child taking his part in a ceremony which, unknown to the participants, dates back to the times of the Druids[19]: '. . . nous formions le cortège avec nos arcs et nos flèches, nous décorant du titre de chevaliers . . .' (*NER*, I, 244). Some years later at Loisy, he again sets out to join the archers; after the enactment of the 'voyage à

Cythère', another leitmotif intertwines with that of archery: a 'couronne', which he had placed on Adrienne's head on the previous occasion, had led to a quarrel and the cooling of his friendship with Sylvie; now, the release of a swan captive under a mass of flowers causes the scattering of garlands and 'couronnes' with which each young man decks the forehead of his companion. This act symbolises a quietus to the uneasy past: 'J'eus le bonheur de saisir une des plus belles, et Sylvie, souriante, se laissa embrasser cette fois plus tendrement que l'autre. Je compris que j'effaçais ainsi le souvenir d'un autre temps' (NER, I, 250). More subtly and enigmatically, the archery theme reappears by an unexpected process of analogy: Sylvie seems to the narrator to have grown in beauty and perhaps the reason is that he associates her with archery: 'sous l'orbite arquée de ses sourcils, son sourire ... avait quelque chose d'athénien ...' (NER, I, 250; cf., also ibid., I, 263).

In the maison du garde, the archery motif predominates and is part of what seems most authentic when the bemused narrator subsequently tries to distinguish between reality and the dream, and test the truth of the apparent visitation by Adrienne within the performance of an allegory. To add to the dream-like quality of details enlisted as proof of verisimilitude, several earlier and recurrent motifs, notably those of the swan and of a clock, reappear dramatically, 'souvenir obsédant' for reader and narrator alike (NER, I, 257). Sylvie's 'sourire athénien' and archery return to haunt the conclusion, and the latter motif is set in details of the utmost prosaic reality, in sharp and ironical contrast to the evocative promise of the words releasing the whole story by a movement of involuntary memory. Now, only nostalgia remains and the final blow falls in the sudden disclosure of Adrienne's death. The leitmotif has served its purpose: staircase, Athenian smile, archery – the latter with its deeper time-dimension – all return as though to mock the narrator whose quest of happiness and attempted re-discovery of the past remain unfulfilled: 'Tandis que ces petits s'exercent, au tir des compagnons de l'arc, à ficher dans la paille les flèches paternelles, nous lisons quelques poésies ou quelques pages de ces livres si courts qu'on ne fait plus guère' (NER, I, 273).

Nerval is justly reputed to be one of the greatest travellers in French literature and it is highly probable that Proust drew from a passage in Voyage en Orient the initial impetus to elaborate the theme of 'Noms de pays'. Unlike Robert de Vigneron, however, I would find it difficult to limit this source of conjectured inspiration to any specific passage in Nerval's account of his travels, so often does the writer seem to develop the Proustian theme of an inner climate created by the mere sound of proper names.[20] Nerval depends on renewed contact with places for revival of his past. Léon Cellier has observed that Châalis, Pontoise, Pontarmé etc. are virtual characters in Nerval's work. Promenades et Souvenirs is rooted in places and for Nerval, as for Proust, affective memory is often released by travel and movement.

56

Anticipating Proust, Nerval exploits the interdependence of time and space (cf., *NER*, I, 132). *Sylvie* is characterised by a constantly fluctuating series of time-levels, and Nerval mirrors this journey through time in terms of space; he enlists place-names to serve memory in the rôle of natural talismans – Châalis, Loisy etc. – before returning us to the authentic present only in the 'dernier feuillet': 'Ces enthousiasmes bizarres que j'avais ressentis depuis si longtemps, ces rêves, ces pleurs, ces désespoirs et ces tendresses . . . ce n'était donc pas l'amour? Mais où donc est-il?' (*NER*, I, 271). This final shifting of the time-element forms a kind of shock-tactics, for we had already thought ourselves in the authentic present of the author at least once in the narrative.[21] Proust himself makes good-humoured comment on the confusion of time-levels in *Sylvie*, shrewdly attributing to Nerval's modern version of a *Carte de Tendre*, to the blurring of distinctions between subjective and objective worlds, the cause of our bafflement as we read the story:

> Il arrive après une nuit d'insomnie, et ce qu'il voit alors, pour ainsi dire détaché de la réalité par cette nuit d'insomnie, par ce retour dans un pays qui est plutôt un passé qui existe au moins autant dans son cœur que sur la carte, est entremêlé si étroitement aux souvenirs qu'il continue à évoquer, qu'on est obligé de tourner les pages qui précèdent pour voir où on se trouve, si c'est présent ou rappel du passé.
>
> (*CSB*, 238)

The basic level or plane on which events are enacted in *Sylvie* is a relative present as in Chapter I – a kind of background or point of reference, in relation to which the other dimensions of time assume meaning and coherence. It dates back to 1852 or 1853, to a period when Gérard was exploring the Valois with the intention of writing his story. In the conclusion, Nerval equates this time-level with fantasy and proceeds to assert a new perspective and recession into the past: 'Telles sont les chimères qui charment et égarent au matin de la vie . . .' (*NER*, I, 271). Distinct from this relative present is the present historic, as within the actual narration of Chapter VII: 'Il est quatre heures du matin; la route plonge dans un pli de terrain: elle remonte . . .' (*NER*,I, 256).

The second level belongs to the writer's youth, 1835 or thereabouts, the time when he loved an actress (in the story, Aurélie). We then move back to the time when Gérard loved Adrienne, in earliest childhood. So is initiated this 'exploration du temps *à reculons*, par sondages successifs opérés de plate-forme en plate-forme. Le récit se présente à nous *en creux* et nous entraîne dans une série *d'emboîtements* qui font penser à des miroirs se reflétant les uns dans les autres. Là encore, il est difficile de ne point retrouver le roman de Proust où, comme l'écrit Georges Poulet, "à peine un mouvement initial est-il posé, que la pensée se met en marche mais en arrière" '.[22]

Proust freely admits the interdependence of time (or memory) and space when he makes his classic comment on the episode of involuntary memory with which *Sylvie* opens: 'Tout à coup ses yeux tombent sur une annonce: "Demain les archers de Loisy [sic] etc." Ces mots évoquent un souvenir ou plutôt deux amours d'enfance: aussitôt le lieu de la nouvelle est déplacé' (*CSB*, 599).

More arresting than the displacement in time and space is the manner in which Nerval ironises the lovers' failure to synchronise the expression of their feelings. He thus provides a masterly variation on the theme of *intermittences*. Sylvie asks Nerval's narrator: ' "Ah, que n'êtes-vous revenu alors!" ', implying that, had he chosen a particular moment, he would have succeeded in winning her.[23] Nerval is supremely skilful in his recalls of the past within the context of the present: there is the parallelism of the 'Voyage à Cythère' and 'Bal de Loisy'; 'le Village' and Ermenonville. Nerval seems to me to anticipate Proust by his vivid sense of the flow of time and the manner in which he underlines the subjectivitiy of love. In the outer scene, Nerval has to admit, 'Je ne retrouvais rien du passé' (*NER*, I, 263), anticipating Proust's insistence that love and art are primarily *cosa mentale*. Proust's narrator fails to rediscover the past in the external surroundings which served this purpose of evocation for Romantic poets. Combray revisited in no way corresponds to the reality which Marcel carries within his mind: 'J'étais désolé de voir combien peu je revivais mes années d'autrefois' (*RTP*, III, 692). Proust's attempt to account for the failure of all but the tangential to restore the essence of the past illuminates our understanding of Nerval's closely related experience in *Sylvie*: 'Mais, séparé des lieux qu'il m'arrivait de retraverser par toute une vie différente, il n'y avait pas entre eux et moi cette contiguïté d'où naît, avant même qu'on s'en soit aperçu, l'immédiate, délicieuse et totale déflagration du souvenir' (*RTP*, III, 692).

Proust draws very close to Nerval by his evocative handling of myth. He associates Oriane and the Guermantes with a race of birds and Swann with Jupiter, who was incarnated in a swan; further, he causes Swann to recall by his illness the myth of the fisher-king. In Nerval's line: 'Suis-je Amour ou Phébus, Lusignan ou Biron?', Lusignan, lover of Mélusine, corresponds to 'Amour'[24] and Proust may have found inspiration here for his own treatment of the myth: Saint-Loup, a member of the Lusignan, loves and marries Gilberte, the new Mélusine, already described as such quite early in the novel, on the score of her dual nature, reflecting now her father, Swann, now her mother, Odette (*RTP*, I, 565). Proust exploits, for its full measure of poetry, all the ambiguity of the myth and notably the image of a swan and Mélusine.[25]

There are moments when Nerval seems to illustrate a Proustian aphorism such as, 'L'homme est cet être sans âge fixe . . .'. Dramatically he juxtaposes youth and age in one person: Sylvie's aunt. The portrait depicts the latter as 'une jeune épouse', while the present moment, as though itself capable of contriving a masque, seems to offer to Sylvie and the narrator a wholly different person in the old aunt. Like Proust, Nerval switches from the remote past to the present and renews the cycle of repetitive pattern. To a greater extent than his successor, however, he elects to think of youth as miraculously surviving beneath the mask of age (*NER*, I, 254–5). Moreover, by attiring herself in the costume of another period, Sylvie becomes for Nerval 'la fée des légendes' and thus renews for him the paradox of eternal youth.[26]

Proust's own awareness of the *correspondances*, and especially of the symbolism of colour, may have been deepened by his reading of Nerval's *Sylvie* and *Aurélia*. Indeed, Proust seems to share Nerval's sense of a hidden, transcendent reality and to use terms strongly reminiscent of the well-known passage concerning the *correspondances* in the latter story (*NER*, I, 403), however vigorously he may protest that such impressions are distinct from all literary preoccupations: '. . . tout d'un coup un toit, un reflet de soleil sur une pierre, l'odeur d'un chemin me faisaient arrêter par un plaisir particulier qu'ils me donnaient, et aussi parce qu'ils avaient l'air de cacher, au delà de ce que je voyais, quelque chose qu'ils m'invitaient à venir prendre . . .' (*RTP*, I, 178–9) (cf., ibid., I, 179). While Nerval had written that 'des combinaisons de cailloux . . . des couleurs, des odeurs et des sons, [il voyait] ressortir des harmonies jusqu'alors inconnues' (*NER*, I, 403), Proust records the following as his reaction to the colours alone of *Sylvie*: 'La couleur juste de chaque chose vous émeut comme une harmonie, on a envie de pleurer de voir que les roses sont roses . . .' (*CSB*, 238).[27]

In common with the Symbolists, Proust conceives of colours as an ideal medium for expression of subjectivity. He notes that the predominant tone of *Sylvie* is 'couleur de rêve' and shades of 'pourpre'. According to his own distinctive *sonnet des voyelles*, the latter colour corresponds to the (*i*) of *Sylvie* as well as to the (*φ*) of 'Les Filles du Feu', and merges with 'une atmosphère bleuâtre'. Overtones of sexual violence and frustration possibly find expression in this colour. *Rouge* also universally implies not only violence but madness (cf., *CSB*, 239). One cannot help recalling Proust's own very subtle use of colour symbolism.[28] The harmonies which he finds in *Sylvie*, especially the 'couleur pourpre, d'une rose pourpre en velours pourpre ou violacé', these anticipate the fusion of shades which he associates with Odette, first introduced to us as 'la dame en rose.' When Odette later (*RTP*, I, 637) appears near the Arc de Triomphe as the incarnation of woman, her beauty enhanced by the rites of spring, symbolically – as on a corresponding appearance (ibid., I, 426) – her dress is dominated by mauve, now (perhaps to reflect her suppressed rôle of *cocotte*) a colour concentrated within 'quelque détail exquis . . . une satinette mauve habituellement cachée aux yeux de tous . . .' (*RTP*, I, 638) and discreetly evident in her sunshade 'comme . . . le reflet d'un berceau de glycines'.

After discerning in the law of 'intermittence' the vital key to an understanding of Nerval's work, and its major theme, as well as an element integral to his own novel, Proust extends the application of this principle to the manifestations of the spirit of poetry in the nineteenth century and throughout the ages. He sees as 'les quatre épreuves . . . d'un même visage' Baudelaire, Hugo, Vigny and Leconte de Lisle, and, for expression of a range of moods, he would no doubt list 'bien d'autres encore'. One can, however, understand why, in the great life-span of this universal poet, it is with a certain endearment that he attributes to Nerval 'les heures vagabondes et innocentes', glimpsing perhaps in this acknowledged precursor a vision of his own 'Moesta et Errabunda', just one image of the poet he might have been – and yet another aspect, never fully realised, of his own rich virtuality.

Notes

[1] L. Cellier: *Gérard de Nerval, l'homme et l'œuvre*, Hatier-Boivin Paris 1956, p. 225.

[2] Compare *Carnet* quoted *CSB* (*FALL*) p. 35.

[3] Compare *NER*, II, 389; similarly the place of Nerval's narrator is usurped by the 'frère de lait' in *Sylvie*.

[4] (Compare Ch. I, p. 19) See Letter to A. Lang (1921) *LR* p. 158. Cf., *RTP*, II, 84–92, for one of Proust's closest approaches to realisation of this ideal. Nerval practises the same kind of intervention most impressively in *Aurélia*.

[5] See note 4 above, *LR* p. 158.

[6] (See Ch. V, p. 87) Compare: 'La seule différence pour moi de la veille au sommeil était que, dans la première, tout se transfigurait à mes yeux . . . les combinaisons des couleurs se décomposaient, de manière à m'entretenir dans une série constante d'impressions . . . dont le rêve, plus dégagé des éléments extérieurs, continuait la probabilité' (*Aurélia NER*, I, 365.) Cf., also, *NER*, II, 131: so convincing is Nerval's impression and presentation of 'une seconde vie' and 'l'épanchement du songe dans la vie réelle' that Proust is baffled in his attempts to distinguish between reality and the dream in *Sylvie* (cf., *CSB*, 237–8); despairingly, he describes the work as 'le rêve d'un rêve' (ibid., 237).

[7] Both Proust and Nerval are fascinated by the way in which dreams reverse time-laws (*RTP*, III, 912; *NER*, I, 368, 392, 412). Dreams are to Nerval what involuntary memory is to Proust. Of dreams Nerval writes: 'Une vie nouvelle commence, affranchie des conditions du temps et de l'espace' (*NER*, I, 412); to involuntary memory Proust refers in comparable terms: 'Une minute affranchie de l'ordre du temps a recréé en nous, pour la sentir, l'homme affranchi de l'ordre du temps' (*RTP*, III, 873), and he clearly

states his reasons for preferring involuntary memory to dreams as a means of recapturing the past (*RTP*, II, 92).

[8] Proust actually wrote in one of his notebooks: 'Allons plus loin que Gérard'. See Cellier: loc. cit.

[9] Cf: 'Je suis persuadé que, si l'on ne changeait pas, les amours seraient éternelles; mais chacun se transforme de son côté: on n'a plus ni les habitudes ni l'humeur, ni la figure même d'un autre temps: comment donc conserverait-on les mêmes affections?' ('Paradoxe et Vérité', *NER*, I, 429). Similarly: 'Je ne demande pas à Dieu de rien changer aux événements, mais de me changer relativement aux choses; de me laisser le pouvoir de créer autour de moi un univers qui m'appartienne, de diriger mon rêve éternel au lieu de le subir. Alors, il est vrai, je serais Dieu.'

[10] Proust detects this principle in art (*RTP*, II, 327), in memory and love (ibid., I, 917), in grief (ibid., III, 476), in society and politics (ibid., III, 669), and Charlus parodies this favourite theory of the narrator and of Proust himself (*RTP*, III, 796 quoted Epilogue, p. 183). Nerval's thought and imagery are Proustian when he reflects, as follows, on the diehard nature of memories in face of destruction: 'C'est qu'il y a un âge, – âge critique, comme on le dit pour les femmes, – où les souvenirs renaissent si vivement, où certains dessins oubliés reparaissent sous la trame froissée de la vie!' ('Promenades et Souvenirs', *NER*, I, 130); cf., *NER*, I, 191, quoted as epigraph to this chapter.

[11] Possibly under the influence of Wagner, Nerval is fully alive to the advantages likely to accrue from the practice of 'une correspondance des arts'. He here anticipates Proust most strikingly as critic and exponent of the technique of leitmotif: 'De même qu'il est bon dans une symphonie même pastorale de faire revenir de temps en temps le motif principal, gracieux, tendre ou terrible, pour enfin le faire tonner au finale avec la tempête graduée de tous les instruments, je crois utile de vous parler encore de l'abbé de Bucquoy . . .' (*NER*, I, 220–1); See also the poem: 'Fantaisie', *NER*, I, 18, for exemplification of this technique.

[12] Cf., J. M. Cocking: *Proust*, Bowes & Bowes, London 1956, pp. 61–6.

[13] Cf., *RTP*, III, 377 ff.

[14] Marie-Jeanne Durry: *Gérard de Nerval et le mythe*, Flammarion, Paris 1956, pp. 15–21.

[15] The latter part of Ch. I, *Sodome et Gomorrhe*, Part II, corresponds to Ch. I, *Le Côté de Guermantes*, Part II: 'Maladie et Mort de ma grand'mère': and, at a further remove, to the account of Marcel's first stay at Balbec with his grandmother: *A l'ombre des jeunes filles en fleurs* Part II, opening section.

[16] A profound psychological truth discerned by Nerval and exploited by Proust, is that memory and emotion attach themselves to the apparently trivial and to the periphery of human experience. (See the letter to René Blum quoted Ch. I, p. 23.)

¹⁷ Cf., 'Rien de plus attrayant que de trouver encore sur le chemin une figure déjà rencontrée, un personnage empreint déjà dans les souvenirs; à sa vue, on recommence par imagination la course achevée ou suspendue . . .' *Le Cabaret de la Mère Saguet*, etc. ed. H. Bachelin, Fr. Bernouard, Paris 1927, p. 95.

¹⁸ Cf., above, note 11.

¹⁹ Nerval subscribes to a belief in a racial, primeval memory. Drugs, particularly hashish (*NER*, II, 362), may well have developed his susceptibility to such experiences: 'Des scènes qui se passaient avant l'apparition des hommes sur la terre me reviennent en mémoire . . .' (*Voyage en Orient*, *NER*, II, 363).

²⁰ Long before Proust, Nerval uses 'noms de pays' to inspire reverie; cf., *Voyage en Orient*, *NER*, II, 63; and 251–3.

²¹ Cf., 'En me retraçant ces détails, j'en suis à me demander s'ils sont réels ou bien si je les ai rêvés.' (*NER*, I, 257).

²² Raymond Jean: *Nerval par lui-même*, Editions du Seuil, Paris 1964, pp. 58-83 especially p. 65.

²³ Compare Marcel's failure to interpret correctly a gesture and so deduce at a crucial moment Gilberte's willingness to love him.

²⁴ Cf., Cellier: op. cit., p. 236

²⁵ Cf., Wallace Fowlie: 'The Esoteric in Proust: symbol and myth', *A Reading of Proust*, Anchor Books, Doubleday & Company Inc., New York 1964, section III, pp. 275–90. As W. Fowlie reminds us: 'When Gilberte marries Robert de Saint-Loup, she becomes heir to the title of duchesse de Guermantes. Mysteriously the cycle is completed, Oriane is the second Mélusine (but Mélusine was also used to describe the girl Gilberte . . .), and Oriane in her cruelty is the female swan who devours her prey . . . These are the two ways Swann's and Guermantes' and they are destined to merge, to fuse one with the other at the end of the cycle, with the appearance of Mlle de Saint-Loup, the daughter of a swan and of a Mélusine.' (op. cit., 280–1)

²⁶ Nerval readily ironises age; witness his narrator's comment on 'ce jeune premier tout ridé' (*NER*, I, 266 and 271).

²⁷ J. M. Cocking observes that Proust has a predilection for pink. (*Proust*, pp. 47–8) It has sensual overtones and recurs constantly in Nerval's *Sylvie*, often in contrast to the 'bleu mystique' associated with Adrienne (cf., *NER*, I, 272, quoted above).

²⁸ Fowlie: op. cit., pp. 94–5, also 280–1. Concerning the colour of Swann's and Oriane's eyes, W. Fowlie finds 'a possible mythological explanation'.

Notes for further reading

Proust pays Nerval the honour of recognising him as his precursor and worthy, in this capacity, to rank beside Chateaubriand and Baudelaire (*RTP*,

III, 919). Proust writes his own commentary on his affinities with Nerval in the following essays and correspondence: 'A propos du "style" de Flaubert' (*CSB*, 599–600); 'Gérard de Nerval' (ibid., 233–42); *CG*, III, 212; IV, 54, 79 (Proust compliments Jean-Louis Vaudoyer on his pastiche of Nerval), 80, 238; *Cahiers Marcel Proust I*, Gallimard, Paris 1927, p. 86.

Proust's appreciation of Nerval, rather than a *rapprochement* between the two writers, preoccupies critics such as W. A. Strauss. *Proust and Literature: the Novelist as Critic*, Harvard University Press 1957, pp 125–8; René de Chantal: *Marcel Proust, Critique littéraire*, University of Montreal 1967, pp. 501–10, *et passim*.

The critics cited next, however, come closer to a literary confrontation proper – Albert Béguin: *L'Ame romantique et le rêve*, Corti 1939, ch XVIII, pp. 358–66 (see especially pp. 356–7); Bernard de Fallois: 'Préface' to *Contre Sainte-Beuve*, Gallimard, Paris 1954, pp. 35–6; Léon Cellier: *Gérard de Nerval: l'homme et l'œuvre*, Hatier-Boivin, Paris 1956, pp. 220 ff. Most interestingly this critic speculates whether Nerval underwent the influence of Novalis and suggests that Heine might have acted as intermediary (p. 174). Parts of *Aurélia*, such as Chapters V, VI, and VIII, bear a strong resemblance to *Heinrich von Ofterdingen*, and others, for instance *Les Mémorables* – undoubtedly influenced by Swedenborg's *Memorabilia* – to Novalis's *Hymnen an die Nacht*.

For Novalis's possible influence on Proust, see Chapter V, pp. 85 ff. of the present work; Raymond Jean: *Nerval par lui-même*, Edition du Seuil 1964, pp. 58–83; *French Studies*, July 1966, pp 253–66, where N. Bailey analyses and compares Nerval's symbolism of colours with Proust's: 'Symbolisme et Composition dans l'œuvre de Proust: essai de "lecture colorée" de *La Recherche du temps perdu*'. See detailed reference to Nerval, ibid., pp. 263–4; also in this connection, L. Cellier: *G. de Nerval, l'homme et l'œuvre*, p. 192. In the present chapter, I attempt to take further some of the *rapprochements* between Proust and Nerval outlined in my book: *Proust's Challenge to Time* M.U.P. 1962, pp. 47, 73, 81 and 117, note 1.

Chapter IV

Baudelaire

A quiconque a perdu ce qui ne se retrouve
Jamais, jamais! ...

('Le Cygne', *BAU*, 83)

... cet air plus pur que les poètes ont vainement essayé de faire
régner dans le Paradis et qui ne pourrait donner cette sensation
profonde de renouvellement que s'il avait été respiré déjà, car les
vrais paradis sont les paradis qu'on a perdus.

(*RTP*, III, 870)

Perhaps it is primarily because Baudelaire may well seem to surpass Chateau-briand and Nerval in the extent to which he finds in involuntary memory a source of metaphysical experience, that Proust senses a closer bond with him than with his other two acknowledged precursors (*RTP*, III, 920). While Proust rates Baudelaire superior to Racine as instructor in the laws of memory, he accounts him inferior to Chateaubriand and Nerval as actual exponent (*CSB*, 641). At a more intimate autobiographical level, he insists on discovering in Baudelaire a fellow homosexual; moreover, each of the two writers has for his mother a love verging on the pathological[1]. Whatever the validity of Proust's assertion that Baudelaire shared an affinity with him in sexual matters, there is no shortage of close resemblances between the two artists in other respects: both are natives and poets of Paris; ailing and 'sédentaire' but correspondingly mobile in thought; consumed by a desire to enjoy the infinite range of imagination while preserving their virtuality intact

65

(BAU, 266). Both are outstanding in their capacity to fashion from sensations recollected or anticipated the warm glow of an inner mental climate, their own Baedeker[2] of 'noms de pays'.

At the deeper level of aesthetics, Proust is immensely reassured to find in the Symbolist, particularly in the Baudelairean practice of transposition, 'la sensation transposée' (RTP, III, 920), a reflection of his own natural capacity to think, feel and finally create by a process of metaphor which here extends memory and prefigures art (RTP, III, 889–90). Most important, both men see art as a complex interpenetration of two adjacent worlds: 'une magie suggestive contenant à la fois l'objet et le sujet, le monde extérieur à l'artiste et l'artiste lui-même' (BAU, 1099), a fusion of landscape or climate and mood, of present and past sensations (RTP, III, 889). In order to reverse the laws of time, both artists have recourse to the power to dream as a function of inner life which feeds memory by increasing the network of communications between past and present, between 'ces sensations et ces souvenirs qui nous entourent simultanément' (RTP, III, 889).[3] Both cherish closely related ideals of art and are ultimately united in favouring the transposition of the external world within the artist's mind (BAU, 254), whatever their fluctuations between irrational transcendentalism and intellectualism in the interval. Finally and perhaps most significantly, there is evident in both authors a power of critical analysis not only intimately associated with the act of artistic creation but actively applied to the themes of evil and suffering. If Baudelaire ranked, in Proust's estimation, with Vigny, as 'le plus grand poète du dix-neuvième siècle', it was probably because Proust so greatly admired his understanding of evil, his 'lucidité dans la souffrance véritable' (CSB, 621), as well as his paradoxical reconciliation not only of sensibility and cruelty but also of 'deux postulations simultanées, l'une vers Dieu, l'autre vers Satan', as illustrated by his 'accents religieux dans les pièces sataniques' (ibid., 621; cf., 618 and 628).

> Cette 'liaison' entre Sodome et Gomorrhe ... il semble que Baudelaire s'y soit de lui-même 'affecté' d'une façon toute privilégiée.
>
> (CSB, 633)

Chief amongst the affinities which exist between the two men in the context of their private lives, but inevitably bound to condition their attitudes as artists, is sexual inversion. Foremost among critics, André Maurois[4] and Lester Mansfield[5] have drawn attention to the possibility that Proust may have found his point of departure for vindicating a portrayal of inversion in Baudelaire's lines which already seem to suggest the theme and title of 'Les jeunes filles en fleurs':

66

Car Lesbos entre tous m'a choisi sur la terre
Pour chanter le secret de ses vierges en fleurs . . .

(BAU, 135)

Further, Proust may well have derived from Baudelaire the initial inspiration to treat an aspect of uranism apparently excluded by Vigny (*CSB*, 632–3), and merely intimated by Baudelaire in the first of the two lines, 'Car Lesbos entre tous m'a choisi sur la terre,' namely the ' "liaison" entre Sodome et Gomorrhe'. Proust's reaction to Saint-Simon's failure to enlighten the reader about 'l'esprit des Mortemart' was to invent 'l'esprit des Guermantes' (*CG*, III,95). By a corresponding wager, he attempts to elucidate in the conduct of 'une brute', Charles Morel, towards Léa and Albertine (*RTP*, III, 214–16, 598–600), as also, on a different level, in that of Odette and Saint-Loup, a liaison which Baudelaire had been content to leave enigmatic in the line quoted:

> Ce rôle, combien il eût été intéressant de savoir pourquoi Baudelaire l'avait choisi, comment il l'avait rempli. Ce qui est compréhensible chez Charles Morel, reste profondément mystérieux chez l'auteur des *Fleurs du Mal*.

(CSB, 633)

W. A. Strauss claims that this passage '. . . warrants the conclusion that certain portions of *RTP*, especially *Sodome et Gomorrhe*, are Baudelairean rather than Balzacian'.[6] George Painter, in turn, claims that Proust 'refrained from announcing to the public the mistaken yet revealing explanation which he gave a few weeks later to Gide, that Baudelaire was himself a practising homosexual. But . . . Proust perhaps inserted at this time and under the influence of these ideas (found in Baudelaire), the relations between male and female inverts . . .'.[7] G. Painter adds that these are certainly late additions, 'for Morel, who elsewhere appears in Proust's manuscript under his earlier name Santois, is here called Morel'.[8] However, I still consider it highly probable that Proust drew upon both Baudelaire and Balzac for inspiration of the homosexual parts of his novel but primarily upon the former for elaboration of the ' "liaison" entre Sodome et Gomorrhe' (See Ch. VI, pp. 102 ff. of the present work).

Gide relates in his *Journal* the conversation which he had with Proust about inversion as a subject for art.[9] In the course of the discussion, Proust expressed to Gide 'la conviction où il est que Baudelaire était uraniste', adding as justification for a thesis which his friend accepted only under protest: 'la manière dont il parle de Lesbos, et déjà le besoin d'en parler, suffiraient seuls à m'en convaincre'.[10] G. Painter (p. 324 fn. 1) has the following illuminating comment to make on Proust's position in the matter: 'In fact, few poets have been as exclusively heterosexual in both life and work as Baudelaire, whose obsession with Lesbianism was caused objectively by the homosexual infidelity of Jeanne Duval and other mistresses, and subjectively by its significance as one of the flowers of evil'.[11] It is interesting that Proust attributes to Marie Dorval's 'amitié pour certaines femmes' the jealousy which Vigny attempts to treat objectively in 'La Colère de Samson': 'La femme aura Gomorrhe et l'homme aura Sodome' (*CSB*, 620). According to these interpretations, Baudelaire's and, at a remove, Vigny's personal and literary attitudes towards sexual perversion would seem to foreshadow with astonishing vividness those of Proust's narrator.

It is highly improbable that, in the treatment of this theme, Baudelaire's fondness for transposition would ever have led the poet to the same lengths as Proust's 'faculté de transposer' did the novelist. In a remarkably frank confrontation with Gide, Proust deplored his own indecision which 'l'a fait, pour nourrir la partie hétérosexuelle de son livre, transposer "à l'ombre des jeunes filles" tout ce que ses souvenirs homosexuels lui proposaient de gracieux, de tendre et de charmant, de sorte qu'il ne lui reste plus pour *Sodome* que du grotesque et de l'abject'[12] (Gide: *Journal* p. 694). In Proust's personal case and possibly in Baudelaire's also (*BAU*, 472) – although we can only speculate about the latter's position in this respect – love, in so far as it was a response to beauty, aesthetic or physical, seems to have diverged from desire, at least if we are to rely on Gide's testimony.[13] Certainly it is true of the narrator's *alter ego*, Swann, that his desire and aesthetic preferences are at variance (*RTP*, I, 224).

Proust reacted vigorously to Gide's reproach that 'il semble avoir voulu stigmatiser l'uranisme' and the older man was forced to the conclusion that, in Proust's case, 'ce que nous trouvons ignoble, objet de rire ou de dégoût, ne lui paraît pas, à lui, si repoussant'.[14] Proust's narrator probably reflects his creator's opinion that 'ce qui l'attire, ce n'est presque jamais la beauté' and that beauty as such 'n'a que peu à voir avec le désir'.[15] Proust vividly exemplifies this viewpoint in his portrayal of inversion in particular, and the narrator implies an interesting possible reason for the power of attraction exerted by ugliness in the Proustian and perhaps in the Baudelairean world (*BAU*, 472), when he switches into reverse the famous Stendhalian *maxime* and, in the process, strikingly renews the theory of crystallisation:

> On a dit que la beaute est une promesse de bonheur. Inversement la possibilité du plaisir peut être un commencement de beauté.
>
> (*RTP*, III, 140; cf. *RTP*, III, 191)

> ' "... un Baudelaire, mieux encore un Dostoïevski ... en trente ans, entre leurs crises d'épilepsie et autres, créent tout ce dont une lignée de mille artistes seulement bien portants n'auraient pu faire un alinéa." '
>
> (*CSB*, 622)

A further important feature which forms a biographical affinity and which has strong repercussions on both artists' work is the condition of *malade*. Proust explicitly associates himself with Baudelaire in making of illness, especially 'la nervosité', a prime element of genius, and in setting 'une secousse nerveuse' at the origin of the creative urge (*BAU*, 1159). If Valéry saw the artist as dramatically curtailing the course of nature by his 'actes éclairés', how much more vividly did Proust conceive of 'quelque malade' as creative in inverse proportion to a drastically reduced expectation of life (*CSB*, 622). It is characteristically on a note of parody that Proust expresses through Docteur du Boulbon his own views on the importance of illness as a part of genius (*RTP*, II, 305).

Baudelaire sees the artist as someone 'qui serait toujours, spirituellement, à l'état du convalescent' (*BAU*, 1158), and 'la convalescence' as subtly related to 'un retour vers l'enfance' (ibid., 1159); Proust, for his part, discerns in illness an inducement to spirituality (*JS*, 6–7) and to an indefinite protraction of desire (*CG*, V, 142), the latter constantly rekindled by memory (ibid., 142) and *vice versa* (*RTP*, III, 27). Illness and consequent confinement within a room confirm Proust in his natural tendency to transpose sensations and, in general, to experience life obliquely.

Baudelaire comes very close to explaining Proust when he states that the proximity of death, the supreme loss, revives the curiosity vital to an artist's vision and gives a heightened sense of existence, for Berenson the criterion of art:

> Revenu récemment des ombres de la mort, il aspire avec délices tous les germes et tous les effluves de la vie; comme il a été sur le point de tout oublier, il se souvient et veut avec ardeur se souvenir de tout. Finalement, il se précipite à travers cette foule à la recherche d'un inconnu dont la physionomie entrevue l'a, en un clin d'œil, fasciné. La curiosité est devenue une passion fatale, irrésistible.
>
> (*BAU*, 1158)

Baudelaire here crystallises the essence of Proust's attitude towards loss: '. . . comme il a été sur le point de tout oublier, il se souvient et veut avec ardeur se souvenir de tout', as well as the Proustian love of 'un être de fuite': '. . . il se précipite . . . à la recherche d'un inconnu dont la physionomie . . . l'a . . . fasciné'. Baudelaire's poem entitled, 'A une passante' – a key line of which is cited by Proust (*CSB*, 258) – brilliantly exemplifies both his own and Proust's conception of the elusive as forming an integral part of beauty: 'une promesse de bonheur' (*RTP*, III, 140). Proust's masterly comment on the human capacity for oblique enjoyment supplements and reinforces Baudelaire's reflections on the subject: 'Tout être aimé, même, dans une certaine mesure, tout être est pour nous comme Janus, nous présentant le front qui nous plaît si cet être nous quitte, le front morne si nous le savons à notre perpétuelle disposition' (*RTP*, III, 181; cf., ibid., III, 458 and 460).

69

Professor Mansell Jones considers that, particularly in 'Le Cygne', Baudelaire conveys by 'incantatory skill' and 'symbols' 'a sense of loss similar to that felt to be suggested by parts of Proust's work' and adds in relation to the title, *A la recherche du temps perdu*:

> *Perdu* suggests the irrevocable, the irretrievable, what is beyond redemption, at least by conscious or voluntary effort. There is some hint of exile from Eden that links Proust's work to Baudelaire's.[16]

This strong sense of loss, of 'ce qui ne se retrouve jamais', accounts for the nostalgia which characterises both writers' work. In Baudelaire, it is deepened by a powerful belief in Original Sin. Constantly the poet expresses his regret for lost innocence, his remorse for past actions deemed irrevocable. The return of the past ('Le Balcon'; 'L'Irréversible'), the recovery of the lost innocence and happiness of childhood ('Moesta et Errabunda') become desirable in direct proportion to the impossibility of their realisation. Baudelaire equals Proust in his power to render the poignancy of this sense of exile from a realm 'interdit à nos sondes'. Some would say that he surpasses Proust in so far as his sense of remorse must exceed regret in intensity. For both, however, the impossibility of the quest is in itself sufficient to command the infinity of desire, the Proustian no less than the Baudelairean 'goût de l'Infini'. Consistently Proust will use the imagery of man's fall from grace but he skilfully transposes the terms to apply to the metaphysical experiences afforded by memory: '. . . les vrais paradis sont les paradis qu'on a perdus' (*RTP*, III, 870); and by art, as when, after hearing the Septet, Marcel declares: 'J'étais vraiment comme un ange qui, déchu des ivresses du Paradis, tombe dans la plus insignifiante réalité . . . je me demandais si la Musique n'était pas l'exemple unique de ce qu'aurait pu être – s'il n'y avait pas eu l'invention du langage, la formation des mots, l'analyse des idées – la communication des âmes' (*RTP*, III, 258).

While Proust regards illness as fundamental to the emergence and character of Baudelaire's genius Baudelaire seems to have anticipated him by declaring that the essence of an artist's originality is latent in his childhood. Significantly it is from an analysis of the rôle of opium in heightening De Quincey's natural propensity to reverie that Baudelaire deduces the power of childhood to contain and determine the man and the quality of his genius. In his commentary on De Quincey's childhood, Baudelaire sketches his theory of 'Le Génie Enfant', to be elaborated in 'Le Peintre de la vie moderne' (*BAU*, 1159), and anticipates Proust's determinism:

> Enfin . . . ne serait-il pas facile de prouver, par une comparaison philosophique entre les ouvrages d'un artiste mûr et l'état de son âme quand il était enfant, que le génie n'est que l'enfance nettement formulée, douée maintenant, pour s'exprimer, d'organes virils et puissants?
>
> (*BAU*, 443)

Baudelaire foreshadows Proust again vividly when he makes several original observations on the importance of the palimpsest in De Quincey's theory of memory. Not only does Baudelaire anticipate Proust by affirming the indestructibility of 'notre incommensurable mémoire' (*BAU*, 451–2), and by calling to witness in this connection the flood of recollections which characterise many persons' dying moments: 'Dans le spirituel non plus que dans le matériel, rien ne se perd' (ibid., 452); he also hints, in imagery which is Proustian *avant la lettre*, at the rôle of oblivion in preserving our memories:

> ... dans la mort peut-être, et généralement dans les excitations intenses créées par l'opium, tout l'immense et compliqué palimpseste de la mémoire se déroule d'un seul coup, avec toutes ses couches superposées de sentiments défunts, mystérieusement embaumés dans ce que nous appelons l'oubli.
>
> (ibid.)

> *Tant de fois, au cours de ma vie, la réalité m'avait déçu parce qu'au moment où je la percevais, mon imagination, qui était mon seul organe pour jouir de la beauté, ne pouvait s'appliquer à elle, en vertu de la loi inévitable qui veut qu'on ne puisse imaginer que ce qui est absent.*
>
> (*RTP*, III, 872)

The question inevitably arises: how far, in theory and in practice, does Proust assign to memory the creative rôle which Baudelaire, in common with most artists, reserves for the imagination?[17] Baudelaire is as quick to recognise the vital connection between memory and art as to discern how closely the former approximates to imagination in the act of artistic creation. In Baudelaire's own terms, does not memory subject the material of experience to 'une idéalisation forcée'? Is not the absence of the 'original' – whether this be an actual experience or, for the artist, a particular model – a prime requisite for the exercise of memory or imagination in life and art?

While Baudelaire subordinates memory to the imagination and unhesitatingly accords first place to this 'reine des facultés', Proust's ultimate position in this matter is much more difficult to determine; he joins Pascal in his awareness of the tyranny exercised by 'cette partie dominante de l'homme' and of its rôle as the accomplice of subjectivity. After noting in *Baudelaire the Critic* that the essential difference between the Baudelairean and the Proustian rôle of memory is that, for Proust, 'the recall is and must be accidental; for Baudelaire it can be provoked',[18] Margaret Gilman declares that, 'when it comes to the rôle of memory in the work of art, the difference is more one of emphasis than anything else'. Both Baudelaire and Proust conceive of the artist as 'déchiffreur' of impressions (*RTP*, III, 890 and *BAU*, 705). However, as Margaret Gilman adds: '. . . Baudelaire's conception is much freer as the passage on Guys shows, *BAU*, 1156 ff.'.[19] Both reflect a conflict between the theory, on one hand, that the artist translates a purely external reality, on the other hand, that he expresses an irreducibly individual vision of an inner world. Proust here perpetuates a paradox which Professor Cocking detects in Hegel and Ruskin[20] and which I have found in Novalis also (see Ch. V, pp. 88–9 of the present work). Baudelaire strikes a Proustian note when he claims that 'Toute notre originalité vient de l'estampille que le temps imprime à nos sensations'.

Margaret Gilman raises the important question whether 'for Proust, the involuntary memory has the predominant rôle that the creative imagination has for Baudelaire'.[21] Benjamin Crémieux seems to answer in the affirmative when he declares that, in Proust, memory is 'la faculté maîtresse' to which all the other faculties are in subjection[22] and particularly when he adds: 'L'acte créateur chez Proust n'est jamais (comme chez les imaginatifs) celui de projeter . . . et de pousser son "idée" comme un cerceau . . . mais c'est celui de retenir, d'entasser, d'enchaîner ce qui voudrait fuir, de rappeler ce qui est resté en arrière, de le haler, de l'extraire, de le fixer hors du temps. Il est tout entier tendu à revivifier, reformer ce qui fut et non pas à vivifier l'informe'. Proust's desire to 'revivifier . . . ce qui fut' rather than to 'vivifier l'informe' is reflected in the narrator's continuing amazement that succession and destruction contain the very principle of creation (cf., Epilogue, p. 191). Memory, defined as the power to re-create the past, will necessarily be judged by its degree of fidelity to the original: imagination, defined as the power to *create*, to 'faire quelque chose de rien', will be measured by the extent to which it enables the artist to transcend any point of departure in reality and 'body forth the forms of things unknown'. While Baudelaire gives priority to imagination in theory, it seems to me that, in practice, his creative memory and corresponding preoccupation with the past are still very much in evidence; Proust, for his part, is divided between the claims made by his strong, at times almost Gidean sense of virtuality, on one hand, and the pull of his creative memory on the other.

Margaret Gilman poses the crucial question, when, after recognising the scope afforded by Baudelaire to the creative imagination in combining and fusing the impressions invoked by memory, she declares: 'What is hard to discover with Proust, I think, is how far he succeeded, in theory and in practice, in dethroning the imagination and in setting up memory in her place'.[23] I agree with this view. It does indeed seem that Proust uses the 'imagination' almost exclusively for 'the faculty of conceiving future experience' – and I quote the instances cited by Margaret Gilman in this connection: *RTP*, I, 115 and 117; 129 and 156; or for the 'reproductive imagination that is practically equivalent to memory': eg., *RTP*, III, 872. I join Margaret Gilman in believing that, to a very considerable degree, Proust's 'memory performs functions that we are accustomed to associate only with the creative imagination'. In my opinion, the action of the 'creative memory' is definitely implied, *RTP*, III, 900–911 and especially *RTP*, III, 908. It is significant how closely Proust associates the two faculties (*RTP*, III, 252).

However, it is important to note that Proust gives us a deep insight into his creative processes when he implies a faculty which seems to approximate to the creative memory but only intermittently, and which ultimately transcends the latter by its sheer power to set man free from the mesh of the past and the particular for experience of virtuality and the general. In Proust's work, the supreme faculty is, in the last resort, not so much memory, basic to the author's experience though this power may be, but imagination understood as a creative force, galvanised into action by suffering, and enabling man to see (and the artist to express) himself as a microcosm of humanity, 'un infini en puissance'.

For Proust, Baudelaire's act of memory is static and allows both the half-remembered, half-imagined world and present reality to exist simultaneously. We are here reminded of Flaubert's 'perception double et simultanée' (*NV*, 288) (see Ch IX, pp. 168 ff. of the present work). Proust possibly indulged in this same technique, once he had made the initial discovery that one experience contains another. The dynamism which sets apart the involuntary memory of his other acknowledged precursors, Chateaubriand and Nerval, must have seemed equally to Proust to distinguish his own act of remembering from what the narrator styles as the Baudelairean 'réminiscences moins fortuites et donc à [son] avis décisives':

> Chez Baudelaire, la réminiscence est à l'état statique, elle existe déjà quand la pièce commence (*Quand les deux yeux fermés* etc. Ô *toison moutonnant*, etc., etc.)
> (*CSB*, 641)

The dynamism which is absent from Baudelaire's act of remembering by most critics' standards and not by Proust's alone, is unmistakably in evidence, according to his successor, both in the 'force extraordinaire, inouïe du verbe' in such a poem as 'Les Petites Vieilles' as well as in the *Pièces condamnées* – for instance in 'Le Rebelle' (*CSB*, 252–3 and 608) – and in his extraordinary sense of renewal, the rebirth of artistic inspiration and impetus reflecting the resurgence of desire in the poems of physical love (*CSB*, 624–5).

It might be claimed that one of the reasons why Baudelaire's act of remembering is static derives from his character and possibly from his use of drugs. The Baudelairean tension between will-power and indolence seems to be resolved in this deliberate search for analogies which, once released, will slowly but surely and without the poet's intervention, restore to him the past and ensure his effortless displacement in time and space; in fact, his penetra-

73

tion of another dimension: 'Tout un monde lointain, absent, presque défunt' contained within the 'vase' of present sensation.

> *Et dans cet univers, un autre plus interne encore, contenu dans les parfums . . .*

(*CSB*, 258)

It is precisely when he is commenting on the richly interlarded nature of human experience, on the multiplicity of peripheral elements which compose its essence, that Proust writes one of his most Baudelairean statements, equivalent to one of Baudelaire's ' "Voix" qui promettent des mondes . . .' (*CSB*, 257): 'Une heure n'est pas qu'une heure, c'est un vase rempli de parfums, de sons, de projets et de climats' (*RTP*, III, 889). Proust inevitably resembles and recalls Baudelaire whenever he touches upon the mystery of evocation, the power of the peripheral to arouse desire by its presence. Baudelaire and Proust play countless variations on the theme which the later writer sums up as follows: 'L'amour d'un être est toujours l'amour d'autre chose'; one could justifiably add: 'et l'amour d'un objet . . .'. Fernand Gregh once described to me Proust's powers of perception as 'polygonal' (cf., Ch. IX, p. 173 of the present work); the term has geometrical overtones but it was intended to convey the insect-like capacity for absorption which Proust could deploy upon any range of sense-stimuli, an ability to register and convey the marginal with as much accuracy as the focal.

Moreover, Proust is so richly endowed with powers of oblique perception, with the capacity to experience one sense-medium in the form of another and generally to associate the senses that, in the transposition of sensation, he becomes Baudelaire's natural successor. Professor S. Ullmann has analysed at length this question of 'transposition of sensations in Proust's imagery'.[24] For both authors, scent and taste are of prime importance in the process of involuntary memory but, as Professor Ullmann states, 'are themselves rarely transcribed in synaesthetic terms'.[25] According to Proust, taste and smell carry 'sur leur gouttelette presque impalpable, l'édifice immense du souvenir' (*RTP*, I, 47). Professor Ullmann quotes (p. 205) the description of Mme Octave's room at Combray, where odours are transcribed mainly in terms of taste.[26] Baudelaire, mostly without elaboration, will powerfully suggest one sense-medium in terms of another: '. . . je hume à longs traits le vin du souvenir' ('La Chevelure' *et passim*). There is a rare if not unique transposition from hearing to scent in the line where one of 'les petites vieilles', catching the strains of a military band,

> . . . droite encor, fière et sentant la règle,
> Humait avidement ce chant vif et guerrier . . .

In the first of the two examples just quoted, the transition by way of the senses to the spiritual, or at least the abstract: 'le vin du souvenir', is typically Baudelairean. Similarly in 'Le Flacon', the sense of smell enables the poet to make contact with the spiritual in the form of memory as if by magic: '. . . D'où jaillit toute vive une âme qui revient'. Baudelaire exploits the spiritual associations of rarefied exotic scents such as that of musk which has become the 'vase' of his love and 'mysticité':

> Grain de musc qui gis, invisible,
> Au fond de mon éternité!

('Hymne', Epaves X, BAU, 146)

The constant interchange, in Baudelaire's poetry, between the sensuous and the spiritual, the one dimension enhancing the effect of the other, results in a distinctive variation on 'Matière et Mémoire' and often powerfully anticipates Proust. In 'La Chevelure' the reader is constantly moving from the one level to the other: '. . . O *parfum* chargé de *nonchaloir*'. 'Infinis bercements du *loisir embaumé* (cf., the 'sentiments défunts, mystérieusement embaumés dans ce que nous appelons l'oubli', *BAU*, 452). This technique, a bold extension of the metaphor, gives rise to a fascinating interplay of overtones and the poet succeeds in enhancing the finite by the suggestion of the infinite and *vice versa*. Proust uses a method strikingly similar when the narrator explains how peripheral associations of climate and atmosphere come to form for each individual an integral part, perhaps even the essence of personalities encountered at any particular time: so the early Swann, his wider social dimension unrecognised, becomes the 'vase' of the after-dinner atmosphere with which he is forever associated in Marcel's and his parents' minds:

> . . . ils (mes parents) avaient pu entasser dans ce visage désaffecté de son prestige, vacant et spacieux, au fond de ces yeux dépréciés, le vague et doux résidu – mi-mémoire, mi-oubli – des heures oisives passées ensemble après nos dîners hebdomadaires, autour de la table de jeu ou au jardin, durant notre vie de bon voisinage campagnard. L'enveloppe corporelle de notre ami en avait été si bien bourrée . . . que j'ai l'impression de quitter une personne pour aller vers une autre qui en est distincte quand, dans ma mémoire, du Swann que j'ai connu plus tard avec exactitude, je passe à ce premier Swann . . . à ce premier Swann rempli de loisir, parfumé par l'odeur du grand marronnier, des paniers de framboises et d'un brin d'estragon.

(RTP, I, 19–20)

Proust often seems to carry further Baudelaire's technique of associating, as in the Paris tone-pictures ('Crépuscule du soir' etc.), 'un cadre d'horizon' with 'un état d'âme'. On his arrival at Doncières, the sight of a hill, 'emmitouflée encore dans sa douce et blanche robe matinale de brouillard', becomes associated for Marcel with the taste of a cup of hot chocolate drunk on this occasion (*RTP*, II, 81). In a subsequent development of this episode (*RTP*, II, 346), as also in connection with 'le Côté de Guermantes', Proust even more interestingly associates intellectual discoveries with certain landscapes.

*... Mes rêves de voyage et d'amour n'étaient que des moments –
que je sépare artificiellement aujourd'hui comme si je pratiquais
des sections à des hauteurs différentes d'un jet d'eau irisé et en
apparence immobile – dans un même et infléchissable jaillissement de toutes les forces de ma vie.*

(*RTP*, I, 87)

Baudelaire rings one of his most rewarding changes on the theme of the
interchangeability of landscape and state of mind when he establishes a
Swedenborgian *correspondance* between woman and her climate or setting.
He demonstrates his power to evoke and enjoy the one in terms of the other.
While brilliantly anticipating Proust, this particular form of analogy affords
parallels with the technique exemplified by Balzac and Fromentin and it is
possible that Baudelaire was influenced by the former in this respect.
Baudelaire fuses woman and setting to the extent that the one becomes the
complete metaphor of the other:

Les soleils mouillés
De ces ciels brouillés
Pour mon esprit ont les charmes
Si mystérieux
De tes traîtres yeux,
Brillant à travers leurs larmes.

('L'Invitation au voyage' LIII, *BAU*, 51)

Proust's fusion of the setting with the woman for whom his fancy is newly
awakening seems to take its origin in a Romantic impulse: in a cult of all that
is associated with one loved from a distance in the sweeping plains of La
Beauce, '... je sentais que ce souffle venait en droite ligne de l'endroit où elle
m'attendait, qu'il avait passé sur son visage avant de venir à moi ...' (*CSB*
(FALL) pp. 83–4). Both Baudelaire and Proust closely associate love and
travel (*RTP*, I, 185; III, 171 and 143). 'L'Invitation au voyage' is equally
'L'Invitation à l'amour', and similarly in Proust's experience the desire for
the woman and her surroundings is at first indivisible (*RTP*, I, 87).

While Baudelaire concentrates his curiosity primarily on the setting as the
analogy in which his mistress is framed (*BAU*, 254–5), the nearest Proust
draws to actual identification of woman and landscape seems to be 'l'encadre-
ment de l'analogie dans la femme', to re-apply the Baudelairean terms. On one
occasion, the sleeping Albertine appears to Marcel to contain a landscape
(*RTP*, III, 70) and, as a result, to come for the first time within his possession.
Proust here succeeds in synchronising and thereby satisfying the two forms of
love which preoccupy him intensely: he conceives of a passion for woman in
terms of her setting and *vice versa*: 'Elle avait rappelé à soi tout ce qui d'elle
était au dehors; elle s'était réfugiée, enclose, résumée, dans son corps' (*RTP*,

III, 70;cf., Ch. VI, pp. 110–11 and Ch. VIII, pp. 148–9). It is interesting that, as a product of nature rather than as an approximation to a work of art, woman finally seems capable of satisfying the narrator and of giving him the closest possible approach to a sense of possession (ibid.). On yet another occasion, the narrator writes of Albertine that she seems to contain her native landscape, to be the medium for his discovery of worlds unknown or rediscovery of the known:

> J'aurais bien voulu, avant de l'embrasser . . . retrouver en elle le pays où elle avait vécu auparavant; à sa place du moins, si je ne le connaissais pas, je pouvais insinuer tous les souvenirs de notre vie à Balbec, le bruit du flot déferlant sous ma fenêtre, les cris des enfants.
>
> (*RTP*, II, 363; cf., ibid., II, 350–5, especially 351 and 352)

The manner in which Proust here makes woman serve as a metaphor of memory and embody what was formerly 'un cadre d'horizon' is distinctly Baudelairean:

> Charme profond, magique, dont nous grise
> Dans le présent le passé restauré!
> Ainsi l'amant sur un corps adoré
> Du souvenir cueille la fleur exquise.
>
> ('Le Parfum', *BAU*, 37)

Contre l'intellectualisme, Proust affirme le primat de l'impression, seul 'critérium de vérité', gage de 'perfection' et de pure 'joie'. Il a le tort d'ériger ce principe en système: 'L'impression est pour l'écrivain ce qu'est l'expérimentation pour le savant'

(RTP, III, 880)

(V.-L. Saulnier: *La Littérature française du siècle romantique.* Paris: Presses Universitaires de France, 1966, p. 117)

As already suggested, Baudelaire and Proust fall prey to a contradiction between, on one hand, the tenet to be found in Symbolism, that forms are interchangeable and benefit from a removal of barriers, and, on the other, the belief in the irreducible individuality of the artist's message. Their entire work reflects a debt both to the *correspondances* which justify free experimentation with form, and to a firm conviction that there is an absolute, ideal form and that each artist is a separate world in himself. It is well-known that Baudelaire's hesitation about form – as between the *Poèmes en prose* and the *Fleurs du Mal* dealing with the same subjects – encouraged Proust to undertake his own novel and realise his vocation. (See extract from Proust's *Carnet, CSB* (FALL) *Contre Sainte-Beuve*, p. 35 and compare *CSB*, Pléiade, 235.) In Proust's work, one of the best illustrations of the conflict between the conception of the artist as decipherer of a reality already in existence, and the belief that the artist's message is capable of only one supreme rendering is to be found in the contrasting attitudes towards music expressed in the Vinteuil passage of *Swann* (*RTP*, I, 349) and in *La Prisonnière* (ibid., III, 256–7).

In so far as he is a Symbolist, Proust will stress the impression; in so far as he is scientific, classical and French, he will make a cult of the intelligence. Indeed, intuition and intelligence have, on occasion, in Proust's work, something of a Pascalian resonance (cf., Ch. I, pp. 17 ff.). It is impossible to determine where the stress finally falls; involuntary memory, the store of impressions accumulated unconsciously, these form the indispensable raw material, the very point of departure without which one can barely conceive of a Proust at all. Critics remain divided on this issue. A. Boase takes a view diametrically opposed to that of V.-L. Saulnier quoted at the head of this section. Professor Boase writes (p. 359) that, in contrast to Gide, 'Proust aspires to the Apollinian ecstasy'[27] (cf., Ch. I of the present work, p. 17).

The whole question whether the act of criticism preceded the creation of Proust's novel or the reverse has been re-opened by M. Pierre Clarac and M. Yves Sandre (*CSB*, 819–29):

> A quelles conclusions nous conduisent les textes que nous venons de rappeler? Aucun d'eux ne nous impose cette idée hors de vraisemblance que le grand roman est sorti de l'essai critique et que l'essai critique n'a eu qu'à se développer pour devenir un grand roman.
>
> (ibid., 827)

At the most then, in the light of the latest discoveries to date concerning Proust's method of procedure, one may well be justified in concluding that the novelist did seriously entertain, but at the end of 1909 finally decided to renounce, a plan to 'souder' what we have come to know as *Contre Sainte-Beuve*, and the actual novel; it still remains a fact, however, that such forms of literary criticism as pastiche and parody – by their very nature more creative and more closely approximating to a work of art in its own right – were always intimately associated by Proust with the act of artistic creation proper. The question whether the critical impulse preceded and even generated the creative process seems to me impossible to determine with absolute certainty; alternation may well be the rule in many cases. In such passages as we find in the 'Réponses à une enquête des *Annales*', notably about the *roman d'aventures* and the 'roman dit d'analyse', Proust is intent upon analysing the subconscious; he attempts throughout to maintain an even balance between impression and analysis, constantly anxious to ensure, however paradoxically, that the two mutually incompatible worlds should not destroy each other:

> Il s'agit de tirer hors de l'inconscient, pour la faire entrer dans le domaine de l'intelligence, mais en tâchant de lui garder sa vie, de [ne pas] la mutiler, de lui faire subir le moins de déperdition possible, une réalité que la seule lumière de l'intelligence suffirait à détruire, semble-t-il.
>
> (ibid., 640–1) (cf., Ch. I and III, pp. 19 and 50)

In the interview with E.-J. Bois (*Le Temps*, 13 November 1913), Proust clearly states that sensibility had provided the elements of his work and that his function had been to convert these musical motifs into an intelligible verbal form. Perhaps Proust goes some way towards fusing the two apparently conflicting conceptions of the artist, as decipherer of an external reality, on one hand, and as expressing an irreducible inner reality, on the other, when, in *Le Temps retrouvé* explicitly but generally elsewhere implicitly, he sets about deciphering the subconscious. Proust readily responds to the challenge extended to the intellect to analyse and classify sensations.[28] Impressions *or* pure intellect, either world on its own would have failed to satisfy Proust's ambivalence. A passion for duality inspires him to apply the principle of self-scrutiny within the act of artistic creation; to use and enjoy both sensation and intellect; in fact, to apply the latter in order to enhance the experience of the former, very much in the spirit of Valéry's Faust[29]; in effect, to fulfil something of Baudelaire's aim to 'transformer la volupté en connaissance'.

The question which we have applied to Proust concerning the order of appearance of the merely critical and the truly creative impulse could be asked of Baudelaire, whose 'christianisme intérieur' and poetic activity are subjected to a relentless analysis and whose concentration of poetry admits an affinity with prose.[30] Baudelaire went so far as to claim that the critic's reaction to a work of art could well be art in its own right, all in perfect consistency with the theory of the *correspondances* and the equivalence of the media. Again, as in Proust's case, it is difficult if not impossible to determine whether criticism precedes artistic creation. Alternation of the two impulses would once more seem to be probable but, as with Proust, impressions have priority despite the *boutade*: 'Comprendre, c'est égaler'.

In yet another respect – one which concerns this time both aesthetics and ethics – Proust reveals affinities with Baudelaire. The selfsame duality of cruelty and sensibility which he admired in his precursor but which may have been one of the factors causing some readers to have reservations (*CSB*, 243 and 250) seems to be evident in Proust's portrayal of Charlus. Moreover, what Proust says of the ambiguous interpretation to which Baudelaire's dichotomy of sensibility and cruelty exposes such poems as 'Les Petites Vieilles' (*CSB*, 250–2; cf., ibid., 608–9), where 'le poète passait la mesure sans le savoir' (ibid., 625–6), could be applied with equal force to his own work, particularly when age, love and homosexuality come under scrutiny. It is at once paradoxical and ironical that, as analyst of inversion, Proust should find himself exposed to two conflicting criticisms: excessive detachment on one hand, excessive involvement on the other. Perhaps one of the principal reasons why Baudelaire ranks so high in Proust's opinion is to be discovered precisely in a certain power of synthesis and quality of tension anticipating Proust's own. One wonders whether Baudelaire's strong sense of division between the two simultaneous pulls of good and evil fascinated Proust as much as it did Gide. For vice, in general, Baudelaire would seem to plead as excuse a misdirected desire for the infinite (*BAU*, 348), and, while singling out duality as fundamental to Baudelaire's genius, Proust shrewdly styles the poet of *Les Fleurs du Mal* as 'l'impur dévot' (*CSB*, 628), and his work as 'ce livre sublime mais grimaçant . . . où la débauche fait le signe de la croix . . .' (*CSB*, 618). Does Proust join Baudelaire in implying that the intensity of man's revolt may correspond to his potentiality for good? Particularly in the characterisation of Charlus and Mlle Vinteuil, also Saint-Loup, he seems to project a strong belief in human ambivalence.

There are further respects in which Baudelaire proves his capacity to fuse elements which might be deemed incompatible: like Proust, he combines a fascination for the irrational and a strong critical faculty; he uses an affinity with prose as a source of evocation in his poetry and thus anticipates Proust's enhancement of art by reality (*RTP*, II, 846–50, 579; III, 200 and 997); in addition, Baudelaire's work reveals features of classicism (*CSB*, 626–8) and Romanticism; Proust comments more than once on the Racinian quality of Baudelaire's poetry (*CSB*, 617 and 641), where the classical force of the style seems to grow in direct proportion to the licentiousness of the subject matter, notably in the *Pièces condamnées* (*CSB*, 609). Finally there is, as already mentioned, the paradox of his intellectualism and irrational transcendentalism. It is open to speculation how far Proust was aware of this contradiction in Baudelaire's work or his own.

Apart from these considerations, Baudelaire must have appealed strongly to Proust by virtue of the extent to which he echoes and transcends Vigny who, in Proust's opinion, as already stated, ties with Baudelaire for the position of 'le plus grand poète du dix-neuvième siècle'. It is generally recognised that Baudelaire both consciously and unconsciously developed aspects of Vigny's work. Governed by his passion for analogy, Proust must have enjoyed reading these two poets in terms of each other. Features which probably appealed to him in both are their interest in inversion; their conception of the 'poète maudit'; their endorsement of the artist's attempts to improve upon corrupt nature; their keen sense of the ephemeral; and – of supreme importance – their intense preoccupation with 'les voluptés des soirs et les biens du mystère' (cf., *CSB*, 621). In at least three major respects, however, it seems probable that Baudelaire would at once rank as Vigny's superior in Proust's eyes and foreshadow the latter's own contribution: by his understanding of the laws of memory (*CSB*, 641); by his anticipation of 'toutes les couleurs vraies, modernes, poétiques . . . pas très poussées mais délicieuses, surtout les roses avec du bleu, de l'or ou du vert . . .' (ibid., 258); and finally by his transposition of a Wagnerian technique of leitmotif, notably in such a poem as 'Le Cygne'.[31] It is often claimed that Baudelaire is dramatically ahead of his time; certainly such a past master in the art of transposition as Proust was one of the first to recognise and appreciate Baudelaire's extraordinary power to transform and renew whatever he touched, and Proust's discovery of so many close affinities with Baudelaire must have marked a decisive stage in his own development as an artist. It is, in every way, appropriate that a poet so intent upon self-scrutiny and the salvaging of the past should have initiated, for the narrator, 'l'histoire d'une vocation' (*RTP*, III, 920).

Notes

[1] W. A. Strauss notes a tendency on the part of critics to 'strain the parallel between Baudelaire's and Proust's Oedipus complexes and to overstress the the Symbolist element in both writers' *Proust and Literature: the Novelist as Critic*, Harvard University Press 1957, p. 61.

[2] See the present author's *Proust's Challenge to Time*, pp. 220–2.

[3] For a detailed treatment of this subject in the work of Baudelaire and Proust, see ibid., pp. 63–93.

[4] André Maurois: *A la recherche de Marcel Proust*, Hachette, Paris 1949, pp. 229–30.

[5] Lester Mansfield: *Le Comique de Marcel Proust: Proust et Baudelaire*, Nizet, Paris 1953, pp. 206–8.

[6] Strauss: op. cit., p. 73.

[7] George Painter: *Marcel Proust, A Biography* (2 vols), Chatto & Windus, London 1966, II, 324.

[8] Ibid., n. 2.

[9] André Gide: *Journal*, 1889–1939 Pléiade, Gallimard, Paris 1951, pp. 691 ff.

[10] Ibid., 14 mai 1921 p. 692

[11] Painter: op. cit., II, 324 n. 1

[12] Gide: op. cit., p. 694

[13] Gide: Ibid., cf., *RTP*, III, 140

[14] Gide: op. cit., p. 694

[15] Ibid.

[16] P. Mansell Jones: *The Assault on French Literature*, Manchester University Press, Manchester 1963, pp. 131–2.

[17] Margaret Gilman: *Baudelaire the Critic*, Columbia University Press, 1943, pp. 195 ff.

[18] Ibid., p. 156

[19] Ibid., p. 246

[20] J. M. Cocking: *Proust*, Bowes & Bowes, London 1956, pp. 64 ff.

[21] Gilman: op. cit., p. 157

[22] Benjamin Crémieux: *Du Côté de Marcel Proust*, Lemarget, Paris 1929, pp. 3–4

[23] Gilman op. cit., p. 247 n. 48

[24] S. Ullmann: *Style in the French Novel*, Cambridge University Press 1957, Ch. V pp. 189-209

[25] Ibid., p. 204

[26] Ibid., p. 205

[27] R. L. Graeme Ritchie: *France: a Companion to French Studies*, Methuen London 1936, Ch. X: A. Boase, p. 359. (Cf., Ch. I of the present book, pp. 17 ff.)

[28] Louis de Robert: *Comment débuta Marcel Proust*, Gallimard, Paris 1969, Lettre V, p. 35

[29] Paul Valéry: *Œuvres* II, Pléiade, Paris 1960, p. 322

[30] A. Thibaudet: *Histoire de la littérature française* II, Stock, Paris 1936, pp. 41 ff.

[31] Baudelaire anticipates Proust's technique of the leitmotif in such a poem as 'Le Cygne'. See Mansell Jones: op, cit., pp. 128–32. Both Baudelaire and Proust may have been strongly influenced by Wagner in their cult of the art of evocation, particularly in their attempts to approximate to music in literature.

Notes for further reading

The subject of Proust's affinities with Baudelaire has been studied by the following:

Justin O'Brien	'La mémoire involontaire avant Marcel Proust' *Revue de littérature comparée*, XIX, Jan, 1939 Ed. Boivin, pp. 19–36
Eméric Fiser	*Le symbole littéraire: Essai sur la signification du symbole chez Wagner, Baudelaire, Mallarmé, Bergson et Proust*, Corti, Paris 1941
René Galand	'Proust et Baudelaire' *PMLA*, 65, Dec. 1950, pp. 1011–35
Lester Mansfield	*Le comique de Marcel Proust: Proust et Baudelaire*, Nizet, Paris 1953
Société des Amis de Proust et de Combray	*Bulletin* no. 20, 1970. Réunion littéraire du 31 août 1969: 'Baudelaire et Proust' pp. 1028–49. (Intervention de M. Larcher; Communication de M. J.

Milly: "Proust et l'image." Extrait de la communication de M. Sandre. Intervention de M. Henri Bonnet).

With special reference to Proust as a literary critic of Baudelaire:

W. A. Strauss   *Proust and Literature: the Novelist as Critic*, Harvard University Press 1957.

René de Chantal   *Marcel Proust, Critique littéraire*, University of Montreal 1967.

Margaret Gilman in *Baudelaire the Critic*, Columbia University Press 1943, seeks to distinguish between Baudelaire's and Proust's conceptions of the creative rôle to be assigned to the imagination and memory respectively. See ibid., 'The poet as critic' pp. 155 ff. and especially the footnotes ibid., pp. 44–8.

Rapprochements between Baudelaire and Proust underlie the discussion of memory and dreams in my book: *Proust's Challenge to Time*, M.U.P. 1962. (See Appendix I: 'Proust and Baudelaire' ibid., pp. 120–9.) The present study is concerned with the further analysis of affinities between the two writers rather than with the question of possible influence.

Chapter V

Novalis

Jeder geliebte Gegenstand ist der Mittelpunkt eines Paradieses.
('Blütenstaub', 51, *NOV*, II, 23)

La vue la plus far reaching *peut-être de Novalis* – what a loss
that he should not have lived to work it out! – *celle qui préfor-
me, qui contient Proust – c'est que cette faculté créatrice, ou plus
exactement chacun de ces innombrables filets, réseaux, projette
un monde possible, et qui de la possibilité n'a besoin pour passer à
l'acte que de l'existence de l'artiste.*
(Charles Du Bos, *Journal*, I, 376, 4 Dec. 1923)

Did Proust ever read Novalis, or is the striking resemblance between the two
men, in thought and approach, nothing more than the result of affinity?
There can be no doubt about the influence exerted by the German writer on
French Symbolism. In Maeterlinck, Novalis found an ardent devotee, who
translated into French, in the *Mercure de France* 1895, *Die Lehrlinge zu Sais
und Fragmente*.[1] Proust greatly admired the Belgian author, and even elected
him to be one of the poets of the 'Six Jardins du Paradis', styling him as 'cet
évolutionniste dans l'absolu . . . [pour qui] science, philosophie et morale sont
sur le même plan, et l'horizon de bonheur et de vérité n'est pas un mirage
résultant des lois de notre optique et de la perspective intellectuelle, mais le
terme d'un idéal réel, dont nous nous rapprochons effectivement'.[2] We know,
moreover, that Proust read Maeterlinck's article on 'La Mort' with keen
interest, when it appeared in serialised form in *Le Figaro*, 1–6 August 1911.[3]

Charles Du Bos first discovered Novalis through Carlyle's essay (1829) included in the *Critical and Miscellaneous Essays*, published 1894, and again a possible source from which Proust may have drawn information about the German author.[4] Four main points made a deep impression on the French critic's mind, the last three closely interrelated. First comes Novalis's predilection for the fragment as a literary form, which the German writer seeks to justify by the assumption that there is one book of knowledge;[5] it is precisely this *genre* of fragment which Du Bos finds at the root of Symbolism in general, and of Mallarmé's and Valéry's aesthetic in particular. Second, he analyses the German's cult of *Verinnerlichung*, the preoccupation with a reality transformed and re-created by the mind. Third, he is impressed by the search for the essential self. Fourth, he is fascinated by the interest in *le règne minéral*, notably in crystal, evident in the work of Novalis, the Symbolists, and Gide, especially the Gide of Symbolism.

Proust never expatiates at the same length as the Symbolists on the function of the fragment nor does he use it as a literary form in the manner of Novalis. He does, however, conceive of works of art as fragments of the artist's own irreducible world or element. This conception, in itself, is an interesting and rewarding variation on the theme of the *Fragmente*, here enriched by a Proustian resonance: to Albertine, the narrator makes a virtual profession of his artistic faith in the principle and the practice of the fragment in the most general terms:

> Vous m'avez dit que vous aviez vu certains tableaux de Ver Meer. Vous vous rendez bien compte que ce sont les fragments d'un même monde, que c'est toujours, quelque génie avec lequel elle soit recréée, la même table, le même tapis, la même femme, la même nouvelle et unique beauté ... Hé bien, cette beauté nouvelle, elle reste identique dans toutes les œuvres de Dostoïevsky.
>
> (*RTP*, III, 377)

Novalis discerns in the broken colours of the spectrum an analogy of 'broken sound'[6] and affirms that art alone affords man scope to express his qualitative essence, that is, his irreducible individuality: 'Poesie ist *Darstellung* des *Gemüts* – der innern *Welt in ihrer Gesamtheit*' (*NOV*, III, No. 244, p. 317). Proust uses the same image of the spectrum to convey his notion that each inner world, as expressed in a work of art, is unique and irreplaceable:

> ... cet ineffable qui différencie qualitativement ce que chacun a senti et qu'il est obligé de laisser au seuil des phrases ... l'art, l'art d'un Vinteuil comme celui d'un Elstir, le fait apparaître, extériorisant dans les couleurs du spectre la composition intime de ces mondes que nous appelons les individus, et que sans l'art nous ne connaîtrions jamais.
>
> (*RTP*, III, 257–8)

As far as *Verinnerlichung* is concerned, Proust was absorbed by this fusion of subject and object, of the artist and the world which he contemplates, or

86

rather, which he refashions from within: 'Die Welt wird Traum, der Traum wird Welt.'[7] According to Proust, the landscape of the mind is a territory irreducibly individual, quite peculiar to its owner and capable of being opened to others only by the medium of art. He subscribes to Novalis's belief that the true reality is always to be found within oneself: 'Nach Innen geht der geheimnisvolle Weg.' After the passer-by has indicated to the lost traveller the path he seeks, it is within himself that the narrator withdraws to discover or rather recover realms deemed lost beyond recall – 'des terres reconquises sur l'oubli . . . je cherche encore mon chemin, je tourne une rue . . . mais c'est dans mon cœur . . .' (*RTP*, I, 67).

Towards the close of *Le Temps retrouvé* (*RTP*, III, 1035), it is in terms of conveying an inner mental landscape that Proust defines his rôle as an artist. He reflects apprehensively that even this inner domain, apparently so safe because of its spirituality, lies under a sentence of time where its expression in art is concerned. The final image of approaching night is strongly biblical and may have been suggested to Proust by his reading of Ruskin:

> L'esprit a ses paysages dont la contemplation ne lui est laissée qu'un temps. J'avais vécu comme un peintre montant un chemin qui surplombe un lac dont un rideau de rochers et d'arbres lui cache la vue. Par une brèche il l'aperçoit, il l'a tout entier devant lui, il prend ses pinceaux. Mais déjà vient la nuit où l'on ne peut plus peindre, et sur laquelle le jour ne se relève pas.
>
> (*RTP*, III, 1035)

This is the essence of Novalis's theme, although the German writer is admittedly free from the Proustian sense of urgency, from the nightmare of the sands of time running out and thereby defeating the artist in his act of creation. Novalis's nostalgia for the spiritual *habitat*, for what the Bible calls man's 'long home', is poignant and implies the act of remembering and re-covering a birthright: 'Alle Märchen sind nur Träume von jener heimatlichen Welt, die überall und nirgends ist' (*NF*, No. 15, p. 411). 'Die Philosophie ist eigentlich Heimweh, Trieb überall zu Hause zu sein' (ibid., p. 422). It is precisely by postulating 'native land,' world of innate spiritual values, that Proust seeks to resolve the enigma of incredibly high human ideals and man's indomitable urge to respond to unwritten laws of another order; here, perhaps, he comes closest to admitting the possibility of immortality: memory and intuition enable us to obey, and reason to apprehend a spiritual authority:

> Toutes ces obligations qui n'ont pas leur sanction dans la vie présente, semblent appartenir à un monde différent . . . de celui-ci, et dont nous sortons pour naître à cette terre, avant peut-être d'y retourner revivre sous l'empire de ces lois inconnues auxquelles nous avons obéi parce que nous en portions l'enseignement en nous, sans savoir qui les y avait tracées, – ces lois dont tout travail profond de l'intelligence nous rapproche et qui sont invisibles seulement – et encore! – pour les sots. De sorte que l'idée que Bergotte n'était pas mort à jamais, est sans invraisemblance.
>
> (*RTP*, III, 188)

Before exploring further Proust's conception of the artist's inner world, I would like to quote what I consider to be Novalis's key passage on the subject of *Verinnerlichung* and the 'native land' of the artist's mind. In this image and interpretation of *Vaterland*, Novalis foreshadows Proust more vividly and profoundly than perhaps even Charles Du Bos had imagined; in fact, Proust would seem simply to annotate and elaborate Novalis's thought as we discover it in this reflection from the *Fragmente und Studien*:

> Die innre Welt ist gleichsam mehr mein als die äußre. Sie ist so innig, so heimlich – Man möchte ganz in ihr leben. – Sie ist so vaterländisch. Schade, daß sie so traumhaft, so ungewiß ist. Muß denn gerade das Beste, das Wahrste so scheinbar – und das Scheinbare so wahr aussehn?
> Was außer mir ist, ist gerade in mir, ist mein – und umgekehrt.
>
> (*NF*, No. 538, p. 518)

Proust extends the range of the landscape projected by the mind and elevates it in status from natural element to native land, 'patrie inconnue', 'patrie intérieure', and finally, by Proustian law, 'patrie perdue'. In a curious and subtle way, this native land of the mind is for Proust bound up with the artist's identity. Intuitively, unconsciously, he will sing in accord with his inner realm or inner self, rejecting all vainglory, even as he seems to fulfil 'obligations' contracted in a former existence and transcending conventional human codes. Memory plays an important part and the artist will experience joy in proportion to the accuracy with which he transcribes the inner message: 'Quand la vision de l'univers . . . devient plus adéquate au souvenir de la patrie intérieure' (*RTP*, III, 257). This exactitude of transcription depends upon the artist's loyalty not only to his sense of vocation but to his innermost qualitative essence, his veritable self so easily overlaid and submerged by the *moi social*. Extensions of our senses – new senses, Novalis would say – are required for perception of these worlds as numerous as individuals, microcosms in fact: 'Der echte Dichter ist allwissend – er ist eine wirkliche Welt im kleinen' (*NF*, No. 17). Adding his particular stress on the necessity of art for communication, Proust seems to echo Novalis's 'Hypothesen über mehrfache Sinne.'[8]

According to Novalis, poetry dissolves the barriers between subject and object, as well as between conventional, man-made divisions of time, especially between past and present: 'Unendlichkeit eines guten Gedichts, die Ewigkeit.' He notes the artist's passive rôle in the hands of destiny, his task of deciphering a message, of being *voyant*, poet, and seer: 'Der Sinn für Poesie hat nahe Verwandtschaft mit dem Sinn der Weissagung, und dem religiösen, dem Sehersinn überhaupt' (*NOV*, III, No. 443, p. 349).

We find, in fact, the stress on the subject: 'Wird nicht die Welt am Ende Gemüt?' and, at the same time, a hint that the poet or artist simply deciphers a reality which already exists independently outside himself, while he serves in some way as a passive instrument. There is thus evident the antinomy between the classical belief in one irreducible form, on the one hand, and on the other, the Symbolist tenet that forms are interchangeable, that a spiritual reality exists outside man and awaits deciphering. It is a conflict between what Professor Cocking has chosen to call 'intellectualism' and 'irrational transcendentalism' respectively, and which he claims to have discovered in German philosophy, as represented by Hegel and Schopenhauer[9] and as continued by Baudelaire, Ruskin, and Proust.

Past and present (the latter extending into the future), and the faculties which we deploy on both respectively, memory and hope – these seem to Novalis to form the essence of poetry and to interweave inextricably to compound the *Stimmung*, that harmony or fusion between man and the material reality which he contemplates: 'Das Wort Stimmung deutet auf musikalische Seelenverhältnisse.' In both authors' moments of illumination, all objects in the external world are capable of releasing magic, of restoring former selves; as Proust writes: '. . . ils avaient l'air de cacher, au delà de ce que je voyais, quelque chose qu'ils m'invitaient à venir prendre . . .' (*RTP*, I, 178). Novalis, equally, moves freely between inner and outer reality and transcends time-laws in the process:

> Alle Erinnerung und Ahndung scheint aus eben dieser Quelle zu sein – So auch diejenige Gegenwart, wo man in Illusion befangen ist – einzelne Stunden, wo man gleichsam in allen Gegenständen, die man betrachtet, steckt und die unendlichen, unbegreiflichen, gleichzeitigen Empfindungen eines zusammenstimmenden Pluralis fühlt.
>
> (*NOV*, III, No. 25, p. 286)

Memory, Novalis conceded, is the communication cord between different parts of the past, through association. The function of this faculty in bringing together objects which are otherwise utterly distinct and separate causes him to go beyond Proust and see in such a pattern of interdependence between the particular and the general evidence of an overriding and transcendental unity:

> In unserm Gemüt ist alles auf die eigenste, gefälligste und lebendigste Weise verknüpft. Die fremdesten Dinge kommen durch *einen* Ort, *eine* Zeit, eine seltsame Ähnlichkeit, einen Irrtum, irgendeinen Zufall zusammen. So entstehn wunderliche Einheiten und eigentümliche Verknüpfungen – und *eins* erinnert an alles – wird das Zeichen vieler und wird selbst von vielen bezeichnet und herbeigerufen.
>
> (*NF*, No. 453, p. 499) (The italics are the author's own.)

On the extent to which we can dilate time, or the present, Novalis is explicit. In fact, he sees this dilation of range as paralleled by the extension of our personality in objects associated with experience. Here he anticipates vividly Proust's cult of objects for their power to recall the past, tangentially as it were, witness the 'vieux gant' which can so unexpectedly revive the power to feel an emotion temporarily suspended by the 'intermittences du cœur',[10] or the talisman-like charm of something as marginal as a book, *François le Champi* – preferably the narrator's personal copy – or the grandmother's copy of Mme de Sévignés' *Lettres*; or the opinion of the Princesse and the Duchesse de Guermantes of *Phèdre*; all these by subtle laws of association rather than for their intrinsic worth, become media for the return of the essence of the past, the part deemed lost beyond recall; they encourage a kind of idolatry. We may well consider Novalis's words on this subject, cited as epigraph to the present chapter: 'Jeder geliebte Gegenstand ist der Mittelpunkt eines Paradieses'. Or again: 'Wir halten einen leblosen Stoff wegen seiner Beziehungen, seiner Formen fest. Wir lieben den Stoff, insofern er zu einem geliebten Wesen gehört, seine Spur trägt, oder Ähnlichkeit mit ihm hat' ('Blütenstaub,' 42). Compare this with Proust's assertion:

> A partir d'un certain âge, nos souvenirs sont tellement entrecroisés, les uns sur les autres que la chose à laquelle on pense, le livre qu'on lit n'a presque plus d'importance. On a mis de soi-même partout, tout est fécond, tout est dangereux, et on peut faire d'aussi précieuses découvertes que dans les *Pensées* de Pascal dans une réclame pour un savon.
>
> (*RTP*, III, 543) (Cf., Ch. VII, pp. 130 ff.)

In time and space we overflow prescribed limits imposed by man and convention. Novalis, like Proust, sees us at the centre of an intricate web of threads dependent on time and space, and affirms that it rests with us to develop our power and range of discovery, although ultimately for both writers, much depends upon chance and upon a combination of mood and circumstance:

> Cet objet, il dépend du hasard que nous le rencontrions avant de mourir ou que nous ne le rencontrions pas.
>
> (*RTP*, I, 44)

> Ce que nous appelons la réalité est un certain rapport entre ces sensations et ces souvenirs qui nous entourent simultanément ...
>
> (ibid., III, 889)

It is remarkable how vividly Novalis's statements about time anticipate Bergson and Proust. The elasticity of time, the dependence of our sense of duration on the extent to which we fill moments with intensity of feeling, the precedence taken by 'temps-qualité' over 'temps-quantité' – does not Novalis record all these phenomena? Before Proust's statement: 'Le temps ... est élastique, les passions que nous ressentons le dilatent, celles que nous inspirons le rétrécissent ...' and Bergson's affirmation of 'durée à élasticité inégale', we find in Novalis a supreme consciousness of time, a shrewd understanding of man's freedom to move at will in past, present, and future:

> Wir stehen in Verhältnissen mit allen Teilen des Universums, sowie mit Zukunft und Vorzeit. Es hängt nur von der Richtung und Dauer unsrer Aufmerksamkeit ab,

welches Verhältnis wir vorzüglich ausbilden wollen, welches für uns vorzüglich wichtig, und wirksam werden soll.

(NOV, II. No. 92, p. 32)

Novalis was intensely alive to the dangers of retrospection as well as to the poetic wealth latent in both memory and anticipation. The former entails crystallisation, and, foreshadowing Bergson, Novalis favours fluidity, a judicious intermingling of all elements of time as the ideal spiritual climate of poetry:

> Daher ist alle Erinnerung wehmütig, alle Ahndung freudig. Jene mäßigt die allzu große Lebhaftigkeit, diese erhebt ein zu schwaches Leben. Die gewöhnliche Gegenwart verknüpft Vergangenheit und Zukunft durch Beschränkung. Es entsteht Kontiguität, durch Erstarrung Kristallisation. Es gibt aber eine geistige Gegenwart, die beide durch Auflösung identifiziert, und diese Mischung ist das Element, die Atmosphäre des Dichters.

(ibid., No. 109, p. 35)

The 'règne minéral', with which Du Bos found Gide and Novalis so intensely preoccupied, fascinates Proust in turn.[11] In the work of all three writers, this interest in geology seems to be intimately associated with the search for the original self, the one activity readily becoming the metaphor of the other. In order to describe the layers of memories, Proust will resort instinctively to the idiom of this science, and as a result he is able to indicate with ease the various levels at which he imagines his memories to be situated, interlarded with strata of intervening time. The imagery is the natural consequence of spatialisation, which ideas of time necessarily undergo: '. . . c'est surtout comme à des gisements profonds de mon sol mental, comme aux terrains résistants sur lesquels je m'appuie encore, que je dois penser au côté de Méséglise et au côté de Guermantes' (RTP, I, 184). The dating of original geological strata is for the geologist what location of memories is for Proust, and the scientist, so powerfully present and alive within him, delights in the attempt at identification. Nothing can be allowed to remain obscure without intelligence having been applied in some guise. The archetype, the original moi (le moi profond), 'le baiser même des Oublis' lies at the term of Proust's as also of Gide's endeavour. Whatever lies 'de l'autre côté de l'horizon' always intrigues Proust, so equally the layer beneath to infinity. Geology is, after all, in the literal sense a dramatic materialisation of time:

> Tous ces souvenirs ajoutés les uns aux autres ne formaient plus qu'une masse, mais non sans qu'on pût distinguer entre eux . . . sinon des fissures, des failles véritables, du moins ces veinures, ces bigarrures de coloration qui, dans certaines roches, dans certains marbres, révèlent des différences d'origine, d'âge, de 'formation'.

(RTP, I, 186)

Novalis associates high mountains with nature's original striving for purity. Proust will find the sealed vases of memory 'disposés sur toute la hauteur de nos années . . . situés à des altitudes bien diverses' (ibid., III, 870) and he is the first to detect Stendhal's association of 'un certain sentiment de l'altitude' with 'la vie spirituelle' (ibid., III, 377). In fact, Proust is quick to discern a preoccupation with geology in other writers; the symmetry of stones has a major significance; of Hardy's novels he writes that they are 'superposables les uns aux autres' and in this respect resemble 'les maisons verticalement entassées en hauteur sur le sol pierreux de l'île . . .' (ibid.).

Péguy describes Bergsonism as a geology.[12] He might justifiably have applied the same metaphor to Proust's attempt to strip away convention and rediscover the personality, but in general can one account for this preoccupation with geology? Did Novalis and others discern in this science a reflection and a symbol of their own search for the philosopher's stone? Certainly, as Charles Du Bos has observed, the fascination of crystallography and mineralogy pervades and, at times, dominates Novalis's writings, expecially *Die Lehrlinge zu Sais*, and, although he does not specifically mention it, *Heinrich von Ofterdingen*, together with the *Fragmente* and *Gedanken*. Furthermore, it extends to the work of the Symbolists: Mallarmé, the early Gide, and Valéry, in particular. Du Bos here ponders, but without ever developing it fully, the fascination of which I speak:

> Si j'en ai le temps, analyser en fonction de Gide et de notre symbolisme – et en m'appuyant sur *Les Disciples à Saïs* – la fascination exercée sur ce type d'esprits par le règne minéral: rattacher ceci (deux textes importants dans le traité du *Narcisse* et du *Philoctète*), à la notion du cristal chez Gide, et montrer dans la prose du premier Gide et dans celle de Novalis que leur idéal est bien celui d'une belle pierre transparente.[13]

In the subterranean grotto, Novalis and others, notably Jean-Paul, symbolised the inner world, man's truly spiritual domain as opposed to the external, finite world of illusion. Lilian Furst sees reflected in the German Romantics' preoccupation with the mine these writers' rejection of external nature in favour of an inner realm of which the subterranean is merely a symbol. She quotes as examples the fifth chapter of *Heinrich von Ofterdingen*, where Heinrich explores the mine: 'as he descends, in his outer journey, into "ein unterirdisches seltsames Reich," he is, in fact, in his inner pilgrimage, groping his way to his "in sich gekehrte Traumwelt" '; or again, Novalis himself in his *Hymnen an die Nacht*, and Tieck in *Der Runenberg*.[14]

Novalis finds a profound *correspondance* between the rôles of poet and miner respectively. It is an analogy rich in nuances and subtlety of variations; the poet resembles the miner in that he 'divines' the source of the inner spiritual world. He may even favour the occult sciences and, as did Novalis, stand in his own right as a seer or *voyant*.

Novalis yearns to re-discover an archetype both of the external and of his own inner world; of the first, the original form; of the second, the original ego.

92

This quest and its accompanying nostalgia are brilliantly resumed when, in *Heinrich von Ofterdingen*, the hermit defines the poet and the miner as being almost 'verkehrte Astrologen' and strikingly develops the latent antithesis:

'Wenn diese Astrologen den Himmel unverwandt betrachten und seine unermeßlichen Räume durchirren: so wendet ihr Euren Blick auf den Erdboden, und erforscht seinen Bau. Jene studieren die Kräfte und Einflüsse der Gestirne, und ihr untersucht die Kräfte der Felsen und Berge und die mannigfaltigen Wirkungen der Erd– und Steinschichten. Jenen ist der Himmel das Buch der Zukunft, während euch die Erde Denkmale der Urwelt zeigt.'

(Heinrich von Ofterdingen, Ch. V, *NOV*, I, 165)

The last sentence with its sharp juxtaposition of future and past, and its insistence that the geologist is necessarily preoccupied with the latter, seems to explain and underlie much of Proust's thought.

Proust, however, goes a stage further than Novalis in his elaboration of the poet-miner analogy. By a process of *dédoublement*, of self-division which he always favoured, he sees himself, the artist, as forming simultaneously the object of analysis and the analyst, here, the mine and the miner: 'Je savais très bien que mon cerveau était un riche bassin minier, où il y avait une étendue immense et fort diverse de gisements précieux' (*RTP*, III, 1037).

Characteristically the sense of time passing adds urgency to the image and engenders in Proust a haunting sense that he is the vessel of inspiration and that, in his capacity as artist, he must husband his resources; such subtlety in self-justification, and the torturing doubt whether he will defeat time – these features are sufficient to distinguish him from Novalis, geological though the point of departure may well have been:

Mais aurais-je le temps de les exploiter? J'étais la seule personne capable de le faire. Pour deux raisons: avec ma mort eût disparu non seulement le seul ouvrier mineur capable d'extraire ces minérais mais encore le gisement lui-même.

(ibid.)

If we subscribe to Werner's Neptunist theory that all geological forms are the result of successive layers of sediment left by the sea and that, by extension, matter represents a falling away from perfection, it is easy to see reasons for the pre-eminence of liquids and finally of crystal. When, in his turn, notably in the *Traité du Narcisse*, Gide seems resolutely intent upon rediscovering the original form or *Urwelt*, and the primitive self, his terms are at once redolent of both Novalis and Proust. The following passage is a spontaneous vindication of crystal and its attraction. Narcisse, as though deliberately practising what Novalis urges in *Die Lehrlinge zu Sais*, is wrapt in contemplation of the river, symbol of time:

Toujours les mêmes formes passent; l'élan du flot, seul les différencie. – Pourquoi plusieurs? ou bien pourquoi les mêmes? – C'est donc qu'elles sont imparfaites, puisqu'elles recommencent toujours ... et toutes, pense-t-il, s'efforcent et s'élancent vers une forme première perdue, paradisiaque et cristalline.[15]

Novalis vividly anticipates not only Gide but Proust, when he stresses the particular distinguishing features of objects or people and tries to discover and characterise their essence. In fact, the German writer's desire to unearth the original layers of reality and identity upon which the past has super-imposed successive strata, concealing the earliest form, is perhaps paralleled by Proust's search for the original *moi*, and by his longing to recover facets of former selves.

Again, like Proust, Novalis considers childhood to be an ideal: 'Wo Kinder sind, da ist ein goldnes Zeitalter.' (*NOV*, II, 'Blütenstaub,' No. 97, p. 33.) He conceives of it as an expression of man's original self, the archetype to which he would return, and such a belief is in perfect harmony with his philosophy, dominated by the cult of essence, original form, *Ur-*, etc., Proust fails to state this quite so explicitly but delights to see in the actions of our earliest years a prefiguration of our entire lives; sobs only give the impression of being repressed; silence and apparent absence or interruption accentuate their essential reality and presence; similarly the 'drame du coucher', symbol-ised by the sound of the bell announcing Swann's arrival, this is, in the deepest sense, 'une sonorité identique', as continuous and irreducible as the disting-uishing colour or quality of an artist's work, or his fundamental identity as a person. However much Proust is inclined to detect disunity and disintegration of the human personality, the fact remains that he never ceases to believe in the existence of a unifying thread. Novalis seems to join Proust in affirming that 'The child is father of the Man', and that 'Heaven lies about us in our infancy': 'Was sind Kinder als erste Menschen? Der frische Blick des Kindes ist überschwenglicher als die Ahndung des entschiedensten Sehers.' (*NF*, No. 18, p. 411. Maeterlinck, *Les Disciples à Saïs . . .*, p. 132). According to Proust and Novalis, the spiritual world constantly intervenes by the medium of memory. The German writer sees this intervention as a survival of the days when the bonds between spirit and matter were closer: 'Die höhern Mächte in uns, die einst als Genien unsern Willen vollbringen werden, sind jetzt Musen, die uns auf dieser mühseligen Laufbahn mit süßen Erinnerungen erquicken' (ibid., No. 15, p. 411. Maeterlinck, op. cit., p. 132).

Proust affirmed that the only true forms of paradise were those which one had lost and which one spent a lifetime trying to recover. Gide has much the same conception of paradise as haunting a man with its image, revealed to him by seers who give him only fragments of the truth; here, too, we discern the reason for the Symbolist cult of the fragment and for Proust's theory that each work affords a glimpse of a spiritual realm more or less perfectly recalled:

Triste race . . . le souvenir du Paradis perdu viendra désoler tes extases, du Paradis que tu rechercheras partout – dont viendront te reparler des prophètes – et des poètes que voici, qui recueilleront pieusement les feuillets déchirés du Livre immémorial où se lisait la vérité qu'il faut connaître.[16]

The recovery of original purity naturally expresses itself in the image of crystal, a lightening of matter: ' . . . formes divines et pérennelles . . . oh! quand, dans quelle nuit, dans quel silence, vous recristalliserez-vous?' Paradise, for the Gide of this Symbolist phase, is virtually everywhere: 'Turn but a stone, and start a wing!' and it is almost always associated with loss and the purity of crystal:

> Le Paradis est toujours à refaire; il n'est point en quelque lointaine Thulé. Il demeure sous l'apparence. Chaque chose détient, virtuelle, l'intime harmonie de son être, comme chaque sel, en lui, l'archétype de son cristal . . . Tout s'efforce vers sa forme perdue.'[17]

Both Gide and Proust see the work of art as a crystal and recognise inspiration and genius by the transparency of the words; Gide writes:

> Car l'œuvre d'art est un cristal – paradis partiel où l'Idée refleurit en sa pureté supérieure . . . où les phrases rythmiques et sûres, symboles encore, mais symboles purs, où les paroles se font transparentes et révélatrices.'[18]

And Proust describes as follows the human reaction to 'la vraie beauté' as opposed to the relative or the approximation with which we are usually confronted and which normally corresponds to what we had imagined; thus by a strange irony, and as a result of the inferiority of our imagination, perfection is likely to disappoint us; a great actor will win less applause than one who is merely skilful:

> Car son geste et sa voix sont si parfaitement décantés de toutes parcelles d'or ou scories qui le troublaient, qu'il semble que c'est seulement l'eau claire, comme un vitrage qui laisse seulement voir l'objet naturel qui est au-delà. C'est à cette pureté, à cette transparence qu'est arrivé le jeu de Saint-Saëns . . .
>
> (*CSB* (FALL) 'Un dimanche au Conservatoire', p. 330)

Virtanen has noted in Proust's work the incidence of images associated with crystallisation.[19] Perhaps the most poetic instance occurs when Marcel describes the afternoons of reading and compares them to crystal in which his memories are enshrined: ' . . . le cristal successif, lentement changeant et traversé de feuillages, de vos heures silencieuses, sonores, odorantes et limpides' (*RTP*, I, 88). More striking in its psychological implications is the reference to crystal and contrasting fluidity within the memory. The process of memory represents for Proust a crystallisation, a gradual transition from flux to solidity. Hence the narrator's surprise on encountering again a certain memory which, during the process of crystallisation was likely to remain inaccessible: 'Tout d'un coup c'était un souvenir que je n'avais pas revu depuis bien longtemps, car il était resté dissous dans la fluide et invisible étendue de ma mémoire, qui se cristallisait' (*RTP*, III, 491; cf., *NOV*, II, No. 109, p. 35).

It is interesting that, apart from sharing Novalis's preoccupation with crystal, Proust seems to provide his own variation on the German writer's belief that spirits live in trees, stone, and landscape. I refer here to the French author's famous 'croyance celtique' (*RTP*, I, 44). Again, the German writer anticipates Proust's erethism in virtually identical form when he identifies a woman with her native landscape and conversely; 'Il faut que l'on sente un paysage comme on sent un corps.'[20]

Finally, about the rôle of music, Novalis is in perfect accord with Proust, even to the mention of the spirit's native land, and what closely approaches a German rendering of 'chanter selon sa patrie'. Within the medium of music, time is captured, the infinite mobility of the human soul. Novalis not only comes near to implying, in common with Herder, the musical origin of language, a theory shared by Proust, but utters in advance Valéry's advice to poets to 'reprendre à la musique leur bien.' This inspired ode to music seems to be at the heart of Symbolism and worthy, in its own right, to rank beside the Proustian conjecture that music was perhaps man's original language, before the drift to the conceptual which leaves the essence of his message 'au seuil des phrases.' I here give Novalis's words in Maeterlinck's translation, since, if Proust read the German author, it was most probably in Maeterlinck's version, and the French form illustrates more vividly than the original any possible features of Proust *avant la lettre*:

> La musique parle une langue universelle, par laquelle l'esprit est excité librement et sans but. Elle lui fait un tel bien, lui est si connue et si familière, qu'en ces courts instants il lui semble qu'il se trouve dans sa patrie. Tout ce qui est amour et bonté, passé et futur, s'élève en lui en même temps que l'espoir et le désir. Notre langue à l'origine était bien plus musicale; ce n'est que peu à peu qu'elle s'est ainsi prosaïsée et assourdie. Elle est devenue un simple bruit, un son, s'il est permis d'avilir ainsi ce mot très beau, il faut qu'elle redevienne un chant.[21]

In conclusion, it would seem that Charles Du Bos had indeed seized upon the virtual affinity between Novalis and Proust when he singled out for analysis the preoccupation of both writers with the threads of relationship which form a web between the self and the outer world. The German author discovers and analyses the complexity of these *Verknüpfungen* or communication chords between the past and the present. Proust, in turn, is intensely preoccupied with 'un certain rapport entre ces sensations et ces souvenirs', with the 'fils mystérieux' which life tirelessly weaves, as if in defiance of death, 'entre les êtres, entre les événements', presenting us with 'une trame' of such subtle texture 'qu'entre le moindre point de notre passé et tous les autres un riche réseau de souvenirs ne laisse que le choix des communications' (*RTP*, III, 1030). No one was more sensitive than Novalis to the interchangeability of inner and outer worlds, to the position of the soul at a kind of crossroads, 'wo sich Innen- und Außenwelt berühren' ('Wo sie sich durchdringen, ist der

Sitz der Seele in jedem Punkte der Durchdringung') – no one was more aware that the conventional division of time is arbitrary. He expresses the new sense of interdependence between inner and outer self conveyed by the freedom of movement in time and inner space; there follows a visionary experience to which transparency is perhaps the key:

> ... die Außenwelt wird durchsichtig, und die Innenwelt mannigfaltig und bedeutungs-voll, und so befindet sich der Mensch in einem innig lebendigen Zustande zwischen zwei Welten in der volkommensten Freiheit und dem freudigsten Machtgefühl.
>
> *(NF, Die Lehrlinge zu Sais*, p. 125; cf., p. 111)

Proust will develop this theme of the interplay between subject and object, stressing that each individual's world is irreducible, and communicable only by art. Here, as already stated, he may be said to extend and complete Novalis, notably the latter's speculations about 'mehrfache Sinne'. Proust and Novalis enjoy a strong sense of virtuality, a heightened awareness of 'mondes possibles', awaiting only the intervention of art for expression (*RTP*, III, 895),[22] and both associate the act of memory intimately with the creative act. However, while Novalis conjectures only tentatively about the extent to which each man can multiply his worlds of experience, Proust goes further. Forever intent upon splitting *ad infinitum* the spectrum of each man's sensi-bility, he triumphantly vindicates and sublimates in himself and in others 'le complexe d'Argus',[23] for, not content with enabling his readers to 'voir l'univers avec les yeux d'un autre, de cent autres, voir les cent univers que chacun d'eux voit, que chacun d'eux est' (*RTP*, III, 258), he sets them well on the way to become, by this very plurality of vision, 'lecteurs d'eux-mêmes' and artists in their own right.

Notes

[1] In the course of this chapter I refer to Maeterlinck's translation, *Les Disciples à Saïs et les fragments de Novalis traduits de l'allemand et précédés d'une introduction par Maurice Maeterlinck* (Brussels, 1895).

[2] '*Les Eblouissements*, par la Comtesse de Noailles' (*CSB*, 537–8). In the novel, the narrator derives bitter satisfaction from observing, on the part of Oriane, 'une complète incompréhension de Maeterlinck' and reflects drily: 'C'est pour une pareille femme que tous les matins je fais tant de kilomètres, vraiment j'ai de la bonté!' (*RTP*, II, 229). So complex is his reaction, however, that he remains reluctant to renounce his boyish admiration of the Duchesse de Guermantes. Ironically Oriane subsequently conforms to fashion to the extent of admiring Maeterlinck's *Les sept princesses*, actually claiming that she had always done so! (ibid., III, 1013). For further reference to Maeterlinck,

see ibid., II, 249; III, 34, 117, 118. Proust wrote a pastiche of Maeterlinck, 'L'Affaire Lemoine par Maeterlinck', 1908: M. Proust, *Textes retrouvés*, pp. 46–50.

[3] See *LAURIS*, Lettre LXXI mid August 1911, p. 222; Maeterlinck interprets death negatively, Proust does the reverse:'... vous verrez que tout mon effort a été en sens inverse pour ne pas considérer la mort comme une négation, ce qui n'a aucun sens et ce qui est contraire à tout ce qu'elle nous fait éprouver. Elle se manifeste d'une façon terriblement positive...' Refer also to the present author's *Proust's Challenge to Time*, Ch. VII, 'Death'.

[4] Thomas Carlyle, *Critical and Miscellaneous Essays*, London 1894. 'Novalis' (1829) I, 421–67. Proust read Izoulet-Loubatière's translation of Carlyle's *Heroes and Hero-worship* at Begmeil in September 1895. We can only conjecture that he may have read also the essay on Novalis. There is one reference to the latter author, on Proust's part, in a letter to Robert de Montesquiou (*CG*, I, 187).

[5] Gide shares this conception with Proust and the Symbolists; see *Le Traité du Narcisse*, *Romans* Pléiade, Paris 1958, p. 7: '... le souvenir du Paradis perdu viendra désoler tes extases, du Paradis que tu rechercheras partout – dont viendront te reparler des prophètes – et des poètes, que voici, qui recueilleront pieusement les feuillets déchirés du Livre immémorial où se lisait la vérité qu'il faut connaître.' See C. Du Bos, 'Fragments sur Novalis III' in A. Béguin: *Le Romantisme allemand*, Cahiers du Sud, Liguré 1949, pp. 145–60. Also C. Du Bos: *Journal* I, 1921–23, Corrêa, Paris 1946, p. 375 ff.

[6] 'Le son paraît n'être autre chose qu'un mouvement brisé dans le même sens que la couleur est de la lumière brisée.' Maeterlinck, op. cit., p. 109; cf., p. 110.

[7] Cf., the interplay of life and the dream in Nerval's work (Ch. III, pp. 50–1). See the present author, op. cit., Ch. VI, 'Dreams,' p. 92; the following passage from *Heinrich von Ofterdingen* is quoted by C. Sénéchal: 'Le Rêve chez les Romantiques,' in *Le Romantisme allemand*, p. 102: 'Chaque rencontre, chaque entretien établit entre l'âme du héros et l'univers environnant un lien nouveau, ou plutôt lui révèle une région encore ignorée de sa propre âme, car l'univers qui le porte n'est en dernière analyse que la partie de lui-même qu'il ignore encore ... sa personnalité s'universalise et le monde du même coup se transforme à ses yeux, "s'intériorise" pour ainsi dire en lui, bref, *devient rêve*.' (The italics are Sénéchal's.) C. Sénéchal quotes also the same 'vers du poème liminaire de la seconde partie de *Heinrich von Ofterdingen*' as worthy to 'servir d'épigraphe à l'œuvre entière de Novalis' (ibid., p. 101).

[8] 'Hypothesen über mehrfache Sinne, – über dunkle, – über neue Sinne, über ihre mögliche Einrichtung,' *NOV*, III, 269 (cf., *RTP*, II, 67). Compare *Heinrich von Ofterdingen*, *NOV*, I, 235: ' "Es ist schwer zu sagen, ob wir

innerhalb der sinnlichen Schranken unsers Körpers wirklich unsre Welt mit neuen Welten, unsre Sinne mit neuen Sinnen vermehren können, oder ob jeder Zuwachs unsrer Erkenntnis, jede neuerworbene Fähigkeit nur zur Ausbildung unsers gegenwärtigen Weltsinns zu rechnen ist."' See C. Du Bos, *Journal*, I, 376, 4 December 1923: 'Certains fragments de Novalis montrent très nettement qu'il croyait qu'il y a autant de ces mondes que nous avons de sens, et qu'il était prêt à penser non seulement que nous avons beaucoup plus de sens que nous ne le croyons, mais presque que nous pouvons nous en donner toujours de nouveaux. Ceci, pas très loin de son admirable aphorisme: *Jeder Gegenstand ist der Mittelpunkt eines Paradieses.*'

[9] Professor Cocking does not mention Novalis. J. M. Cocking: *Proust*, Bowes & Bowes, London 1956, pp. 62 ff.

[10] Letter to René Blum. See 'Lettres à René Blum' ed. Léon Pierre-Quint, *Proust et la stratégie littéraire*, Corrêa, Paris 1954, p. 51: '... (... nous croyons ne plus aimer les morts, mais c'est parce que nous ne nous les rappelons pas; revoyons-nous tout d'un coup un vieux gant et nous fondons en larmes) par une grâce, un pédoncule de réminiscences.' Cf., Novalis, 'Blütenstaub' No. 42 quoted later. See C. Du Bos, 'Fragments sur Novalis' III, *Le Romantisme allemand*, pp. 152–3. (See p. 61, n. 16 of the present work.)

[11] Most recently David Mendelson has written about the Proustian fascination with transparency in *Le Verre et les objets de verre dans l'univers imaginaire de Marcel Proust*, Paris 1968.

[12] Ch. Péguy: *Œuvres en prose*, 1909–14, Pléiade, Paris 1957, p. 1260.

[13] C. Du Bos, *Journal* I, p. 381. Cf., Maeterlinck, op. cit., p. v.

[14] Lilian R. Furst: *Romanticism in Perspective*, London 1969, p. 95. See also pp. 93–6. Cf., Werner Vordtriede: *Novalis und die französischen Symbolisten*, Stuttgart 1963, p. 102: 'Bei Novalis ist der Abstieg ins Unterreich zugleich der Abstieg in das Reich des Wortes und damit auch in das der Erinnerung, wodurch das grosse Romanwerk Marcel Prousts sich auch als eine mögliche Form symbolistischer Welterfahrung erweist.'

[15] Gide, op. cit., p. 4

[16] Ibid. p. 7. See n. 5 above.

[17] Ibid., p. 7

[18] Ibid., p. 10

[19] Reino Virtanen: 'Proust's Metaphors from the Natural and the Exact Sciences,' *PMLA*, LXIX (1954), pp. 1038–59.

[20] Maeterlinck, op. cit., p. 104. The rest of the fragment bears a close resemblance to Proust's reflections on the 'croyance celtique'.

[21] Ibid., p. 106.

[22] Cf., C. Du Bos, *Journal* I, 376, 4 Dec. 1923, quoted as epigraph to the present chapter.

[23] 'Il faut que chaque armée soit un Argus aux cent yeux.' (*RTP*, III, 981).

Notes for further reading

This chapter forms a development of the theme which I broach in my book: *Proust's Challenge to Time*, M.U.P. 1962, pp. 60, 64, 92; Charles Du Bos was fascinated by the affinity between Proust and Novalis and intended to explore the matter further. In the absence of any detailed study of this *rapprochement* by Du Bos or any other critics, and intrigued by the words of Du Bos which I have selected to serve as epigraph to the chapter, I decided to investigate personally the affinities between Proust and Novalis.

Chapter VI

Balzac

Aimer Balzac! Sainte-Beuve qui aimait tant définir ce que c'était que d'aimer quelqu'un aurait eu là un joli morceau à faire . . . Balzac, on sait toutes ses vulgarités, elles vous ont souvent rebuté au début; puis on a commencé à l'aimer, alors on sourit à toutes ces naïvetés qui sont si bien lui-même; on l'aime, avec un tout petit peu d'ironie qui se mêle à la tendresse; on connaît ses travers, ses petitesses, et on les aime parce qu'elles le caractérisent fortement.

('Sainte-Beuve et Balzac', *CSB*, 271–2)

Proust's relationship to Balzac is a subject as absorbing as it is complex. The laws of attraction and repulsion seem to operate in turn, to condition the later writer's reactions to his predecessor. By a singular irony, it is in an author of whom he can disparagingly declare: 'Il ne cache rien, il dit tout' (*CSB* (FALL) 210), that Proust is drawn to admire an arresting power to evoke. In Proust's opinion, Balzac's lacunae have as much power to convey to the reader intimations about the novelist's characters as the blanks of Flaubert to render the flow of time (*CSB*, 595; see Ch. IX, p.162 of the present work). If the latter writer seemed to Proust to fall from grace and recall Balzac at his worst by a momentary equation of art and life, conversely one of Balzac's redeeming features in Proust's eyes will be an evocative power worthy of Flaubert.[1] For Proust, however, Balzac is only by exception evocative. A capacity to seize upon the contingent, the coincidences and 'hardiesses' of life, seems ironically to be also his limitation. Proust experiences a keen sense of disappointment on discovering the restricted terms of reference of novels

101

whose titles are as evocative as any *noms de pays*. If, in fact, he fuses elements of two such titles: *La Recherche de l'absolu* and *Illusions perdues*, to form his own version – admittedly a debatable conjecture but no less intriguing for that – it may well have been in answer to the challenge which he considered his predecessor had failed to meet (*CSB*, 269*). In the following pages, I attempt to discover the nature of the inspiration which Proust undoubtedly found in Balzac's work, to judge only by his perpetual desire to multiply viewpoints of the novelist concerned. Even while he is in apparent revolt against certain Balzacian practices, he seems incapable of exorcising similar tendencies in himself, for instance the urge to enhance reality by art and conversely; Proust at once continues and renews certain Balzacian techniques such as *le retour des personnages* or the suggestion of *correspondances* between plant, animal and human life and milieu; finally it is of great significance that he develops his own distinctive variations on the art of the memorialist as practised by Saint-Simon and Balzac in particular, perhaps his most notable predecessors in this *genre*.

Albert Thibaudet finds his chief justification for a *rapprochement* between the two authors in Proust's power to act as Balzac's amanuensis and commentator in the study of homosexuality, to go beyond what may well have begun as a Balzacian 'reconstruction' of Vautrin, to the creation of a character owning an independent right to existence: Charlus.[2] Bernard de Fallois prefaced the publication of *Le Balzac de Monsieur de Guermantes* with a statement that Proust set himself to re-create, in the encounter of Charlus and Morel on the platform of Doncières station, the already famous meeting of Balzacian tradition: 'Et d'ailleurs son admiration va si loin, il est si persuadé d'avoir seul pénétré la signification de cette scène'.[3] In the encounter with Morel, M. de Charlus expresses the unconscious twist of motive which Proust had attributed to Vautrin: 'le sens très différent et très précis des théories de domination, d'alliance à deux dans la vie etc., dont le faux chanoine colore aux yeux de Lucien, et peut-être aux siens mêmes, *une pensée inavouée*' (*CSB*, 273); there is an important difference, however, in that it is now Charlus who, in contrast to his Balzacian prototype, desires to be dominated (*RTP*, II, 863–4).

Proust the analyst, forever preoccupied with deducing the laws of human behaviour, seems to delight in making explicit the discoveries which Balzac is content to set before the reader in a relatively untransformed state, rather as he might interpret a book of nature awaiting further glossing but already deliberately opened (by the critic) at the most significant pages, where the contingent has already assumed something of literary form and value without undergoing the complete metamorphosis into art proper. Balzac, in fact, would seem to have just that quality of the rough-hewn which inspires Proust not only to disengage in the world of his precursor's invention implicit laws of

102

conduct but to create in turn his own determinism in the form of an inexorable fatality of emotions and the flesh, with the result that one can apply with equal force to the later work Proust's comment on *La Comédie humaine*:

> Là, sous l'action apparente et extérieure du drame, circulent de mystérieuses lois de la chair et du sentiment.

(CSB, 277)

'Autant de têtes, autant d'avis'

It is significant that there is hardly any other author (admitted within the framework of *A la recherche du temps perdu*) whom Proust has refracted through such a multiplicity of viewpoints or *optiques* as Balzac. A. Thibaudet has gone so far as to describe Proust as 'le plus balzacien des écrivains français après Balzac'[4] adding, in his chapter on Proust, that, 'ce que Balzac a fait pour la durée historique, Proust l'a fait pour la durée psychologique'.[5] What other author within *A la recherche du temps perdu* becomes such a cynosure as Balzac and thereby affords Proust such scope to indulge his passion for seeing an artist and his creation 'avec les yeux d'un autre, avec les yeux de cent autres . . .'? Perhaps we come closest to a *Balzac par lui-même* in Proust's work, when the author of *La Comédie humaine* is conceived as deriving from the nineteenth-century capacity for self-contemplation 'une beauté nouvelle extérieure et supérieure à l'œuvre, lui imposant rétroactivement une unité, une grandeur qu'elle n'a pas' (*RTP*, III, 160). Even here, however, it is difficult to disengage fact from Proustian fiction within the body of what purports to be literary criticism. The power to watch himself at work and to unite indissolubly the rôles of artist and critic seems to have been more of a Proustian than a Balzacian attribute. Yet the fact remains that Proust continues to act as the optician at Combray in the sphere of literary criticism in showing us Balzac through the eyes of Sainte-Beuve, not only in the essay proper '*Sainte-Beuve et Balzac*' (*CSB*, 263–98), but even more subtly by the medium of Mme de Villeparisis, at times a living pastiche of the critic whom she quotes instinctively. It is possible to arrive at some conception of Proust's passion for plurality of vision if one considers, in addition to the pastiche of Balzac in *L'Affaire Lemoine* series, and parallel to that of Flaubert as reviewed by Sainte-Beuve,[6] another of Balzac as seen by Mme de Villeparisis (*RTP*, I, 722),[7] Sainte-Beuve's disciple. There is a further virtual pastiche of Sainte-Beuve's views on Balzac, in the opinions expressed by Brichot in dialogue with Charlus (*RTP*, II, 1050–6 ff.). The Guermantes, with the notable exception of their aunt, make a cult of Balzac far more convincingly in the novel[8] than in *Le Balzac de M. de Guermantes* (*CSB*, 279–98). Marcel, a novelist in the making, reflects the phases of his own development in his reactions to this

103

writer, the preference for *Le Lys dans la vallée* corresponding to the ideals of his adolescence.[9] Thus it comes about that 'This pattern of multiple viewpoints enables one to view Balzac critically in a typically Proustian fashion'.[10]

Sainte-Beuve gives point to Proust's central accusation, namely a failure to comprehend the creative act, by stating, in his review of *La Recherche de l'absolu*, that Balzac 'devine les mystères de la vie de province, il les invente parfois'.[11] In the pastiche, Sainte-Beuve is seen to imply that art is nothing more than a direct transcription of reality; thus Proust has him again demonstrate that he would have made of Balzac a far more passive 'secrétaire de l'histoire' than is compatible with an artist's creative rôle (*CSB*, 19).

Throughout the debate between Charlus and Brichot, Proust closely identifies himself with the former character. He shares undoubtedly at least two of the Baron's reasons for holding a preference for Balzac: an interest in homosexuality and a passion for vicarious experience, especially for 'la transposition mentale' (*RTP*, II, 1058-9). Early in the debate, Charlus praises eloquently, in virtually the same terms as Proust, in the essay: 'Sainte-Beuve et Balzac' (*CSB*, 273-4), the moment in *Illusions perdues*, described by Swann as the 'Tristesse d'Olympio' of pederasty (*RTP*, II, 1050), and alludes obliquely to the irony of Oscar Wilde's admiration for Lucien de Rubempré. At this point, Brichot intervenes with an *idée reçue* of Balzacian criticism, worthy of Mme de Villeparisis herself. His total lack of subtlety distinguishes him sharply from Charlus with grotesque effect:

> 'Je sais que Balzac se porte beaucoup cette année, comme l'an passé le pessimisme,'[12] interrompit Brichot.

Brichot returns to the charge later in the debate, voicing Sainte-Beuve's well-known line of criticism that Balzac lacks authenticity: '. . . j'aime qu'un livre donne l'impression de la sincérité et de la vie' (*RTP*, II, 1051). Ironically such a reaction is at variance with Proust's generally accepted judgement that Balzac's style is 'trop peu transformé' and inconsistent with Sainte-Beuve's own description of it as 'ce style si souvent chatouilleux et dissolvant, énervé, rosé, et veiné de toutes les teintes, ce style d'une corruption délicieuse, tout asiatique comme disaient nos maîtres, plus brisé par places et plus amolli que le corps d'un mime antique . . .'.[13]

Proust disdains what one might be tempted to call Balzac's special technique of *diurama*, or the enhancement of art by reality, here history, as tantamount to the artist's admission of a failure of creative power. However, he concedes the point that there is mutual enhancement between art and historical reality, as in the process of *composition en abyme*:

> Œuvre d'art tout de même et qui, si elle s'adultère un peu de tous ces détails trop réels de tout ce côté Musée Grévin, les tire à elle aussi, en fait un peu de l'art.
>
> (*CSB*, 290)

104

Did Proust, in fact, escape completely a similar tendency in himself? H. Levin has detected[14] traces of the Balzacian technique in such a sentence as the following:

> 'O audace' (s'écrie Swann à l'audition d'une phrase musicale), 'aussi géniale peut-être que celle d'un Lavoisier, d'un Ampère, l'audace d'un Vinteuil expérimentant, découvrant les lois secrètes d'une force inconnue, menant à travers l'inexploré, vers le seul but possible, l'attelage invisible auquel il se fie et qu'il n'apercevra jamais!'
>
> (*RTP*, I, 351)

The introduction of the *gouvernante*, Céleste Albaret, almost as part of Proust's autobiography, untransformed and life-size (*RTP*, II, 846–50), gives a curiously dramatic relief to the re-created figure of Françoise. When the latter devises a system of papers to be threaded on a string, Proust records obliquely for posterity one of his greatest debts to Céleste: her discovery of a system whereby his notes could be interpolated *ad infinitum* (*RTP*, III, 1034) (*CG*, III, 9).

The presence of a character in the dimensions of both life and art is sometimes less pronounced, as when Proust leaves, rather as a painter might, a trace of the original, or key to his portrait (*RTP*, II, 579; III, 200); Charles Haas is cited as having some of Swann's traits. Again, the effect is one of dramatic relief and, although not identical with Balzac's method of juxtaposing characters of his own imagination with historical figures proper, the Proustian technique here reveals a hint of the Balzacian enhancement of art by life or history. Proust modifies and re-distributes the proportions between his point of departure in reality and his point of arrival in fiction. For instance, he obviously has in mind Réjane throughout his portrayal of the closing scenes in La Berma's life but, as George Painter states:

> Proust can have had neither the fear nor the intention of seeming to portray (Réjane's son and daughter-in-law), Porel and Anne-Marie, except by contrast, and the appalling cruelty of the last days of La Berma, the final turn of the screw which completes the ruin of the Narrator's world, was enforced by aesthetic necessity.[15]

Such is Proust's creative power that Réjane becomes a shadowy figure as seen by this device, an illusion of perspective:

> Bien plus, comme à la même époque Réjane, dans tout l'éblouissement de son talent, donna à l'étranger des représentations qui eurent un succès énorme, le gendre trouva que la Berma ne devait pas se laisser éclipser, voulut que la famille ramassât la même profusion de gloire, et força la Berma à des tournées où on était obligé de la piquer à la morphine, ce qui pouvait la faire mourir à cause de l'état de ses reins.
>
> (*RTP*, III, 997)

Proust gives us the key both to his outlook as a memorialist and to his desire to experiment, often in Balzac's style, with the laws of historical perspective ('Journées de lecture', *CSB*, 527–33). Indeed, he seems to draw

105

much closer to his predecessor in the enhancement of the fictional by the historical and conversely than he would sometimes be prepared to admit. Does he not, in turn, resemble 'ces peintres de panorama, qui mêlent aux premiers plans de leur œuvre, les figures en relief réel, et le trompe-l'œil du décor'? ('Sainte-Beuve et Balzac', *CSB*, 268). Jacques Truelle has affirmed that, however contrary to the declarations contained in 'Sainte-Beuve et Balzac', Proust did openly unite with Balzac in 'l'habitude de parler de ses personnages comme s'ils avaient réellement vécu', proclaiming as 'des personnages coexistants', whom he associated 'dans la confusion des siècles et des pays', Colonel Chabert, Cardinal Fleury and Dr Cottard.[16]

However, while Balzac places the stress on life, conceding to the latter the victory over art in the last resort, Proust always has in mind the enhancement of art as his prime objective. He does not hesitate to use an artistic term of reference in order to enhance a description, while remaining fully aware of the dangers to which this *idolâtrie esthétique*, however sublimated, must necessarily expose his creative power. Although he parodies ruthlessly Balzac's extremely general portrayal of a character in terms of a work of art,[17] he uses exactly the same technique, only far more subtly, in his depiction of Swann's compromise of art. The latter remains content to enhance his love of Odette by likening her to a Botticelli painting and to revitalise his experience of art in the process. Independently of character portrayal, Proust is only too ready to continue to see life through the eyes of his admired artists: 'Des femmes . . . différentes de celles d'autrefois, puisque ce sont des Renoir . . . Les voitures aussi sont des Renoir, et l'eau, et le ciel . . .' (*RTP*, II, 327). Despite all his attempts to exorcise the demon of mime, a certain tendency to 'faire toute sa vie du pastiche involontaire' (*CSB*, 594) lingers still in his frequent introduction of the terms of reference of a painter, Mantegna or another, not only when Swann[18] but also when the narrator holds the stage (*RTP*, II, 572–3). No doubt, Proust could attempt to clear himself of this charge of artistic heresy by pointing to the narrator's protracted struggle to realise his vocation and become truly creative.

Within Balzac's work, Proust admires the added depth, the continuity and virtual dimension of the extra-temporal[19] conferred by the device of *le retour des personnages*. Before Proust's advent, Balzac had realised that the impression of continuity conveyed by nature could be reproduced in art by the reappearance of characters whom readers like Marcel were so anxious to see live beyond the confines of 'une journée de lecture'. It remains for Proust, however, to use the device intensively as a means of revealing the materialisation of time and, in the process, numerous successive facets of personality. In both respects, he goes far beyond Balzac.[20] Admittedly, Balzac was operating the device from one book to another of the vast *Comédie humaine* but, within the exceptionally wide compass of his own novel, Proust no doubt desired and achieved a comparable effect. While conscious of following in Balzac's traces by his use of this device, Proust sees his own originality as springing paradoxically from a variation which he will devise on the Balzacian *retour des personnages*; his predecessor's use of this technique may well have inspired Proust with the desire to analyse the 'return of impressions' as a virtual leitmotif of the subconscious:

> Ce ne sont pas seulement les mêmes personnages qui réapparaîtront au cours de cette œuvre sous des aspects divers, comme dans certains cycles de Balzac, mais en un même personnage, nous dit M. Proust, certaines impressions profondes, presque inconscientes.[21]

Proust's selection of 'livres de chevet' from Balzac

While retaining always a special regard for the 'grandes fresques' of *Illusions perdues*, Proust seems to have greatly admired Balzac's technique in the *nouvelle*. Works enlisted to serve the mirror-technique of character-revelation within the novel, *A la recherche du temps perdu*, may often hold a further fascination for Proust the artist. One is tempted to apply to Proust himself the test to which he subjected his characters, that is, to investigate his artistic and particularly his literary preferences. Mostly, however, in this respect, he personally acts as our guide:

> Bien montrer pour Balzac (*Fille aux yeux d'or, Sarrazine, La Duchesse de Langeais, etc.*) les lentes préparations, le sujet qu'on ligote peu à peu, puis l'étranglement foudroyant de la fin. Et aussi l'interpolation des temps (*Duchesse de Langeais, Sarrazine*), comme dans un terrain où les laves d'époques différentes sont mêlées.
>
> (*CSB*, 289 – Proust spells *Sarrazine* with a 'z', whereas the editors of the Pléiade edition of Balzac's novels give *Sarrasine*.)

After satisfying our curiosity about why *La Fille aux yeux d'or* should be in Swann's library and why Gilberte reads it with such interest, we feel impelled to press the inquiry further: Which qualities inspired Proust's admiration for such *nouvelles* as *La Duchesse de Langeais* and *Sarrasine*?

The opening situation of the former story, as a dramatic *entrée en pleine matière*, was calculated to appeal to Proust strongly.[22] The Rossini air as well as the *Te Deum* in a French rendering – played by a nun in 'une ville espagnole située sur une île de la Méditerranée' – reveals to the General, who is the chief protagonist of the *nouvelle*, the identity of one whom he had loved, and his suspicion is confirmed by the 'vague rappel' of 'l'air de Fleuve du Tage',[23] associated with the same person:

> Terrible sensation! Espérer la résurrection d'un amour perdu, le retrouver encore perdu, l'entrevoir mystérieusement, après cinqe années pendant lesquelles la passion s'était irritée dans le vide . . .
>
> (*LANGEAIS*, 56)

After a dramatic interview between the 'exilée' and her former lover under the eyes of the Mother Superior, the General decides to abduct the nun and, with the intention of drawing up his plans, returns to France. The opening is intriguing and only now does Balzac give us a flashback:

> Voici maintenant l'aventure qui avait déterminé la situation respective où se trouvaient alors les deux personnages de cette scène.
>
> (ibid., 61)

There follows a displacement in space reflecting the return to the past and, plunged into the Faubourg Saint-Germain of the Restoration, the reader takes up the threads of the Duchesse de Langeais's earlier life. The story of her relationship with Montriveau is marked by syncopation; in fact, it is a history of syncopation, of 'intermittences', Proustian *avant la lettre*: while Montriveau responds, the Duchesse fails to do so and conversely. Some of the most potent irony with which the *nouvelle* is charged stems from the fact that the General fails to return to his home in time to have a chance to respect the ultimatum which the person whom he loves has imposed. The result is that the Duchesse enters the convent as she had vowed she would, if her lover did not intervene within certain time-limits. The sense of precipitousness and inevitability is dramatic in the extreme. This flash-back enables the reader to appreciate the lovers' feelings at the moment of the confrontation in the Carmelite convent; the technique allows different time-levels to be skilfully interlarded; while he is reading of the period at Saint-Germain which coincides with the beginning of the love-affair, the reader is absorbed by his attempts to explain retrospectively the opening of the story, an 'interpolation des *temps*' indeed. The story now proceeds swiftly and inexorably to the *dénouement*. The subject is fully 'ligoté' and we enter upon 'l'étranglement foudroyant de la fin'. As previously noted, the precipitation in time is strikingly reflected in the displacement in space: the General goes to Marseilles and thence to Cadiz; a few months later he sets sail and, almost in the manner of a leitmotif, Balzac re-introduces the sacred music which had given such an impetus to the opening of the story; from the ship, Montriveau hears the music of the convent and thinks he can distinguish Antoinette de Navarrein's voice:

> Terribles souvenirs pour Armand, dont l'amour reflorissait tout entier dans cette brise de musique, où il voulut trouver d'aériennes promesses de bonheur.
>
> (ibid., 102)

There follow two further stresses on characteristically human syncopations of the heart: the General loves with far greater intensity a nun 'dépérie dans les élancements de l'amour, consumée par les larmes, les jeûnes . . . la femme de vingt-neuf ans, la sylphide' (ibid.) By an irony of fate, the Duchesse has died by the time the General reaches her and it is a dead woman whom he finally abducts. It is left to the General's friend to formulate the supreme syncopation in lapidary terms: a Balzacian aphorism already present in *Les Secrets de la Princesse de Cadignan* and anticipating the Proustian anatomy of love:

> ... il n'y a que le dernier amour d'une femme qui satisfasse le premier amour d'un homme
>
> (ibid., 103)

In *Sarrasine*, we rediscover all the features which must have fascinated Proust in the short story just discussed: the dramatic exposition, the creation of suspense and the interplay of time-levels. The opening coincides with M. de Lanty's ball, the occasion of a brilliant gathering, mysteriously dominated by the figure of an old man. By way of explanation to his younger companion of this sinister presence, the narrator embarks upon an incursion into the past. Here, much as in the *Duchesse de Langeais*, but with fewer clues at their disposal, the reader and the listener within the framework of the story try to conjecture the identity of the old man in the flash-back afforded. Only at the very end of this inset within the past does it become perfectly clear that the dancer of ambiguous sex, La Zambinella, is the curious figure haunting the present of the narrator and his young companion. It is evident that the ambiguity of sex in the character of the dancer, and Balzac's portrayal of the equally equivocal reactions on the part of Sarrasine, the would-be lover of La Zambinella, may well have been the central interest which the story offered Proust apart from the artistic issues of narrative technique. Characteristically, Balzac leaves it mostly to the reader to analyse the theme of equivocal sex and passion. Again, the fact that Sarrasine was confused by the ambiguity of sex and loved La Zambinella, believing the latter to be a woman, means that the protagonist, listener and reader are involved in a retrospective analysis of the former artist's passion. The revelation of sex is reserved for the moment of climax and marks the point at which we return to the question of the old man's identity:

> – Mais ce ou cette Zambinella?
> – Ne saurait être, Madame, que le grand-oncle de Marianina.
>
> (*SARR*, 275)

The story ends not so much on a *maxime* as on an impassioned cry of regret that love and friendship cannot exist in purity.

As already noted, *La Fille aux yeux d'or* serves an important mirror-function in Proust's novel, since it is one of Gilberte's 'livres de chevet' and prefigures the theme of *La Prisonnière*. Proust finds in this short story the same qualities of slow exposition and dramatic *dénouement* as in *Sarrasine* and *La Duchesse de Langeais*. In addition, he discerns in this *nouvelle* one of the 'profound' and 'mysterious' 'lois de la chair et du sentiment', 'comme Paquita Valdès aimant précisément l'homme qui ressemble à la femme avec qui elle vit' (*CSB*, 277). One wonders whether Proust would have wished to imply the same reasons for Albertine loving the narrator. He suggests that a physical resemblance is possibly responsible for Saint-Loup's choice of Morel as successor to Rachel (*RTP*, III, 682–3).

> *Ainsi un pays était suspendu à un visage. Peut-être aussi ce visage était-il suspendu à un pays.*
>
> 'Journées', *CSB* (FALL) 84

Apart from their interest in such laws, the two novelists have further common ground. Professor Cocking has stated that there are many subtle *correspondances* between the landscapes of *Le Lys dans la vallée* and those of Proust in his novel,[24] Clochegourde embodies the rich feudal past which is France's heritage, and the riverside fastnesses of Novepont, Clairefontaine, Martinville-le-Sec, Bailleau-l'Exempt seem to Proust to serve the same function. Both writers develop a *correspondance* between a woman loved and the landscape which is her setting. While Balzac ranks as Proust's precursor in this respect, Swedenborg may well be the original source of this particular *correspondance* and perhaps Baudelaire acted as intermediary (see Ch. VIII, pp. 147–9). There is a profound analogy between the narrator as he invests the river and landscape of the Vivonne with the mysterious charm of the Duchesse de Guermantes, on one hand, and Félix de Vandenesse as he discovers that Mme de Mortsauf is reflected in the scenery of Clochegourde, on the other. Before Proust, Balzac exemplifies 'Un paysage est un état d'*amour*' but peculiar to the later writer is the commentary on the erethism which accompanied Marcel's loving of a woman in terms of her setting and conversely. (ibid., p. 148). Literary associations enhance 'un pays de rêve' and Proust's reading of *Le Lys dans la vallée* inspires in him a love for certain flowers 'en quenouille', 'dépassant verticalement de leur grappe aux sombres couleurs un chemin fleuri'.[25]

Perhaps Proust does little more than renew a Romantic tradition in contriving a scene of seduction by flowers, since jasmine serves this purpose in *Edouard* of Mme de Duras, violets in Fromentin's *Dominique*, and a selection cunningly compounded is intended to express the lovers' unassuaged longing in *Le Lys dans la vallée* (cf., *RTP*, I, 126). Here again, however, Proust's variation on the theme is much more subtle than anything that has gone before, witness the coining of the phrase, rich in psychological overtones: 'faire catleya', destined to an ironically swift growth and wane as a living metaphor (*RTP*, I, 234).

The *correspondance* between woman and landscape is supplemented by another, more distinctively Proustian, between woman and the flowers of her choice. These no longer serve simply as the medium of love but in the rôle of 'un livre de chevet', 'le titre du volume encore ouvert' to reveal that elusive essence of personality which can only ever be expressed obliquely. The violets of Mme Swann seem to Marcel to disclose the 'luxe secret' of a *cocotte* and to partake of that element of the unknown which is her inner life, forever beyond the reach of physical possession (*RTP*, I, 594).

> . . . ces fleurs qui n'avaient pas été préparées pour les visiteurs d'Odette mais comme oubliées là par elle, avaient eu et auraient encore avec elle des entretiens particuliers qu'on avait peur de déranger et dont on essayait en vain de lire le secret, en fixant des yeux la couleur délavée, liquide, mauve et dissolue des violettes de Parme.
>
> (ibid.)

By his stress on the *correspondances* between plants and human beings, as also by his naturalist's delight in collating and comparing phenomena from both worlds, Balzac often seems to anticipate Proust and to impart a conviction that human passion is ineluctable. Proust may be indebted to Darwin and possibly to Zola, when he subjects human behaviour to the laws of plant and animal life,[26] particularly in his dramatic account of the Baron de Charlus's first encounter with Jupien. Whether or not Balzac was inspired in his study of the *correspondances* between plant and human life, by the writings of Père Louis-Bertrand Castel (1688–1757), he already gives the reader a foretaste of Proust's clinical attribution of power to natural laws, despite the unrestrainedly Romantic tone which prevails throughout his description of 'l'ivresse de la fécondation' in the world of flowers (*LYS*, 330).

A lineage of memoir-writers: Saint-Simon, Balzac and Proust

While powerfully attracted by a naturalist's preoccupations, Proust believed that one of his major functions in writing his novel was to serve as memorialist (at times even as 'mémorialiste de la nature,' *RTP*, I, 184), and the work abounds in indications that he set great store by this particular facet of his vocation. He reflects this conviction by constant references to Saint-Simon (*RTP*, III, 1044 *et passim*) and aspires to continue the tradition of the very writer whom A. Thibaudet has described as 'le plus balzacien des écrivains français avant Balzac, comme Proust sera le plus balzacien après Balzac'.[27] Thibaudet could with impunity have shifted the stress slightly and qualified Balzac as 'saint-simonien'. The 'côté saint-simonien' of Balzac must have preoccupied Proust intensely, especially since his immediate precursor's span of recorded history already anticipates the generation of 1850 and influences that of 1885. Thibaudet would plot the end of this truly Napoleonic span as falling in 1914, the date at which Proust would seem to be timed to enter: 'Avec la génération de 1914, la *Comédie humaine* prend figure de roman ou de

111

cycle historique'.[28] Proust must have felt inspired to do for the generations of 1885 and 1914 what Balzac had already done for that of 1820, and – with reservations for the bare *droit de cité* accorded to the 'paysans' – he could have joined his predecessor in making the following claim for his own 'memoirs':

> Mon ouvrage a sa géographie comme il a sa généalogie, et ses familles, ses lieux et ses choses, ses personnes et ses faits comme il a son armorial, ses nobles et ses bourgeois, ses artisans, et ses paysans, ses politiques et ses dandies, son armée, tout son monde enfin.

Moreover, Proust consciously reflects his sense of kinship with Balzac as a memorialist, for, like his predecessor, he enlists what Thibaudet has termed 'les natures mères', 'la collaboration des femmes, une maternité de génie'. Beside the women to whom Balzac had recourse as to the memoirs of his age: Mmes de Berny, d'Abrantès and de Castries, Thibaudet ranges the good *genii* presiding over Proust's world of society, 'Ici Villeparisis . . . Verdurin et Guermantes' and he implies that Proust intends perhaps a conscious *rapprochement* between Mme de Villeparisis and Balzac's Mme de Berny.[29]

As a further facet of the mirror-technique which he favours, Proust has set, within his own memoirs of French society, a figure who anticipates the memorialist and in W. Strauss's words, 'takes the place of a modern Mme de Boigne'.[30] Proust's choice for this rôle has fallen on Mme de Villeparisis. A faithful disciple of Sainte-Beuve, as already mentioned, brought up on the latter critic's *Lundis*, and, like Mme de Boigne, a reader of the *Constitutionnel*, she naïvely reproaches Balzac 'd'avoir prétendu peindre une société "où il n'était pas reçu", et dont il a raconté mille invraisemblances' (*RTP*, I, 722).[31] Yet, by an arresting irony, while Mme de Villeparisis experienced only rebuffs and rejection the moment she sought to attract to her own *salon* those 'dames brillantes' who frequented that of Mme Leroi, and while, for her own part, she could lay no claim to 'un salon véritablement élégant':

> . . . cette nuance n'est pas perceptible dans ses Mémoires, où certaines relations médiocres qu'avait l'auteur disparaissent, parce qu'elles n'ont pas l'occasion d'y être citées; et des visiteuses qu'il n'avait pas n'y font pas faute, parce que dans l'espace forcément restreint qu'offrent ces Mémoires, peu de personnes peuvent figurer et que, si ces personnes sont des personnages princiers, des personnalités historiques, l'impression maximum d'élégance que des Mémoires puissent donner au public se trouve atteinte . . .
>
> (*RTP*, II, 194)

Proust conceives of social rejection as having been at the heart of the inspiration and style of Mme de Villeparisis's *Mémoires*. He imagines that, as a blue-stocking, the authoress was possibly scorned by 'telle snob comme Mme Leroi', and perhaps he has Balzac and himself in mind as he clinically deduces:

Et entre certaines qualités littéraires et l'insuccès mondain, la connexité est si nécessaire . . .

(RTP, II, 186)

Proust undoubtedly fashions the Marquise memorialist in his own image and goes beyond any initial Balzacian analogy, firstly when he portrays her as attempting, during her period of withdrawal, to recover in the form of writing 'ce qui dans la deuxième [période] avait été si gaîment jeté au vent' (*RTP*, II, 187); and secondly, when, having admitted that the Marquise has only a limited amount of literary talent, he sees social rejection as an incentive to the potential writer:

> Et si les dispositions littéraires de Mme de Villeparisis sont la cause du dédain des Mme Leroi, à son tour le dédain des Mme Leroi sert singulièrement les dispositions littéraires de Mme de Villeparisis en faisant aux dames bas bleus le loisir que réclame la carrière des lettres.

(RTP, II, 195)

C'est un plaisir qui n'est vraiment pas très pur. Il essaye de nous prendre comme la vie par un tas de mauvaises choses et il lui ressemble.

(JS, 200)

The novelist C. of *Jean Santeuil* discerned in Balzac a certain earthiness, a rough-hewn quality which attracted and at the same time repelled the artist, since it was calculated to challenge the latter's creative powers and yet fall short of his conception of a finished work of art. We may assume that we are here very close to Proust's personal view of Balzac as opposed to the superficial one held by the Guermantes, 'les gens qui le connaissent bien', the latter category to be distinguished from the enlightened minority who, for all their awareness of the novelist's shortcomings, continue to admire him, despite and perhaps because of 'ses travers, ses petitesses'. Of these readers – and Proust includes in this minority the artists – we are told:

> Mais vous savez qu'ils l'aiment bien tout de même. Et au fond, c'est bien curieux, car il semble que rien ne devrait nous sembler plus bas. Car, au fond, tout le temps, ce n'est pas par l'art que cela nous prend.

(JS, 200)

'Vulgarité de ses sentiments, vulgarité de son langage', this is the most pertinent criticism which Proust levels against Balzac, explicitly in the essay: 'Sainte-Beuve et Balzac', of *Contre Sainte-Beuve*, by parody in *Pastiches et mélanges*. D'Arthez's astonishment, so crudely expressed by Balzac: 'Il avait froid dans le dos' (*CSB*, 264**), Proust mischievously transfers to the Baron

113

de Nucingen in the pastiche: 'Le baron, se sentant joué, avait froid dans le dos' (*CSB*, 10). The resentment felt by Félix's former women friends at the hero's present happiness with Mme Marie de Vandenesse, inspires the most commonplace of all Balzac's images:

> ... elles auraient volontiers donné *leurs plus jolies pantoufles* pour qu'il lui arrivât malheur'
>
> (Quoted *CSB*, 264*) (The italics are Proust's own.)

Proust parodies this banality with admirable verve in the pastiche, and the fact that such a vulgar expression of heat follows immediately the Baron's chilling shock, heightens the effect to the point of hilarity (at the same time, Balzac's passion for expanding detail comes under attack):

> Mme Firmiani suait dans ses pantoufles, un des chefs-d'œuvre de l'industrie polonaise.
>
> (*CSB*, 10)

Hyperbole is satirised as well as Balzac's addiction to explanations inter-calated in brackets (*CSB*, 10) and references to his other novels as a means of advertising *La Comédie humaine* (ibid., 9, 11 and 12). His naïveté and vulgarity of sentiment are both treated with equal ruthlessness in one sentence which proves to be a masterpiece of syntax:

> D'Arthez fit semblant de ne pas s'être aperçu de la comédie qui venait de se jouer, telle que la vie de Paris peut seule en offrir d'aussi profonde (ce qui explique pourquoi la province a toujours donné si peu de grands hommes d'Etat à la France) et sans s'arrêter à la belle Négrepelisse, se tournant vers Mme de Sérizy avec cet effrayant sang-froid qui peut triompher des plus grands obstacles (en est-il pour les belles âmes de comparables à ceux du cœur?)
>
> (ibid., 10)

'Vulgarité', then, Proust comes to set at the very source of Balzac's strength and to rank as an integral part of this novelist's genius (*CSB*, 265); in the course of his reflections on the mysteries of artistic creation, Proust will voice conjectures about the interdependence of vulgarity and creative power, as previously about the closely interwoven nature of vice and art in Vinteuil, Charlus and Morel. In the former matter, he contrasts Swann and Balzac and accepts only with difficulty that this creative force should seem so arbitrarily to lie in a generally recognised weakness, in short, to be accompanied by an apparently inevitable inferiority of the *moi social* to the *moi œuvrant* (*RTP*, III, 720).

Perhaps Proust has Balzac uppermost in mind when he attempts to find in the creative process a means of deliverance from passions, and to make art serve as a catharsis, transcending the purgation of pity and fear envisaged by the Ancients. He expresses the theory that art should purge us of life: '. . .

114

notre mondanité y est purgée comme dirait Aristote; dans Balzac, nous avons presque une satisfaction mondaine à y assister [à une soirée dans le grand monde'] (*CSB*, 268–9). Similarly he states on the register of morality, that if Charlus had become an artist, we would have seen 'sa valeur spirituelle isolée, décantée du mal' (*RTP*, III, 209*). The problem of the relationship between life and art never ceases to preoccupy Proust and perhaps here is to be discovered the paramount reason why he was always so powerfully fascinated by Balzac's work, in itself a vivid incarnation of this very question. While he is still in search of his literary vocation, the narrator hesitates whether he should accord priority to life or art, and ultimately Proust may well have extended to Balzac the recognition which he formally makes of the function performed by the Goncourts in redressing the balance between life and art. Once recovered from the despondency which had first assailed him upon his reading of the Goncourts' *Journal* and made him doubt his own vocation, the narrator conceives of life as redeemed, if only by virtue of its contribution to art. Thus Proust emerges finally triumphant from his en-counter with the double-edged sword not only of this diary but of any other work which, by disparaging the private identity of the artist, would threaten to discredit the latter's act of creation. The name of Balzac, mentioned only in the asterisked footnote, seems to be strongly implied through this defence of the genius who represents 'une force de la nature':

> Quel malheur que – alors que j'étais seulement préoccupé de retrouver Gilberte ou Albertine – je n'aie pas fait plus attention à ce monsieur! Je l'avais pris pour un raseur du monde, pour un simple figurant, c'était une Figure!' Cette disposition-là, les pages de Goncourt que je lus me la firent regretter. Car peut-être j'aurais pu conclure d'elles que la vie apprend à rabaisser le prix de la lecture, et nous montre que ce que l'écrivain nous vante ne valait pas grand' chose; mais je pouvais tout aussi bien en conclure que la lecture au contraire nous apprend à relever la valeur de la vie, valeur que nous n'avons pas su apprécier et dont nous nous rendons compte seule-ment par le livre combien elle était grande.
>
> (*RTP*, III, 720)

In Proust's opinion, it is, above all, Balzac's work which poses for each reader, according to his lights, the choice between two possibilities: artistic sterility and artistic fulfilment, in themselves the essence of the narrator's drama. 'Cette réalité selon la vie des romans de Balzac', precisely by conferring upon the merest contingencies of life 'une sorte de valeur littéraire', en-courages the race of Charlus, Swann and that forerunner of Gilberte: 'la jeune Marquise de Cardaillec, née Forcheville',[32] simply to live vicariously and to equate, in their turn, art and life. Paradoxically, it is this selfsame Balzacian quality of the true to life which seems to have been decisive in inspir-ing Proust to pass beyond parody – conscious or unconscious – and equally literary criticism, to the creation of a world irreducible in its individuality.

Notes

[1] Flaubert is Balzacian when he states: 'Il me faut une fin splendide pour Félicité' (*CSB*, 276). Balzac's evocative power underlies not so much his treatment of time as of the twist and turn of human motives: 'Aussi est-on étonné de voir que cependant il y a de beaux effets de *silence* dans son œuvre: Goncourt s'étonnait pour *L'Education*, moi, je m'étonne bien plus des *dessous* de l'œuvre de Balzac. "Vous connaissez Rastignac? Vrai?" ' (*CSB* (FALL) 210). The italics are Proust's.

[2] A. Thibaudet: *Histoire de la littérature française de 1789 à nos jours*, Stock 1936, II, 294: 'Il y a un monde proustien, original et peuplé, comme il y a un monde balzacien et beaucoup plus qu'il n'y a un monde flaubertien. Il y a une *Comédie Proustienne* des années 1890–1910. Peut-être Proust a-t-il contribué depuis 1920 à nous éclairer et à nous approfondir Balzac; Charlus n'a comme substance, épaisseur, puissance, radiations terribles, qu'un équivalent dans le roman: Vautrin.'

[3] *Le Balzac de M. de Guermantes*, ed. Bernard de Fallois: Ides et Calendes Neuchâtel 1950, pp. 16–17. Cf. '... la rencontre de Vautrin et de Rubempré, ce sera à peine transposée, celle de Charlus et de Morel, sur le quai de la gare à Doncières...' (Preface to *CSB* (FALL) 39).

[4] Thibaudet: op. cit., I, 286.

[5] Ibid., II, 294.

[6] 'Critique du roman de M. Gustave Flaubert sur L' "Affaire Lemoine" par Sainte-Beuve, dans son Feuilleton du *Constitutionnel*'; L'Affaire 'Lemoine', III, (*CSB*, 16–21).

[7] If Valéry, possessed by an equally strong desire for a refinement of self-division, deplored the fact that 'se voir' could not be doubled to become 'se voir se voir', at least Proust achieves the feat of portraying one angle of vision within another by the medium of such pastiche as mentioned above, and an impressive multiplication of viewpoint within viewpoint. His characters reveal themselves obliquely in their artistic tastes: Valéry, Gide and Proust find in the act of artistic creation – and the latter two writers notably in the elaboration of characters – the supreme opportunity for self-scrutiny and self-appraisal.

[8] In the 'red-slippers scene', where they unconsciously parody Balzac (*RTP*, II, 596). Just as the 'Bal de Mme de Beauséant' had taken priority over the Père Goriot's dying moments, so now, the 'dîner de Mme de Saint-Euverte' is judged more important than Swann's impending death.

[9] See 'Un des premiers états de "Swann" ' *Textes retrouvés*, p. 176.

[10] W. A. Strauss: *Proust and Literature: the Novelist as Critic*, Harvard University Press 1957, p. 85.

116

[11] C. A. Sainte-Beuve: *Portraits contemporains*, nouvelle édition, (5 vols), Paris 1855–74, I, 442.

[12] Cf., *Le Balzac de M. du Guermantes*. See *CSB*, 279–98 especially p. 284, where the Marquise, forerunner of Mme de Villeparisis, expresses the following view: ' "Du reste, ce Balzac c'était un mauvais homme. Il n'y a pas un bon sentiment dans ce qu'il écrit, il n'y a pas de bonnes natures. C'est toujours désagréable à lire, il ne voit jamais que le mauvais côté de tout. Toujours le mal. Même s'il peint un pauvre curé, il faut qu'il soit malheureux, que tout le monde soit contre lui . . ." '.

[13] C. A. Sainte-Beuve: *Causeries du lundi*, Garnier, n.d. II, 449. With this opinion of Sainte-Beuve, Proust sharply disagrees. His comment on the above quotation from the *Causeries* is emphatic: 'Rien n'est plus faux' (*CSB*, 269).

[14] H. Levin: 'Balzac et Proust', in *Hommage à Balzac*, Paris 1950, p. 307.

[15] George Painter: *Marcel Proust. A Biography*. (2 vols), Chatto & Windus, London 1965, II, 291.

[16] Levin: op. cit., p. 286.

[17] Of 'un regard sublime' on the part of Diane, he writes in the Balzac pastiche: 'Seul Raphaël eût été capable de le peindre' (*L'Affaire* 'dans un roman de Balzac', *CSB*, 10).

[18] On his way up the staircase at the *Soirée* of Mme de Saint-Euverte, Swann sees the servants as in a painting of Mantegna, Dürer, Goya or a sculpture of Cellini, in turn (*RTP*, I, 324–5).

[19] Levin: op. cit., p. 307. Proust attributes the evocative effect of the first meeting between Vautrin and Lucien to a still powerful recollection of the past and a presentiment that Rubempré is destined to become Eugène's ill-fated successor. (*CSB* (FALL) 219)

[20] '. . . Heretofore no novelist had made it [*le retour des personnages*] an instrument for catching the facets of the personality, for recording the passage of years, for registering the shifts and compromises and re-alignments that interrelate a series of careers. If psychology added a third dimension to the flat, old-fashioned technique of characterisation, Balzac's system of cross-reference added a fourth – the dimension of time and change in which Proust was going to move.' (H. Levin: *Toward Balzac*, New Directions, Norfolk 1947, p. 62.)

[21] *Choix de lettres*, ed. P. Kolb: Plon, Paris 1965. Appendice: pp. 283–9 and p. 286. Interview avec Elie-Joseph Bois (parue dans *Le Temps* 13 novembre 1913, p. 4). Much of the material is identical with that to be found in *Lettres de M. Proust à Bibesco*, Guilde du Livre, Lausanne 1949, pp. 175–7 etc.

[22] For a brilliant study of the Balzacian feature: 'l'interpolation des temps' see Geneviève Delattre, 'Le retour en arrière chez Balzac', *Romanic Review*, April 1966, pp. 88–98. I should like to state that I had written my own analysis of *La Duchesse de Langeais* and *Sarrasine* before discovering the above-mentioned article.

[23] 'Mélodie de Pollet, très à la mode vers 1820' (*LANGEAIS*, 56).

[24] J. M. Cocking: *Proust*, Bowes & Bowes, London 1956, p. 45.

[25] *Textes retrouvés*: p. 176 (and compare *RTP*, I, 172). About the literary enhancement of 'un pays de rêve', Proust is explicit in the early draft of *Swann* just quoted, where the narrator describes himself as '. . . cherchant à identifier au paysage lu le paysage contemplé pour lui donner la dignité que déjà la littérature conférait pour moi à la réalité en me manifestant son essence et en m'enseignant sa beauté' (Ibid: 'Un des premiers états de "Swann"' (cf. note 9)). See G. Tupinier: 'La digitale de *JS*' *RHLF* No. 5–6, 1971.

[26] For further details about Darwin's possible influence on Proust, see the present author's article: 'Le thème de l'hérédité dans l'œuvre de Proust', *Europe*: 'Proust (II)' February–March 1971, pp. 94 and 96–8. In this same article, I discuss at greater length determinism in Proust's work.

[27] Thibaudet: op. cit., I, 286–7. For the importance of Saint-Simon's work as one of the favourite books of Swann and Charlus, see J. Rousset: *Forme et signification*, Corti, Paris 1962, pp. 154–6. For a detailed study of Proust's affinities, I refer again, as already in the Prologue, to Herbert de Ley: *Marcel Proust et le Duc de Saint-Simon*, University of Illinois Press, Urbana 1966. In addition to Saint-Simon and Balzac, Chateaubriand should be mentioned, since he is a memorialist whom Proust openly acknowledges as one of his precursors. See Ch. II of the present work, pp. 35 and 38 ff.

[28] Thibaudet: op. cit., I, 285.

[29] '. . . Villeparisis, (justement le pays de Mme de Berny) . . .' (Thibaudet: op. cit., II, 295). Cf., 'J'avais été frappé en apprenant que le nom Ville-parisis était faux' (*RTP*, III, 294). See also the *Guide littéraire de la France*, Hachette, Paris 1964, for the following information: 'A cette localité s'attache le souvenir de Balzac et de la "Dilecta". C'est là que le jeune homme rencontra pour la première fois Mme de Berny.'

[30] Strauss: op. cit., p. 154.

[31] Compare the view expressed by the Marquise in *Le Balzac de M. de Guermantes*: 'Elle niait l'exactitude de ses peintures . . . Mais surtout, ce qu'elle ne pouvait pas admettre, c'est qu'il eût prétendu peindre la société: "D'abord il n'y était pas allé, on ne le recevait pas, qu'est-ce qu'il pouvait en savoir? . . ." ' (*CSB*, 283).

[32] 'Le lecteur de Balzac sur qui son influence se fit le plus sentir fut la jeune marquise de Cardaillec, née Forcheville' (*CSB*, 293). As one would expect, Proust implies disapproval of Mme de Cardaillec's attempts to reconstitute 'l'hôtel d'Alençon', and characteristically he traces the cause of the young woman's conduct to heredity, 'le sang Swann' (ibid., 294). The importance which he attaches to the act of artistic creation obliges Proust to deplore this form of aesthetic idolatry; he writes of 'la petite évocation' as follows: 'Mais pour ma part, j'en fus un peu déçu. Quand j'avais appris que Mme de

Cardaillec habitait à Alençon l'hôtel de Mlle Cormon ou de Mme de Bargeton, de savoir qu'existait ce que je voyais si bien dans ma pensée, m'avait donné une trop forte impression pour que les disparates de la réalité puissent la reconstituer' (ibid., 294).

Notes for further reading

Proust's relationship and debt to Balzac have been assessed by:

Pierre Abraham	*Proust: Recherches sur la création intellectuelle*, Rieder, Paris, 1930 pp. 50–7.
H. Bonnet	'Proust, Sainte-Beuve et Balzac', *BMP*, no. 1, 1950, pp. 34–45; idem: 'Le problème du roman chez Proust à la lumière de ses réflexions sur Balzac', *Le Disque vert*, 'Hommage à Marcel Proust', December 1952, Paris-Brussels, pp. 73–83.
B. de Fallois	Preface to Proust: *Le Balzac de M. de Guermantes*, Neuchâtel and Paris, Ides et Calendes, 1950, pp. 13–27.
H. Levin	*Toward Balzac*, Norfolk, New Directions, 1947; idem: 'Balzac et Proust', Hommage à Balzac, Unesco, Mercure de France, Paris 1950, pp. 281–308.
Laurent LeSage	'A great reader of Balzac: Marcel Proust', University of Toronto Quarterly, Oct. 1952, pp. 26–34.
W. A. Strauss	*Proust and Literature*, Harvard University Press, 1957, pp. 84–105.
R. Vigneron	'Structure de *Swann*: Balzac, Wagner et Proust', *French Review*, XIX, no. 6, May 1946, pp. 370–84.
J. Rousset	*Forme et signification: Essai sur les structures littéraires de Corneille à Claudel*, Corti, Paris 1962, pp. 150–4.
Ch. Daudet	*Répertoire des personnages de 'A la recherche du temps perdu'* Gallimard, Paris 1928 (see Ramon Fernandez's introduction which compares Proust's social world to that of Balzac).
P. Kolb	*Choix de lettres*, Plon, Paris 1965, no. 121, pp. 263–4, peu après le 14 mai 1921: A J.-L. Vaudoyer, where Proust speaks of 'ce projet de dictionnaire balzacien' and adds '(je rougis devant cette comparaison écrasante pour moi)'.

P. A. Spalding	*A Reader's Handbook to Proust*, Chatto & Windus, 1952.
B. Guyon	'Proust et Balzac', *Entretiens sur Proust*, Décade de Cerisy, Mouton, Paris 1966, pp. 129–55. (M. Guyon refers *en passant* to the work of A. Maurois, E.-R. Curtius, B. de Fallois and G. Picon on this subject.)
M. Zeraffa	'Personnage et personne dans le roman français', *Revue d'Esthétique*, T. XII, Jan.-Feb. 1959.

However, as W. A. Strauss states (*Proust and Literature* p. 85): 'The most Balzacian treatment of Proust's novel occurs in the *Répertoire des personnages de 'A la recherche du temps perdu'* inspired by the Balzacian *Répertoire* of Cerfberr and Christophe, Calmann-Lévy, Paris 1887'. See also M. Bardèche: 'Balzac et Proust' *RDM*, Dec. 1971.

Chapter VII

George Eliot

... a certain consciousness of our entire past and our imagined future blends itself with all our moments of keen sensibility ... The secret of our emotions never lies in the bare object but in its subtle relations to our own past.

(*Adam* Ch. XVIII, p. 194)

A partir d'un certain âge nos souvenirs sont tellement entre-croisés les uns sur les autres que la chose à laquelle on pense, le livre qu'on lit n'a presque plus d'importance. On a mis de soi-même partout, tout est fécond, tout est dangereux, et on peut faire d'aussi précieuses découvertes que dans les Pensées *de Pascal dans une réclame pour un savon.*

(*RTP*, III, 543)

A. Thibaudet thought that he found exemplified in the English novel, particularly in the works of George Eliot, a Bergsonian conception of time and memory, normally absent from the French novel in so far as the latter tended to favour the concentration of French Classical tragedy: 'Justement, c'est que *L'Evolution créatrice* est un roman, un beau roman. C'est surtout qu'un roman d'Eliot est profondément une évolution créatrice'.[1] While Proust might have been reluctant to concede the first statement, he would probably have had little hesitation in accepting the second claim, with or without its Bergsonian overtones. Certainly (if he read Thibaudet's article), he would have agreed that 'le roman anglais ... sait se donner le temps' and no one more vigorously than Proust was to emulate this expansiveness. Quite apart from the major Bergsonian concept that all our acts of perception are conditioned or, rather, orchestrated by our past experience, there was much in George Eliot's novels to suggest to Proust the presence of a spirit and aims akin to his own. J. P. Couch has remarked[2] that most of Proust's 'Notes sur George Eliot' (*CSB*, 656–7) could be applied, with only minor changes, to *A la recherche du temps perdu*, notably the recognition that George Eliot has a superb mastery of dialogue, a sensitive response to nature and an intense awareness of the process of change as well as of a higher spiritual order which constantly intrigues novelist and characters alike. Here, in the 'Notes sur George Eliot', as elsewhere, Proust tends to use literary criticism as a means of self-scrutiny and, in any examination of his literary relationship to George Eliot, it is particularly difficult to distinguish between affinity and influence.

In common with George Eliot, Proust finds, in the novel, ideal scope to debate the question of free-will and the rôle of chance; it is significant that both authors reflect elements of Darwinism when they ring the changes on an aphorism of Novalis which George Eliot, for her part, strongly contested: 'Character is destiny' (*The Mill* Book VI, Ch. 6, p. 378). While Proust is preoccupied mainly with the psychological effects of suffering and the creative impulse which it affords the artist, George Eliot consistently adopts a strongly didactic approach which Proust readily recognises, at the same time, perhaps, inwardly noting a different scale of values from his own: 'Sentiment de l'utilité de la souffrance, du progrès moral . . .' (*CSB*, 657). Lucien Daudet testifies to Proust's liking for Tolstoy, Dostoievsky and George Eliot 'et même pour leur morale'.[3] Both George Eliot and Proust write memoirs of society, the former novelist showing a strong bias towards study of the provincial strata, and both see in 'la sagesse des familles' (*RTP*, III, 675) a microcosm of history. Like the Dutch painters whom they admire, they discover poetry in the unheroic and in apparently insignificant material. The fact that the cult of associations, on the part of George Eliot and her characters, is even more than usually strong in *The Mill on the Floss*, where it is inextricably interwoven with sentiment, may have been crucial in giving this novel first place in Proust's hierarchy of preferences for English novels about childhood, with Dickens's *David Copperfield* a very close second. One wonders whether, like Thibaudet, Proust discerned affinities between George Eliot and that favourite author of his own and Marcel's childhood, George Sand. One of George Eliot's acquaintances, Ch. El. Norton, thought he saw a physical resemblance between the two novelists,[4] but he was judging mainly by the Burton portrait of George Eliot and the drawing of George Sand by Thomas Couture (1815–79) done in 1879 and now in the Carnavalet Museum. Another correspondent, John Fiske, expressed the view that 'George Eliot is *much* better looking then George Sand' (23 Nov. 1873). At a

122

deeper level, George Eliot, for her part, attributes both to Rousseau and to his 'spiritual daughter' George Sand the power to stimulate her creative urge but she never renounces the right to preserve her own independence of judgement. (Letter of G. Eliot to S. Hennell 9 Feb. 1849, *CORR. HAI.* I, 277.)

Who knows whether Proust may have detected another parallel, equally fascinating, between George Eliot and one of her favourite poets: Wordsworth? Such discoveries would be consistent with Proust's conception of literary criticism as an extended application of metaphor and as ultimately dependent for renewal on multiplication of viewpoint. Traces of Ruskin's influence evident in George Eliot's cult of realism must have afforded Proust a special sense of delight not unmixed with irony: 'Je sais que Ruskin exécrait ce roman-là (*Le Moulin sur la Floss*) mais je réconcilie tous ces dieux dans le Panthéon de mon admiration'.[5] In so far as Bergotte incorporates characteristics of Ruskin, it is natural that Proust should attribute to him a dislike of George Eliot. (It is significant that Bergotte dislikes also Tolstoy and Dostoievsky.) The fact that Proust does not stop there but is bold enough to invest Bergotte with qualities which we might associate with George Eliot (and Ruskin?), such as a liking for 'les expressions rares, presque archaïques' and a combination of realism with 'une philosophie idéaliste', is vivid proof of his intention to reflect in art the element of self-contradiction which he considered to prevail in life. One of the essentially 'modern' aspects of George Eliot is her intense preoccupation with the complexity and inconsistency of human nature inevitably mirrored in the social structure.

During Proust's childhood and youth, George Eliot's works had considerable vogue in France, in translation. Although, after 1900, her following in France decreased from the strength which it had known in the 1880s and 1890s, she was already receiving official acclaim from such writers as were to attain international eminence and become her devoted followers: Proust, Gide, the Abbé Bremond, A. Thibaudet, Charles Du Bos and E. Jaloux; and, among the philosophers, Bergson.[6] Both Georges de Lauris[7] and Marie Nordlinger[8] record that, with the exception of Ruskin, Proust was dependent on translations for his reading of English literature, especially the English novel. No doubt Proust intends more than a tinge of irony when he contrives that, within his novel, at least one of the characters should make up for his own shortcomings in this respect: '... Andrée me disait que ... ses meilleures heures étaient celles où elle traduisait un roman de George Eliot' (*RTP*, I, 943). Franklin Gary observes[9] that R. de Billy assigns the date 1910 to the letter in which Proust confesses to a veritable passion for English and American literature in general and for one of George Eliot's novels in particular: '... deux pages du *Moulin sur la Floss* me font pleurer', and that, by this time, Proust had already written a large part of *A l'ombre des jeunes*

123

filles en fleurs; with Gary we cannot help wondering whether the novel of George Eliot which Andrée is translating, is *The Mill on the Floss*.

Proust refers to Albert Durade's translations of *Middlemarch*, *Scenes of Clerical Life* and *Adam Bede* in quotations from these novels in *Pastiches et mélanges* (*CSB*, 72–4), and it is highly probable that he read *The Mill on the Floss* rendered by the same translator. Does the fact that he had recourse to the translation mean that Proust never browsed in the original? If he had been tempted in this direction, he would have had his attention drawn to a question which often preoccupies him – the literary use of dialect which he always found a source of fascination, if only because here, in archaic forms, the past seemed to him to be miraculously preserved. In Chapter VIII (pp. 146–7), I refer to Oriane's use of Old French forms in her speech, particularly when she narrates anecdotes. Proust believed he had discovered a paradoxical compromise between colloquial and mannered speech in certain tales of Chateaubriand (*Mémoires d'Outre-Tombe*), in George Sand's rustic novels and in the turbulent speech-rhythms of Céleste and her sister Gineste (*RTP*, III, 35), and he repeated the feat at first hand in his own novel, in the speech of Oriane. It is precisely the question of how to effect this kind of compromise in French which George Eliot discusses with her translator, A. Durade, in a letter of 29 Jan. 1861, after he had told her that he was experiencing greater difficulty in translating *The Mill* than *Adam*: '. . . il n'y a pas de dialecte; mais il y a des différences de couleur de style, suivant le caractère et la position sociale des auteurs, que le français se refuse à rendre' (24 Jan. 1861). To which George Eliot replied with a request which revealed, on her part, a deeply sensitive reaction to the character of the French language. It is significant that she is just as keenly aware of George Sand's innovation in making the spoken idiom an integral part of literary style as Proust would be later in his capacity as critic, as *pasticheur* of Céleste Albaret and her sister, and finally as creator of Oriane de Guermantes. The most cursory reading of the original texts would have sufficed to convince him of George Eliot's audacity and success in using colloquial English to treat serious, often potentially tragic, subject matter. Proust will give his answer to the question which she had every right to ask her translator:

> But it would be inadmissible to represent in French, at least in some degree, these 'intermédiaires entre le style commun et le style élégant' to which you refer? It seems to me that I have discerned such shades very strikingly rendered in Balzac and occasionally in George Sand. Balzac, I think, dares to be thoroughly colloquial in spite of French strait-lacing. Even in English this daring is far from general. The writers who dare to be thoroughly familiar are Shakespeare, Fielding, Scott (where he is expressing the popular life with which he is familiar) and indeed every other writer of fiction of the first class [sic].

One wonders how far Proust was inspired consciously or unconsciously to emulate George Eliot's use of this 'very accent of living men' in both dialogue and 'style indirect libre'. We know that he greatly admired her 'manière exacte, pittoresque, spirituelle, éloquente de faire parler les personnages caricaturaux sans caricature, avec la pointe de bien dire qu'il y a dans France' (*CSB*, 656), and his own use of conversation as a means of engaging in lively interchange personalities of intriguing complexity owes much of its power to the fact that he only narrowly avoids parody, witness the family conversations at Combray in particular, which invite comparison with the domestic scenes involving such characters as Uncle and Aunt Glegg, Uncle and Aunt Pullet etc., and, in *Adam Bede*, the inimitable Mrs Poyser; Proust's and George Eliot's family figures often owe their verisimilitude to their near self-parody.

Robert Dreyfus vouches for Proust's familiarity with George Eliot's novels when, as young boys, they played in the Champs-Elysées. André Ferré relates[10] that, from the age of thirteen or fourteen to seventeen, Proust 'lisait et relisait *Le Moulin sur la Floss*'. He tells us also that *Middlemarch* was another of the books which Proust admired while he was still at the *lycée*. However, according to J. P. Couch, such an early acquaintance with *Middlemarch*, on Proust's part, would have been impossible, since the French translation did not appear until 1890, the year after Proust had completed his *année de philosophie*. Once again one is driven back upon the conjecture that Proust's enthusiasm may have been so great as to impel him to read *Middlemarch* in the original. André Maurois traces Proust's *eliotisme* back still further to the time at Illiers. Between 1896 and 1910 Proust frequently mentions George Eliot in his correspondence with his mother, Georges de Lauris, Marie Nordlinger and Robert de Billy. However much Proust continued to be absorbed by George Eliot's works later in life, the formative influence which she exerted upon him seems to have been crucial in the period 1896–1904, to which most critics refer the 'Notes sur George Eliot' (*CSB*, 656–7) and part of *Jean Santeuil*. To judge by the allusions in his correspondence, 'En mémoire des églises assassinées', *Sésame et les lys* (Mercure de France, Paris, n.d., pp. 78–9 n. 2.) and *Contre Sainte-Beuve*, Proust seems to have known at least five of her novels in depth: *Scenes of Clerical Life* (1857), *Adam Bede* (1859), *The Mill on the Floss* (1860), *Silas Marner* (1861), and *Middlemarch* (1871–72). George Eliot, for her part, was well acquainted with French literature and her letters contain references to Molière, Pascal, Rousseau, Vauvenargues, Mme de Staël, Balzac, George Sand and Renan.

In his introduction to *Jean Santeuil*[11] André Maurois states that he finds reflected in the novelist C.'s love of English literature Proust's admiration for Dickens, Eliot and Hardy. More important, he thinks he detects veiled allusions to George Eliot specifically, as for instance, in such a feature as an implied approval of authorial intervention. C.'s two youthful admirers like to hear the author's voice within his work and it is their belief that passages of authorial intervention are tantamount to theatrical asides or monologues on the part of a novelist and disclose the private individual as opposed to the artist, a dichotomy which seems to have fascinated Proust from boyhood to maturity. Such a device obviously increases scope for psychological analysis but Proust no doubt appreciated its exploitation by Stendhal, Balzac and Anatole France. It remains therefore a matter for speculation how far George Eliot's practice, in this respect, inspired Proust to create the rôle of the narrator, dual in the sense that he is also protagonist, and Proust enhances such complexity by bringing into play the narrator's interlarded time-levels. It is characteristic of Proust that he will never directly intervene in the narrative but, in consistency with his Protean quality and strong sense of multiplicity, always choose an alibi. Germaine Brée considers that Proust's use of the omniscient narrator in *Jean Santeuil* is particularly interesting in its flexibility and she concludes that the 'presence of the narrator within the fiction itself and his ambiguous relation to both Proust and the reader seems to have been deliberately adopted as a conscious device'.[12]

In *Jean Santeuil*, some of the interventions which reveal a sensuousness lyrical in tone (*JS*, 460–1) closely resemble certain passages where George Eliot interrupts the mainstream of the narrative with what strikes the reader as a personal confidence: for instance, in *Adam Bede*, she cannot resist the temptation to give us the benefit of her own reactions to the evocative taste of whey, in an inset which becomes an incident of involuntary memory:

> Ah! I think I taste that whey now with a flavour so delicate that one can hardly distinguish it from an odour, and with that soft gliding warmth that fills one's imagination with a still, happy dreaminess. And the light music of the dropping whey is in my ears, mingling with the twittering of a bird outside the wire network window – the window overlooking the garden and shaded by tall Gueldres roses.
>
> (*Adam* Ch. XX, p. 211)

J. P. Couch finds numerous parallels between *Jean Santeuil* and *The Mill on the Floss*, notably between the characters of Jean Santeuil and Maggie Tulliver. Franklin Gary had already noted a particularly interesting analogy between Aunt Pullet and Tante Léonie, since both are studies in hypochondria. George Eliot and Proust are masterly in their use of comedy and in their power to blend laughter and tears, a quality which the former writer admires in George Sand. The strong emotive appeal of both novels is in large part due to the fact that they are intensely autobiographical in origin and amongst the least transposed works of their respective authors. Illiers and many of the Breton scenes, no less than Dorlcote Mill and St. Oggs, are 'familiar with forgotten years'. Both novels treat the theme of childhood rediscovered and convey it to the reader with a controlled but still vibrant intensity of emotion. George Eliot confessed that her absorption in this childhood 'recollected in tranquillity' had adversely affected the balance of the whole work: 'My love of the childhood scenes made me linger over them, so that I could not develop as fully as I wished the concluding "Book" in which the tragedy occurs'. It is highly probable that she projected much of her own unresolved conflict between conservatism and rebellion in a Maggie Tulliver divided between the claims of loyalty to the past and a spontaneous passion. Both Maggie Tulliver and Jean Santeuil (*JS*, 692–3) experience the bitterness of rejection at the hands of a society to which they ironically still feel themselves powerfully drawn. The tragedy of *The Mill on the Floss* lies in the impossibility of preserving, within the present, allegiance to the past, since growth itself is dependent on destruction, and a process of natural selection operates for the individual as well as for the race. Professor Cocking sums up the universal problem of this novel as follows: 'Sentiment binds; self-realisation tears apart'.[13] I would add: 'The past binds; the present and the future tear apart.' Proust must have been strongly attracted by George Eliot's analysis of a dilemma so closely resembling his own. Like his precursor, he came perhaps as near as possible to achieving catharsis by projecting in art his division between loyalty to the past and the desire for self-realisation. Both *Jean Santeuil* and *A la recherche* reveal a conflict between the generations, and the idealist's anguish when faced with the inevitability of betraying the past. George Eliot points a dramatic contrast between the destructive and the creative aspects of time in Maggie and Tom respectively. When Maggie alludes to the powerful attraction which she sees in the prospect of a relationship with Stephen, she voices George Eliot's constant sense of duality: 'It seems right . . . but then such feelings come continually across the ties that all our former lives have made for us' (*The Mill* Book VI, Ch. 11, p. 423; cf., ibid., p. 223); or again, this time in words which seem to answer in advance Gide and Montherlant: 'If the past is not to bind us, where can duty lie? We should have no law but the inclination of the moment' (ibid., Book VI, Ch. 14, p. 448). Very early in the narrative, George Eliot foreshadows in Darwinian terms the kind of *intermittence* within heredity which will bring about the tragic reversal of rôles between Maggie and Tom in the conclusion: 'Simple people think they can see through her [Nature] quite well, and all the while she is secretly preparing a refutation of their confident prophecies. Under these average boyish physiognomies that she seems to turn off by the gross, she conceals some of her most rigid, inflexible purposes, some of her most unmodifiable characters; and the dark-eyed, demonstrative, rebellious girl may after all turn out to be a passive being compared with this pink and white bit of masculinity with the indeterminate features' (ibid., Book I, Ch. 5, p.28).

Everywhere in *The Mill on the Floss* and frequently in her other novels, George Eliot shows herself intensely preoccupied with the ephemeral nature of childhood, especially with the adult's difficulty in remembering or imagining its unique quality of vision 'when the golden gates have been passed':

Every one of those keen moments has left its trace, and lives in us still, but such traces have blent themselves irrecoverably with the firmer texture of our youth and manhood; and so it comes that we can look on at the troubles of our children with a smiling disbelief in the reality of their pain'.

(ibid., Book I, Ch. 7, p. 59)

The notion that the past 'lives in us still' but blended with the substance of a later phase is extremely Proustian in content and imagery.

When Maggie Tulliver pushes her cousin Lucy into the mud and runs away to the gipsies, the episode might seem to foreshadow the pattern of her later life in much the same way as the 'drame du coucher' in *Du côté de chez Swann* anticipates Marcel's destiny in the rest of the novel. Maggie's relationship to her father, for whom she remains to the last 'the little wench', has many of the emotional overtones of Marcel's bond of understanding with his mother (already subtly sketched in *Jean Santeuil*); some would claim that the brother-sister relationship is of even greater importance than the one between father and daughter in George Eliot's novel. It is a measure of the destructive power of time that, like Jean and, later, Marcel, Maggie finds herself driven to 'kill the thing she loves'. Bankruptcy and the loss of personal possessions seem to imply in George Eliot's works much the same profanation of ideals as auctions in Flaubert's novels, and symbolise the same conception of a world in the throes of disintegration. George Eliot anticipates Proust in her power to convey the poignancy of loss and the overwhelming sadness imparted by the absence of familiar objects, when Tulliver goes bankrupt; similarly in *Middlemarch*, when Lydgate's and Rosamond's possessions are seized.

Ironically and paradoxically the flood which, in *The Mill on the Floss*, symbolises the destructive aspect of time, acts also as liberator, since it re-unites brother and sister. Perhaps death alone could put an end to Maggie's state of division between past and present. However strongly the conclusion of *The Mill on the Floss* may still be criticised for its elements of Victorian melodrama and sentimentality, it may well have seemed to George Eliot and, at a remove, to Proust, to be the ideal artistic solution of a problem ultimately insoluble in terms of life.

Perhaps it is because both the sense of change and the resignation to its inevitability are greater in Proust than in George Eliot that as early a work as *Jean Santeuil* has a greater time-span than *The Mill on the Floss*. *Jean Santeuil* bridges four generations and contains speculations on their interplay. In contrast to Proust, George Eliot is more concerned to stress continuity and uphold the authority of the past than to surrender even elegiacally to the law of flux, although she is capable of such a mood on occasion, witness the close of *The Mill*, but even here her lament for the past is not unmixed with defiance: '... if there is a new growth, the trees are not the same as the old ... To the

128

eyes that have dwelt on the past, there is no thorough repair' (Book VII, Conclusion). This reluctance to accept change without reserve prevents George Eliot from subscribing completely to the Darwinian philosophy. As already suggested, when she speculates on the caprices of heredity, it is usually in Darwinian terms. There is a dramatic example in *Adam Bede* where she reflects on the complicated pattern of tensions caused by the laws of heredity: 'Nature, that great tragic dramatist, knits us together by bone and muscle and divides us by the subtler web of our brains, blends yearning and repulsion, and ties us by our heart-strings to the beings that jar us at every moment' (*Adam* p. 40). Although both writers share a profound interest in heredity, George Eliot never presses her inquiry into this subject to the same lengths as Proust. One cannot help wondering how she would have reacted to Proust's suggestion, in *Jean Santeuil*, that one generation may grow into the likeness of its successor by virtue of a retroactive influence (*JS*, 873). The fact remains that George Eliot presents an interesting affinity with Proust in some of her notions of continuity, possibly because both authors shared with Emerson a belief in a universal spirit or 'oversoul' which uses human beings as its intermediaries (cf., *JS* pp. 720–1 and *Adam* p. 275).

George Eliot is masterly in her power to render time tangible in the form of change. There is not only the striking example of Lydgate whom E. Jaloux compares to Swann in his transformations. She shows dramatically in *Adam Bede* 'le changement de nos cœurs et des choses dans la vie'. Arthur Donnithorne and Hetty undergo profound changes of heart (*Adam* pp. 306, 309 and 348), and George Eliot sounds a Proustian note when she claims that, in Hetty's case, the child is present in the woman, the present illumined by the past (ibid., p. 391). After his fight with Arthur Donnithorne, Adam experiences a Proustian *intermittence du cœur*: he finds himself reacting to Arthur as he used to know him before the quarrel about Hetty, and then suddenly, he synchronises with the present at the realisation: 'It was affection for the dead, *that* Arthur existed no longer' (ibid., p. 449). George Eliot conveys an equally powerful sense of change when, at the trial, Adam sees in Hetty a ghost of her former self. According to George Eliot and Proust, love induces a subjective quality of vision, a Stendhalian 'crystallisation' which invests the other person with a beauty present only in the mind of the beholder. Like Proust, George Eliot conceives of each man's love as following a certain pattern; it is therefore hardly surprising but potentially dramatic that, after Hetty's tragedy, Arthur Donnithorne should again feel himself drawn towards the same woman as Adam, namely Dinah. Proustian also is the belief that one love-affair contains another: 'And Dinah was so bound up with the sad memories of his first passion that he [Adam] was not forsaking them, but rather giving them a new sacredness by loving her. Nay, his love for her had grown out of that past . . .' (ibid., p. 482). Proust had seized upon the essence of *Adam Bede* (as well as *Silas Marner*) when he noted that loss is a condition of gain, an aphorism which has strong biblical overtones: 'Adam perd Hetty et cela était nécessaire pour qu'il trouvât Dinah' (*CSB*, 656). If George Eliot seems to re-cast a French proverb: 'Partir c'est toujours mourir un peu' when she writes: 'In every parting there is an image of death' (*Scenes*: 'Amos Barton' Ch. X), she gives a strongly Proustian resonance to a dominant tension of her philosophy when she coins, with Adam's words, her own version of a universal truth so close to paradox:

> 'I suppose it's a bit hard to us to think anything's over and gone in our lives: *and there's a parting at the root of all our joys*. It's like what I feel about Dinah: I should never ha' come to know that her love 'ud be the greatest o' blessings to me, if what I counted a blessing hadn't been wrenched and torn away from me . . .'
>
> (*Adam* p. 494)

I have been pressing my elbows on the arms of my chair, and dreaming that I was standing on the bridge in front of Dorlcote Mill, as it looked one February afternoon many years ago.
(*The Mill* Ch. 1.)

It is above all as analyst of the laws of memory that George Eliot anticipates Proust. The opening of *The Mill on the Floss* is formed by a notable incident of involuntary memory. The analogy of a present with a past sensation is the key to re-discovery of childhood here, as in Proust; the numbness of the narrator's elbows, as she sits in an armchair, causes her to experience a visionary rebirth of the past when she rested her elbows against the cold parapet of the stone bridge by Dorlcote Mill. The past effectively becomes the present as the narrator sees what we take to be an image of her childhood self. Perhaps Proust was inspired by his reading of this incident to set the opening of his own novel in an atmosphere of half waking, half sleeping, in which impressions of rooms where Marcel had once slept are released by 'la mémoire du corps, la mémoire de ses côtes', by what he chose to call elsewhere 'une mémoire involontaire des membres' (*RTP*, III, 699). Perhaps, too, the dramatic manner in which George Eliot seems to see her childhood self projected before her as a distinct entity may have led Proust to discover the circular technique which distinguishes his novel, where the ending is already contained in the beginning.

Proust may well have noted some of the other occasions on which George Eliot invetsigates this physical memory. She closely associates such experiences with a strong awareness of the companionship of objects but the limbs concerned seem to command a power of memory entirely their own; a

130

conjecture which Proust reflects humorously by making each relevant part of the body the subject of a mental action:

> ... mon corps se rappelait pour chacun [chaque logis] le genre du lit, la place des portes etc. ... Mon côté ankylosé ... s'imaginait par exemple allongé face au mur dans un grand lit à baldaquin.
>
> (*RTP*, I, 6)

When, in *The Mill on the Floss*, after a quarrel, Bob throws a penknife in the direction of Tom's retreating figure, a physical reaction takes possession of his mind and begins to dictate a course of action calculated to offset an acute physical sense of loss: 'His very fingers sent entreating thrills that he would go and clutch that familiar rough buck's-horn handle, which they had so often grasped for mere affection as it lay idle in his pocket' (*The Mill* Book I, Ch. 6, p. 46). He experiences intense pleasure once he grasps it again after this temporary separation.

A similar episode involving the sense of touch provides the metaphor with which George Eliot expresses Tulliver's love of the 'spot where all his memories centred, and where life seemed like a familiar smooth-handled tool that the fingers clutch with loving ease' (ibid. Book III, Ch. 9, p. 245). Most vivid of all is the occasion when, for an acutely homesick Tom, the mere feel of old familiar objects in his pocket releases a whole succession of memories so feverish as to suggest a comparison with delirium, witness the choice of the term 'calenture'; here, in this instance, the sense of touch both arouses and sustains nostalgia:

> And then the mill, and the river, and Yap pricking up his ears, ready to obey the least sign when Tom said, 'Hoigh!' would all come before him in a sort of a calenture, when his fingers played absently in his pocket with his great knife and his coil of whipcord, and other relics of the past.
>
> (ibid. Book II, Ch. 1, p. 132)

However, the most dramatic incident of involuntary memory in *The Mill on the Floss* relates not to the sense of touch but to that of hearing. It occurs when Mr Glegg and Tom, anxious to find and destroy Mr Moss's 'note-of-hand for three hundred pounds' in face of the imminent threat that Mr Tulliver will be made bankrupt, open the old oak chest and prop the lid with the iron holder. While they are engaged in lifting out the deeds from the tin box, 'the iron holder gave way, and the heavy lid fell with a loud bang, that resounded over the house'. George Eliot refers to the 'sanative effect of the strong vibration' which temporarily relieves Mr Tulliver's paralysis but only in certain respects. She is careful to point out that the noise brought a flash of memory or a 'vanishing gleam' which lit up only prominent ideas, and that it derived much of its power from its highly individual associations. The analysis of the connection between sound and memory is masterly and throws

131

into relief George Eliot's belief in a human sense of kinship with the outer world in so far as the latter 'seems only an extension of our own personality' through the sheer force of associations born of long familiarity (ibid. Book II, Ch. 2, p. 141 and cf., *Silas* Ch. 2, p. 24, and Ch. 5, p. 54). (Proust records a similar sense of union, on the part of Jean Santeuil, with the outer world: *JS*, 392–6.) It is not surprising that George Eliot is a regional novelist or that she entertains an almost superstitious awe for all familiar surroundings. Here, the stress is on familiarity with sounds:

> All long-known objects, even a mere window-fastening or a particular door-latch, have sounds which are a sort of recognised voice to us, – a voice that will thrill and awaken, when it has been used to touch deep-lying fibres.
>
> (*The Mill* Book III, Ch. 4, p. 206)

Similarly the young Proust, reflected in Jean Santeuil, found natural sounds such as the buzzing of flies more evocative of the past than a melody of Schumann which could never become such an integral part of the listener's deepest consciousness, or so the narrator of this early novel argues, before Proust's scruples are fully awakened to the dangers of according the preference to life over art (*JS*, 293–5).

A closely related episode of involuntary memory, again inspired by sound, occurs in *Scenes of Clerical Life*: 'Mr Gilfil's Love-story'. When Caterina lies ill, heedless of life around her, her former playmate Ozzy, 'in quest of a forbidden pleasure', strikes the handle of his whip on a deep bass note of the harpsichord which Maynard Gilfil has had installed in the room in the hope of reviving the young girl's interest in music. The effect of this random sound is again inextricably bound up with associations and, symbolical of music generally in George Eliot's novels, especially *The Mill*, restores the listener spiritually:

> The vibration rushed through Caterina like an electric shock; it seemed as if at that instant a new soul were entering into her and filling her with a deeper, more significant life.
>
> (*Scenes*: 'Mr Gilfil's Love-story' Ch. XX, p. 30)

It may be more than a mere coincidence that what M. P. Clarac considers to be perhaps the earliest example of an incident of involuntary memory in Proust's writings is inspired by the 'power of sound' and bears a close resemblance to the two episodes which I have quoted above from *The Mill on the Floss* and *Scenes of Clerical Life*, both of which novels Proust had read by the time he wrote *Jean Santeuil*. In the episode concerned, Proust seems to hesitate between the power of a sound and a musical phrase, no doubt the earliest version of 'la petite phrase', and finally to favour a 'sonorité' as responsible for releasing a flood of memory in his hero, Jean:

> Et cette sonorité ah! oui la voilà, il l'entend, et il l'a reconnue, c'était celle du vieux piano aigre de chez M. Sandré. Par hasard, en accrochant un peu, les doigts de T. ont

tiré de ce bon piano un son juste aussi aigre que celui du piano de M. Sandré. Sans cela jamais sans doute Jean n'y eût repensé . . .

(JS, 898)

However, Proust's indebtedness to George Eliot may go much further. He may owe to her the inspiration to use music at once as yardstick of human emotion and as leitmotif within the fabric of a novel. George Eliot employs the device of *livres de chevet* as a means of reflecting characters and their moods in most of her novels but in 'Mr Gilfil's Love-story', as later in *The Mill on the Floss* and *Middlemarch*, she opens the way for Proust by enlisting music in the rôle of *livre de chevet* in its own right. She contrives that Gluck's *Orfeo*, in particular the air *Che farò* and *Ho perduto il bel sembiante* by Paesiello (in both of which 'the singer pours out his yearning after his lost love'), should serve most beautifully as mirror-compositions to the entire story. The experience of Orpheus is echoed by that of Caterina in losing Anthony and even more tragically by Maynard when Caterina dies; in fact, George Eliot deliberately but no less subtly allows the theme of Orpheus's sorrow to underlie Maynard's expression (in free indirect style) of his own desolation which becomes a variation on the theme of *Che farò* (*Scenes*: Vol. 2 'Mr Gilfil's Love-story' Ch. XIX, p. 10). The chance vibration marks only the first stage in Caterina's rebirth to life and it is only the familiar air from Gluck which, by recapturing the essence of the singer's childhood, can restore her sense of identity, anticipating the Proustian rôle of sound and music in recovering time lost:

> Caterina was singing the very air from *Orfeo* which we heard her singing so many months ago at the beginning of her sorrows. It was *Che farò*, Sir Christopher's favourite, and its notes seemed to carry on their wings all the tenderest memories of her life, when Cheverel Manor was still an untroubled home. The long happy days of childhood and girlhood recovered all their rightful predominance over the short interval of sin and sorrow.

> *We could never have loved the earth so well if we had had no childhood in it . . . What novelty is worth that sweet monotony where everything is known and* loved *because it is known.*

(The Mill Book I, Ch. 5, p. 35)

On the subject of childhood and memory there are, in *The Mill on the Floss*, two key passages which frequently inspire critics to draw parallels with Proust's novel and, since its publication in 1952, with *Jean Santeuil* which, as already stated, was written at a time when George Eliot's influence on Proust was strikingly evident. One of these passages relates to the way in which the act of perception is intensified by past experience, present sensation extended by the spiritual dimension of memory: 'l'heure qui s'écoulait était

133

devenue comme de l'âme' or, as George Eliot describes the process in *Adam Bede*, the present is 'enriched with your most precious past'. It is not surprising that the following extract from *The Mill* should have distinctly Wordsworthian overtones and echo the 'Ode: Intimations of Immortality from recollections of early childhood':

> These familiar flowers, these well-remembered bird-notes, . . . such things as these are the mother tongue of our imagination, the language that is laden with all the subtle inextricable associations the fleeting hours of our childhood left behind them. Our delight in the sunshine on the deep-bladed grass to-day might be no more than the faint perception of wearied souls, if it were not for the sunshine and the grass in the far-off years, which still live in us and transform our perception into love.
>
> (Book I, Ch. 5, p. 36)

It vividly anticipates the following passage in *Jean Santeuil*:

> On dit qu'en vieillissant nos sensations s'affaiblissent. Peut-être, mais elles s'accompagnent de l'écho de sensations plus anciennes, comme ces grandes chanteuses un peu vieilles dont un chœur invisible renforce la voix affaiblie.
>
> (*JS*, 476)

As already stated, George Eliot is Bergsonian in her belief that past experience enriches present perception. Professor Cocking asserts that 'if, on the intellectual plane, the three statements are very closely related, indeed, on the plane of literature . . . all three formulations are different, and the distance between Bergson's and Proust's is perceptibly greater than the distance between George Eliot's and Proust's'.[14] I agree with Professor Cocking that Bergson tends to stand apart from both George Eliot and Proust by virtue of his insistence on the need for 'forward-looking thoughts' and action. (Cf., Chapter IX, p. 176 of the present work.) There is, however, a strong reservation to be made to this grouping of George Eliot and Proust, apart from the one which Professor Cocking makes when he sees reflected in the Proustian image of the prima donna the priority which Proust gives to art, and when he contrasts these markedly aesthetic overtones with the primarily emotional appeal and universality of George Eliot's message. By her repeated stress on childhood and by her characterisation of children (her novels teem with lively children and animals) she gives a much more balanced picture of the extremes of youth and age, and, in the process, expresses a much less elegiac attitude to the inevitability of loss than does Proust. As epigraph for *Silas Marner* she characteristically chooses lines from Wordsworth which are eminently positive and crystallise the power of childhood to draw even the shrunken, introspective thoughts of a miser outwards and in ever widening circles away from himself:

> A child, more than all other gifts
> That earth can offer to declining man,
> Brings hope with it and forward-looking thoughts.

Again, her attitude to love is much more positive than anything we find in Proust except the mother-son relationship in *Jean Santeuil* and in *A la recherche*, supplemented this time by another generation in the grandmother. When she portrays the growth of love between Adam and Dinah, George Eliot extols the dynamic power of subjectivity to transform the nondescript terms of language into poetry, and such idealism sets her in a category apart from Proust by the sheer force of its creative aspect and relates her rather to the Wordsworth of *Michael* (lines 198–203):

> I am of the opinion that love is a great and beautiful thing too; and, if you agree with me, the smallest signs of it will not be chips and sawdust to you; they will rather be like those little words, 'light' and 'music', stirring the long-winding fibres of your memory and enriching your present with your most precious past.
>
> (Adam p. 473)

The theory that the familiar impressions of childhood are 'the mother tongue of the imagination', that the early patterns of behaviour continue, like the 'primitive tissue' of individual and society (see pp. 128, 138 ff. of the present work) to evolve into maturity and beyond, such notions may have illuminated Proust's understanding of his own experience, but it should be noted that, consciously or unconsciously, George Eliot is echoing Wordsworth who 'raises the song of thanks and praise'

> . . . for those first affections,
> Those shadowy recollections,
> Which, be they what they may,
> Are yet the fountain-light of all our day,
> Are yet the master-light of all our seeing
>
> ('Ode: Intimations of Immortality . . .' lines 152–6)

The second passage cited by Franklin Gary, Professor Bisson and Professor Cocking bears an equally close resemblance to Proust's thought, particularly as expressed in *Jean Santeuil*. On account of its associations with the past, George Eliot prefers an elderberry bush to the more exotic fuchsia (*The Mill* Book II, Ch. 1, p. 141). Jean Santeuil and, later, Marcel prefer may-blossom for the same reason (*JS*, 330–3). Thus George Eliot raises a matter which, on the plane of aesthetics, becomes a major Proustian issue: the love of an object (or a work of art) for its associations rather than for its intrinsic worth. We see the origins of aesthetic idolatry of which Ruskin also was guilty, however much he deplored such an overthrow of priorities. Proust attributes to this false sense of values the failure of such potential artists as Swann and Charlus, both of whom attempt to equate life and art and carry the practice over into their love-affairs: Swann loves Odette in terms of art; Charlus finds his own love-affair with Morel enhanced by its Balzacian overtones and anticipates this stage when he admires Albertine's grey dress because of its affinity with the one worn by the protagonist in Balzac's short story, *Les Secrets de la*

Princesse de Cadignan. In his youth, Marcel tends to admire a painting for what it represents rather than for truly aesthetic reasons, thus allowing life, in terms of sentimental associations, to invade the preserve of art. Marcel reaches the moment of crisis when he has to choose between an Albertine, loved in terms of art, and art itself. His sense of vocation triumphs over the rival attractions of love and social ambition, in both of which activities associations play a major rôle, particularly in the second, where they are fundamental to *snobisme*.

There is one notable occasion in *Middlemarch* when George Eliot's preoccupation with the connection between associations and the act of memory causes her to break fresh ground in psychological analysis. At the time of Featherstone's funeral, an analogy between a past and a present mood recalls, for Dorothea, associated past impressions:

> But for her visitors, Dorothea too might have been shut up in the library and would not have witnessed the scene of old Featherstone's funeral, which, aloof as it seemed to be from the tenor of her life, always afterwards came back to her at the touch of certain sensitive points in memory, just as the vision of St. Peter's at Rome was inwoven with moods of despondency. Scenes which make vital changes in our neighbours' lot are but the background of our own, yet, like a particular aspect of the fields and trees, they become associated for us with the epochs of our own history, and make part of that unity which lies in the selection of our keenest consciousness.
> (*M* Vol. 1, Book IV, Ch. 34, pp. 285–6)

George Eliot believes that the peripheral elements of an experience may survive indefinitely as a landscape to the innumerable 'moods of memory', which 'shifts its scenery like a diorama'[15] (*M* Vol. 2. Book V, Ch. 53, p. 83). In the above description of Dorothea's reactions, she suggests that one mood can recall another by analogy and bring in its train impressions associated with a past experience. For Proust, on the other hand, it is usually impressions which recall each other and, in the process, re-create an associated mood or evoke an entirely new one. While George Eliot here gives the priority to mood, Proust usually conceives of an analogy between impressions as the decisive factor in reviving the past. Apart from this fundamental difference, namely a switch of the level on which analogy operates (a mood here evoking impressions which were previously associated with the protagonist's experiences by the mere chance of contiguity), the atmosphere and general tone of the narrative, including such terms as 'sensitive points in memory', are strikingly Proustian and the final description of inner continuity as 'that unity which lies in the selection of our keenest consciousness' might be considered to savour of Proust and Bergson in equal proportions.

The experience at St. Peter's, Rome, to which George Eliot alludes is distinguished by a similar chance association of mood and external reality: Dorothea's despondency and the jarring impact of an alien Rome on her

136

young consciousness. The incident anticipates the linking of outer and inner worlds at the time of Featherstone's funeral and, as in the later episode, George Eliot gives to the mood the right of precedence over external impressions which merely happen to coincide with an exceptionally vulnerable and receptive state of mind, on the part of Dorothea:

> Our moods are apt to bring with them images which succeed each other like the magic-lantern pictures of a doze; and in certain states of dull forlornness Dorothea all her life continued to see the vastness of St. Peter's, the huge bronze canopy, the excited intention in the attitudes and garments of the prophets and evangelists in the mosaics above, and the red drapery which was being hung for Christmas spreading itself everywhere like a disease of the retina.
>
> (*M* Vol. 1, Book II, Ch. 20, p. 170)

This kind of experience seems to resemble a spontaneous combustion of memory operating independently of any analogy between impressions, in the first instance, and to form a separate category within the sphere of involuntary memory proper.

Wordsworth may have recorded the same sort of experience in which mood has the ascendancy:

> For oft, when on my couch I lie
> In vacant or in pensive mood,
> They flash upon that inward eye
> Which is the bliss of solitude
>
> ('I wandered lonely as a cloud' *Poems of the Imagination* No. XII)

Jerome Thale actually classifies as Wordsworthian George Eliot's 'use of imagery' and he adds: 'In Middlemarch, for example, places, things and people quietly and easily gather emotional value and meaning, become charged with natural piety'.[16] In Dorothea's attitude towards the 'blue-green boudoir', George Eliot probably reflects her own as well as the heroine's intense 'inward life', when she subtly analyses the tendency for such natures to associate (perhaps at first arbitrarily) impressions with emotional overtones:

> While the summer had gradually advanced . . . , the bare room had gathered within it those memories of an inward life which fill the air . . . the invisible yet active forms of our spiritual triumphs or our spiritual falls . . .
>
> (*M* Vol. 1, Book, IV, Ch. 37, p. 327)

I, at least, have so much to do in unravelling certain human lots, and seeing how they were woven and interwoven, that all the light I can command must be concentrated on this particular web, and not dispersed over that tempting range of relevancies called the universe.

(*M* Vol. 1, Book, II, Ch. 15, p. 122)

Certes, s'il s'agit uniquement de nos cœurs, le poète a eu raison de parler des 'fils mystérieux' que la vie brise. Mais il est encore plus vrai qu'elle en tisse sans cesse entre les êtres, entre les événements, qu'elle entre-croise ces fils, qu'elle les redouble pour épaissir la trame, si bien qu'entre le moindre point de notre passé et tous les autres un riche réseau de souvenirs ne laisse que le choix des communications.

(*RTP*, III, 1030)

A major respect in which George Eliot anticipates Proust would seem to be suggested in what Professor Q. Anderson considers to be two of the complementary key-images of *Middlemarch*: the web of human relationships and the metal mirror.[17] The first of these two images is paralleled by the 'primitive tissue' which Lydgate, the Middlemarch surgeon, is intent upon discovering. It could be said of George Eliot and Proust that they give this medical image a twofold figurative dimension by seeking to lay bare the 'primitive tissue' in individual and society. The image of the web suggests the interweaving of past, present and future (cf., epigraph of present chapter, *RTP*, III, 543). This image, together with the related figure of the metal mirror in which a lighted candle creates the illusion of concentric circles from irregular scratches on the surface, implies subjectivity of vision and symbolises the unity of the entire novel conceived as a series of characters' successive views of each other. A highly dramatic effect is derived from showing the discrepancy between a character's opinion of himself and the image or sequence of images which he presents to others. In *Middlemarch*, both Lydgate and Rosamond are impressive examples of George Eliot's skill in using this technique.

In *Jean Santeuil*, is not Proust already engaged in showing the difference between illusion and reality, but in an episodic manner? In *A la recherche*, one of his principal aims is to reveal each character as he sees himself and as he is seen by others at different stages of the action. Everyone in the novel seems to be subjected to this process, in proportion as Proust seeks to fulfil, particularly in the social context, his desire to 'voir l'univers avec les yeux d'un autre, avec les yeux de cent autres . . .' and to multiply viewpoints to infinity. Amongst the most striking examples of what Professor Anderson calls the 'disparity between the intentions of agents and the opinions of observers' is the disillusionment which Marcel experiences some time after an early encounter with M. de Norpois (*RTP*, I, 477–8): 'Ce "potin" m'éclaira sur les proportions inattendues de distraction et de présence d'esprit, de mémoire et d'oubli dont est fait l'esprit humain'. There is a parallel episode which concerns Charlus. The latter is perhaps the most baffling of all the characters in *A la recherche* by reason of the multiplicity of images which he presents to the others, defying the narrator's and finally the reader's attempts to synthesise viewpoints. (For instance, Proust leaves unresolved the question of Charlus's possible heterosexuality.) In poignant contrast to Marcel, Charlus fails tragically to realise the utter discrepancy between his own notion of his public image and the harsh reality (*RTP*, III, 1047–9). To George Eliot's symbol of the metal mirror corresponds, in Proust, that of the 'pavillon', of necessity dual:

> ... en face de celui que nous croyons être l'unique, il y a l'autre qui nous est habitu-ellement invisible, le vrai, symétrique avec celui que nous connaissons, mais bien différent ... Quelle stupeur pour M. de Charlus, s'il avait pénétré dans un de ces pavillons adverses, grâce à quelque potin ... Mais ... nous manquons du sens de la visibilité comme nous manquons de celui de la distance ....
>
> (*RTP*, III, 1048–9)

Although it would be impossible to prove that George Eliot influenced Proust in this matter of studying a web of ever-shifting relationships (cf., *RTP*, III, 972–3 and 1029–30), the two images of web and mirror would seem to be equally applicable to both *Middlemarch* and *A la recherche* and, since Proust had certainly read *Middlemarch* – in which he was quick to seize upon the theme of vocation[18] – the conjecture of influence cannot be dismissed as wholly unrealistic.

By leaving the characters of her novel relatively free to determine their fate, George Eliot aligns herself with Bergson's conception of personality as opposed to the philosophy of determinism towards which Proust was attracted by his scientific interests, his predilection for laws, a stronger sympathy than that attested by George Eliot for the ideas of Darwin (*CORR. HAI.* III, 227) and, perhaps, finally by the influence of Balzac and Zola which militated against that of Idealism. The novel *Silas Marner* exemplifies the idealistic twist which George Eliot gives to a potentially Balzacian (or Zola-like?) theme: the weaver's subjection to the loom, and Silas is miraculously saved from the ultimate degradation in the process of *la déformation professionnelle*. Chance and involuntary memory join forces to change the course of Silas's life since the child's golden hair at first deceives him into thinking that he has recovered his lost gold and then, more important, but once again by analogy, revives his recollections of a dearly loved sister.

Both George Eliot and Proust have a strong sense of virtuality and attach great importance to the interplay of elements outside human control: ' "Character ... is destiny" but not the whole of our destiny, ...' (*The Mill* Book VI, Ch. 6). Bulstrode in *Middlemarch* might so easily not have allowed himself to become a passive accomplice in the killing of Raffles: Dorothea's decision to comply with Casaubon's demands hangs on chance and ironically comes after his death. In *Adam Bede*, Irwine and Arthur weigh the importance

139

of character and circumstance, respectively, concluding that it is better to have struggled against a fault and lost than never to have struggled at all (*Adam* p. 168). For Proust, chance often governs the course of a love-affair, witness Marcel's strong sense of interchangeability in his relationship with the 'jeunes filles en fleurs' and Mme de Stermaria. More important for the narrator, chance determines even the fulfilment of a vocation against all odds!

The ineluctable relationship which George Eliot establishes between human deeds and their consequences (*Adam* p. 168; cf., *CSB*, 656) fascinates Proust throughout his novel. Not only does he symbolise in the *soirée* organised by Charlus at the Verdurins 'cette union profonde entre le génie, (le talent aussi, et même la vertu) et la gaine de vices' (*RTP*, III, 264), he goes so far as to parody in Charlus an obsession with the sequence of events, reflecting this idiosyncrasy in the tic of a recurrent phrase and an associated comic gesture; by such parody he may be exorcising an excessive preoccupation with 'l'enchaînement de circonstances' on his own part (*RTP*, II, 287). While stressing art as a channel for human redemption and recognising suffering as the supreme stimulus of creative power, Proust demonstrates in his novel (cf., *RTP*, III, 187–8) his own version of the higher order which he finds operative in George Eliot's world:

> C'est aussi par-dessus l'enchaînement de nos vices et de nos malheurs, une sorte d'ordre supérieur de providence puissante qui fait de notre mal l'instrument incompréhensible de notre bien (cf., *Silas Marner*).
>
> (*CSB*, 656)

Important amongst the features which Proust admired in George Eliot are a vein of poetic realism in the portrayal of humble subjects and human relationships; a remarkable skill in conveying the beauty of nature in her range of changing moods; the ability to trace the moral repercussions of ordinary events; 'd'une passée ici, d'une allée à l'église là, d'une lessive ailleurs' (*CSB*, 657); finally a strong sense of the social structure, of the deceptive nature of social appearances and of the subjection of all institutions to the process of change. Proust must have noted with keen approval George Eliot's practice of setting back in time the events of the narrative in order to intensify the reader's sense of nostalgia for a lost past. Inspired by her example, he cultivated comparable powers and insights in *Jean Santeuil* and in *A la recherche*. Probably the greatest affinity between George Eliot and Proust, however, lies in the rôle which both these writers assign to memory, not only as a theme within their works but as a force vital to the functioning of imagination in the act of artistic creation itself. Indeed, this affinity affords the key to an understanding of both novelists and goes a considerable way towards explaining why each may provide an equally illuminating approach to the other.

140

Notes

[1] A. Thibaudet: *Réflexions sur le roman*, Gallimard, Paris 1938. p. 96.

[2] J. P. Couch: *George Eliot in France*, University of North Carolina Press, Chapel Hill 1967, p. 151.

[3] Lucien Daudet; 'Autour de soixante lettres de M. Proust', *Les Cahiers Marcel Proust*, 5, Gallimard, Paris 1929.

[4] Ch. El. Norton to G. Will Curtis, London, 29 January 1869.

[5] Letter to Robert de Billy 1910, *Hommage à Marcel Proust*, NRF, Paris 1923, p. 38.

[6] Couch: op. cit., pp. 135 and 147.

[7] *LAURIS*, p. 22.

[8] M. Proust: *Lettres à une amie. Recueil de Quarante-et-une lettres inédites adressées à Marie Nordlinger*, 1899–1908 ed. Marie Nordlinger, Editions du Calame, Manchester 1942 Preface, p. vii.

[9] Franklin Gary; 'In search of George Eliot: An Approach through Marcel Proust' *Symposium*, IV, 1933, p. 184.

[10] André Ferré: *Années de collège de Marcel Proust*, Gallimard, Paris 1959, p. 67.

[11] André Maurois: M. Proust. *Jean Santeuil* (3 vols), Gallimard, Paris 1952, Vol. I, p. 14.

[12] Germaine Brée: *The World of Marcel Proust*, Chatto & Windus 1967, pp. 59–60.

[13] J. M. Cocking: 'Some English influences on Proust' *Adam* 1957, p. 96.

[14] Cocking: op. cit., p. 97.

[15] Intense physical activity can also produce this effect of diorama: 'While his [Adam's] muscles were working lustily, his mind seemed as passive as a spectator at a diorama: scenes of the sad past, and probably sad future, floating before him, and giving place one to the other in swift succession' (*Adam* Ch. IV, p. 48).

[16] Jerome Thale: *The Novels of George Eliot*, Columbia University Press 1959, p. 158.

[17] Q. Anderson: 'George Eliot in "Middlemarch"' *Pelican Guide to English Literature*, vol. 6, Penguin Books 1958, p. 227.

[18] Nordlinger: op. cit., pp. 5 and 50.

Notes for further reading

For details of the editions used, see the note on abbreviations, p. X.

Q. D. Leavis's edition of *Silas Marner*, in the Penguin English Library, 1967, contains in the 'Introduction' and especially in the 'Notes' (see Appendix: 'A note on dialect' pp. 245–7) some interesting observations on George

Eliot's affinities with other writers such as Wordsworth and George Sand. The subject of affinities between Proust and George Eliot has been treated by the following:

E. Jaloux   'Sur la psychologie de M. Proust' *Hommage à M. Proust* NRF, Paris 1923.

F. Gary   'In search of George Eliot: An approach through Marcel Proust' *Symposium*, IV, 1933, pp. 182–206.

L. A. Bisson   'Proust, Bergson and George Eliot' *Modern Language Review*, XL, April 1945, pp. 104–14.

A. Maurois   *A la recherche de Marcel Proust*, Hachette, Paris 1949.

J. P. Hulin   'Du *Moulin sur la Floss* à *Jean Santeuil*' *Etudes anglaises*, VI, Feb. 1953.

J. M. Cocking   'Some English Influences on Proust' *Adam*, Proust number, 1957, pp. 92–9.

W. A. Strauss   *Proust and Literature*, Harvard University Press, 1957, especially pp. 174–7.

Q. Anderson   'George Eliot in *Middlemarch*', *The Pelican Guide to English Literature* 1958, pp. 274–93.

J. Thale   *The Novels of George Eliot*, Columbia University Press, 1959.

G. Brée   *The World of Marcel Proust*, Chatto & Windus, 1967.

J. P. Couch   *George Eliot in France: A French appraisal of George Eliot's writings* 1850–1960. *Studies in Comparative Literature* (4) University of North Carolina Press, Chapel Hill 1967.

R. de Chantal   *Marcel Proust, Critique littéraire* 2 vols. Montreal Press 1967, especially pp. 532–6.

Chapter VIII

Fromentin

... l'état du ciel règle ... celui de mon esprit ... Je me livre corps et âme à la merci de cette nature extérieure que j'aime, qui a toujours disposé de moi ... J'essaye les cordes les plus sensibles et les plus fatiguées de mon cerveau pour savoir si rien n'y est brisé et si le clavier en est toujours d'accord. Je suis heureux de l'entendre résonner juste; j'en conclus que ma jeunesse n'est pas finie ...

(*A*, 57)

... j'entendais avec ivresse un son nouveau rendu par le violon intérieur. Ses cordes sont serrées ou détendues par de simples différences de la température, de la lumière extérieures. En notre être, que l'uniformité de l'habitude a rendu silencieux, le chant naît de ces écarts, de ces variations, source de toute musique: le temps qu'il fait certains jours nous fait aussitôt passer d'une note à une autre. Nous retrouvons l'air oublié.

(*RTP*, III, 25)

A nineteenth-century artist combining Janus-wise the rôles of painter and novelist, and with whom Proust shows marked affinities, is Eugène Fromentin. The latter's *Les Maîtres d'Autrefois* (1876) presents art criticism in the form of a travel-journal and it was appreciated by writers such as Flaubert and Edmond de Goncourt as well as by painters, notably Van Gogh and Odilon Redon. Within Proust's novel, Charlus refers to Fromentin's painting of Eastern scenes (*RTP*, III, 809) and there are allusions to *Les Maîtres d'Autrefois* in the pastiche of the Goncourt diary (*RTP*, III, 709). Proust hastens to dissociate himself from Montesquiou's attitude of unqualified admiration for Fromentin, the art critic (*CG*, III, 123). His chief grievance against the latter seems to be an alleged neglect of Vermeer.[1] He is no more charitable in his judgement of Fromentin the painter, since he adds, in the same letter to Jacques-Emile Blanche (ibid.) in support of a title for the latter's art criticism: '*Les Maîtres d'Aujourd'hui* par Jacques-Emile Blanche, en symétrie avec *les Maîtres d'Autrefois* par Fromentin (bien entendu je ne vous égale pas ce peintre!)'. On the other hand, we find him in 1904 anxious to borrow *Le Sahara et le Sahel* from Georges de Lauris but convinced that the latter does not possess a copy.[2]

Fromentin, for his part, seems to have had greater confidence in his powers as a writer and probably as a novelist than as a painter.[3] We know that Proust had read *Dominique*: Fromentin figures at a remove, almost by his 'absence', in the pastiche of the Goncourt diary, where we learn that Mme Verdurin, the snob, is the 'Madeleine' of Fromentin's novel (*RTP*, III, 709). Did Proust intend here to underline the subjectivity of love on the part of the author Fromentin and his hero, and to stress the gulf between life and art? Certainly the interest shown by the Goncourt Brothers in Fromentin's technique as painter, art critic, writer and novelist, and the patronage extended to him in the latter capacity by George Sand, could not have failed to attract Proust's attention. Fromentin, no less than his patron, was absorbed by an issue central to Proust's preoccupations: the problem of the relationship between nature and art.

Baudelaire had allowed himself to linger for a moment in conjecture about Fromentin's expertise in two media: 'Tout le monde sait que M. Fromentin raconte ses voyages d'une manière double, et qu'il les écrit aussi bien qu'il les peint . . .'. ('Salon de 1859', *BAU*, 1067.) This was a tribute to be expected from an exponent of the *correspondances*. Moreover, the painter's technique is everywhere discernible in Fromentin's writing, particularly in *Dominique*, in the detailed accuracy of observation, in the 'ideal' form of a scene remembered, and in an interplay of land- and sea-scapes, although Fromentin never takes this last-mentioned procedure to the point of metaphor, as does Elstir in the painting of the Port de Carquethuit.

The closest Fromentin comes to using the land as a metaphor of the sea and vice versa is in the following passage, where the immobility of the land and the mobility of the sea seem alike to the eye. This 'intime analogie' might also imply that the sea often presents the immobility of the land and conversely; the movement of a spinning-top can give the appearance of immobility, so for Proust the effect produced by the movement of memory is 'le reflet neutre où se confond l'insaisissable tourbillon des couleurs remuées' (*RTP*, I, 46; Cf., Ch. IX, p. 171 of the present work), and this analogy between the immobility of the land and the mobility of the sea would become more pronounced, the greater the height of the observer's vantage-point: the lighthouse in *Dominique*, La Raspelière in Proust's novel. There is a further nuance: symbolically Dominique, as a would-be *terrien*, has renounced the 'vie aventureuse' offered by society and by the love-affair with Madeleine, of which the restless sea becomes the veritable leitmotif, forming as it does the virtual 'cadre d'horizon' of this 'souvenir' in the lighthouse scene. I incline to the belief that the 'intime analogie' is between (*a*) the calm of the land as 'alternative' to the eternal restlessness of the sea, on one hand, and (*b*) Dominique's rôle of *terrien* assumed as an evasion of passion on the other:

> Et puis, dans ce contraste du mouvement des vagues et de l'immobilité de la plaine, dans cette alternative de bateaux qui passent et de maisons qui demeurent, de la vie aventureuse et de la vie fixée, il y avait une intime analogie dont il devait être frappé plus que tout autre, et qu'il savourait secrètement, avec l'âcre jouissance propre aux voluptés d'esprit qui font souffrir.
>
> (*D*, 19)

George Sand, to whom Fromentin dedicated *Dominique*, confessed to a profound sense of kinship with the hero of the novel; she wrote to the author, 18 April 1862: 'Et comme votre Dominique, avec qui d'ailleurs je me suis trouvée en contact étonnant dans mes *Souvenirs d'enfance*, je sens beaucoup plus que je ne sais . . .'. With George Sand, Fromentin shares certain ideals, especially the belief in a *correspondance* between atmosphere and 'les heures obscures de l'âme'. Nowhere does Proust explicitly link the authoress with her *protégé* but the reader need only be aware of these two writers' mutual affinities and the relevance of both to the Proustian cult of the past, to penetrate to 'un autre univers plus interne encore', made possible by their introduction within the Proustian context.

Marcel's grandmother gives the child for his *fête* the four rustic novels of George Sand (*RTP*, I, 39); the donor's predilection for this novelist (ibid., III, 14) is but a facet of her passion for the past, a propensity which can equally express itself in the form of a cult of old furniture, too frail to be used! Mme Ceyssac in *Dominique* is the prototype of Marcel's grandmother. Fromentin endows the character in question with 'le génie de sa province, l'amour des choses surannées, la peur des changements, l'horreur des nouveautés qui font du bruit' (*D*, 50).

In another sphere, these novels of George Sand satisfy the perennial human desire for the past, if only in the purity of their archaisms which, threatened by time, are destined, by a strange irony, to enjoy a new lease of imagery: are they not 'pleins, ainsi qu'un mobilier ancien, d'expressions tombées en désuétude et redevenues imagées, comme on n'en trouve plus qu'à la campagne' (*RTP*, I, 41)? It is not far from old furniture to effaced metaphor. Old pigeon-cotes, archaic words, and, Proust would add, the

145

enrichment of a book by the aura of the reader's past – all have in common the power to inspire 'la nostalgie d'impossibles voyages dans le temps' (ibid.).

Fromentin's Dominique is, like Swann, an *artiste manqué*, yet, in contrast to Proust's character, he renounces the woman he loves when physical possession is within reach. George Sand had urged Fromentin to explain the hero's motives here: '. . . respecter Madeleine quand peut-être elle eût voulu des brutalités pour l'absoudre, était-ce le fait d'un scruple bien méritoire ou un acte de pure imbécillité?[4] In my opinion, however, this renunciation sets the love of Dominique and Madeleine beyond the reach of disillusionment in a realm of virtuality where imagination can reign supreme, and thus tends to impart to the relationship the quality of art. Professor Cocking points a contrast between Marcel and Dominique in this matter of renunciation. He describes the latter's sacrifice as 'dismal' and 'effected not as the joyful choice of a greater good but as the repression of a feared indiscipline'.[5]

Yet the fact remains that Dominique the *terrien* conveys to the reader a way of life and perhaps even a veritable aesthetic. The novel *Dominique* seems to reflect and continue the inspiration of George Sand's *romans champêtres*, especially *François le Champi*. In both works, one detects the cult of a region, poetry deriving directly from local colour and local customs; and an extensive use of country speech and archaisms. Fromentin perhaps as well as his hero is attracted all the more powerfully by a rustic setting with its cult of the *terroir*, its undying allegiance to habits and traditions – born, in turn, of the rhythmic succession of seasons – because such a background of the unchanging would seem to present the ideal foil to offset the ebb and flow of passions. 'La peur des changements'[6] explains Dominique's and Fromentin's reasons for preferring the land to the sea and motivates the former's withdrawal into a microcosm where 'Tout est dans tout' (*A*, 7) and 'la sagesse des familles' proves to be a facet of history itself, as Proust will later affirm in a characteristic gesture of loyalty to the particular (*RTP*, III, 675).

The language of George Sand's peasants is of the same origin as Oriane's *parler* 'savoureux' and lives on in Fromentin's renewal of the prose narrative at the spoken sources of country dialect: *chattières, biniou, bots, treuillée, treuils*, etc. Whether one is reading Oriane or Fromentin, one is constantly reminded of George Sand's rustic characters who do not hesitate to use such words as *cestuy-là, mêmement, mémorieux, assavoir, pastour, avenant*; rich with Old French associations. To Proust's delight, Oriane's language of the *terroir* brings her close to the peasants, her social inferiors, whenever she relates her tales (*RTP*, III, 35). Proust may well have associated with the Duchess's colourful, earthy style of narration not only the purity of idiom cultivated by *la dame de Nohant*, but the experience awaiting him when he turned to Fromentin, whose novel *Dominique* is, after all, of the same

tradition as the rustic novels. Proust had written of the Duchesse de Guermantes as though Oriane served as a kind of intermediary between natural
speech and art, performing orally the feat of writers such as George Sand and
Fromentin, or even acting as an Old French chronicler:

> ... c'est presque avec le tranquille sans-gêne qu'on a quand on est tout seul, les
> pieds sur les chenets, que je l'écoutais, comme j'aurais lu un livre écrit en langage
> d'autrefois ... J'écoutais sa conversation comme une chanson populaire délicieuse-
> ment française.
>
> (*RTP*, III, 34)

One cannot help wondering whether Proust's mother admired *Dominique* as
she did *François le Champi*. Certainly in the French Romantic novel, a
mystique attaches to the life and custom of a small community centred in the
manor and the tradition runs from Clarens through Clochegourde to 'le
Château des Trembles'.

Fromentin never tires of stressing Dominique's sense of unity with the
setting, with the earth, almost as though it were part of his character's
dependence on the elements, on the finest modulations of wind and sunlight.
Such a determinism explains, if it does not vindicate, his hero's cult of the
past. When the protagonist speaks of his instinctive sense of unity with the
earth from which he has sprung, he expresses his allegiance in language which
anticipates the animated Proustian idiom from 'les mille liens indéracinables'
onwards; the stay in Paris is an evasion, but:

> Le campagnard en outre persistait et ne pouvait se résoudre à se dépouiller de lui-
> même, parce qu'il avait changé de milieu. N'en déplaise à ceux qui pourraient nier
> l'influence du terroir, je sentais qu'il y avait en moi je ne sais quoi de local et de
> résistant que je ne transplanterais jamais qu'à demi, et si le désir de m'acclimater
> m'était venu, les mille liens indéracinables des origines m'auraient averti par de
> continuelles et vaines souffrances que c'était peine inutile.
>
> (*D*, 100)

Although not directly associated with Swann or Marcel as a redemptive
facet, there is nevertheless a corresponding cult of the *terrien* in Proust's
work: Oriane is not alone in revealing a 'côté terrien et quasi paysan' for she
is joined in this respect by the mother of Saint-Loup, by Françoise and
Céleste and by the latter's sister, Mlle Marie Gineste. Oriane has, in fact,
achieved a compromise between 'ce qui eût semblé trop involontairement
provincial, ou au contraire artificiellement lettré' (*RTP*, III, 35), the kind of
compromise – Proust adds – favoured by George Sand in *La Petite Fadette*,
and by Chateaubriand in certain stories of the *Mémoires d'Outre-Tombe*.

Fromentin's association of character with setting anticipates Proust's
identification of a woman with the landscape, often in a Dionysian situation
full of eroticism. Both writers demonstrate the capacity of vision to spill over
from the focal centre to the setting: 'Et la terre et les êtres, je ne les séparais

pas' (*RTP*, I, 157). Proust finds that erethism is enhanced by the scope which nature affords the imagination (ibid., I, 156 and 157). For Proust, it is necessary to take possession of the landscape in which a woman lives, although for 'quelques êtres', these natural settings, 'plus utiles pour leur imagination que le plaisir sensuel, n'eussent pas suffi pourtant, sans lui, à les attirer' (ibid., I, 690). In *Dominique*, Madeleine's discovery of the hero's native setting gives an extra dimension to her love.

In Fromentin's novel, the interdependence of man and nature is reflected on two levels: in the structure of the work and in the testimony of the characters, especially of Dominique. The action takes place against a background of sense impressions recorded with a naturalist's powers of fine perception. The presentation of this natural *décor* is classical in its apparent detachment but it is as closely associated with the human drama as wind and sunlight with the words of a book which Proust's narrator is reading (ibid., III, 885 and 889): 'Tel nom lu dans un livre autrefois, contient entre ses syllabes le vent rapide et le soleil brillant qu'il faisait quand nous le lisions'.

Fromentin's characters acknowledge this interdependence of man and nature. Perhaps the most striking instance occurs where Madeleine resumes unforgettably the *correspondance* between Dominique and the Aunis landscape. Speaking for both Dominique and Fromentin, she exclaims: 'Votre pays vous ressemble'. Having known Aunis first by the medium of Dominique's personal recollections, Madeleine is ideally equipped to discover and analyse the affinity between the man and his province; the result is a metaphor of man and landscape, a variation of Proust's identification of a woman with her native setting (ibid., I, 87). Concerning Dominique's place of origin, she adds:

> Je me serais doutée de ce qu'il était, rien qu'en vous voyant. Il est soucieux, paisible et d'une chaleur douce. La vie doit y être très-calme et réfléchie. Et je m'explique maintenant beaucoup mieux certaines bizarreries de votre esprit, qui sont les vrais caractères de votre pays natal.
>
> (*D*, 117)

Baudelaire's 'L'invitation au Voyage' may well have served as point of departure for both Fromentin and Proust. As the poet evokes an infinitely nostalgic *correspondance* between the woman he loves and the land of his dreams,[7] we behold through his eyes the woman in terms of the landscape and conversely, both merging, and enhancing each other's beauty like sea and land in the Proustian metaphor:

> Aimer et mourir
> Au pays qui te ressemble;
> Les soleils mouillés
> De ces ciels brouillés

Pour mon esprit ont les charmes
    Si mystérieux
    De tes traîtres yeux
Brillant à travers leurs larmes.
        (*Les Fleurs du Mal*, LIII, 'L'invitation au Voyage', *BAU*, 51)

Fromentin associates emotions and events with places and re-discovers in the scenes of childhood and adolescence the essence of his identity. In a distinctly Proustian passage, Dominique confesses that he fears the magical power of names to evoke the past. Fromentin here writes the opening of *un sonnet de noms* but applicable to the past in contrast to Proust's *noms de pays* which anticipate the future:

> Et ne vous étonnez pas si je divague en vous parlant de réminiscences qui ont la puissance certaine de me rajeunir au point de me rendre enfant. Aussi bien il y a des noms, des noms de lieux surtout, que je n'ai jamais pu prononcer de sang-froid: Le nom des Trembles est de ce nombre.
>
>   (*D*, 35)

The name Ormesson has the same power over Madeleine as Trembles over Dominique, possibly as a result of associations. Her lover has revealed Aunis to her as a part of the landscape of his own mind, his 'patrie intérieure' (ibid., 117). He would certainly have told her that the first break with Les Trembles was his exile to Ormesson. The sound of the name thus conjures up a whole inner realm of shared experience: 'Ce mot d'Ormesson sembla réveiller en elle une série de souvenirs déjà affaiblis ... "Cette fois", reprit-elle, "vous n'y voyagerez plus seul" ' (ibid., 126–7).

The Goncourt Brothers marvelled at Fromentin's 'mémoire locale extraordinaire'.[8] This same 'mémoire spéciale' is described by its owner as 'assez peu sensible aux faits mais d'une aptitude singulière à se pénétrer des impressions' (*D*, 33). Both Fromentin and Proust testify that peripheral impressions blend into a kind of harmony which ensures their survival in memory: 'Je m'en souviens [de cette soirée], surtout à cause d'un certain accord d'impressions qui fixe à la fois les souvenirs, même les moins frappants, sur tous les points sensibles de la mémoire' (*D*, 7). These peripheral sensations seem to be a condition of memory for both writers, and to harmonise in defiance of all laws of relevance and reasoning.

> ... le geste le plus insignifiant que nous avons fait était entouré, portait sur lui le reflet de choses qui logiquement ne tenaient pas à lui, en ont été séparées par l'intelligence ... mais au milieu desquelles – ici reflet rose du soir sur le mur fleuri d'un restaurant champêtre, *sensation de faim*, désir des femmes, plaisir du luxe; *là volutes bleues de la mer matinale enveloppant des phrases musicales* qui en émergent partiellement comme les épaules des ondines ...
>
>   (*RTP*, III, 870)

Proust's sense of reality as 'un certain rapport entre ces sensations et ces souvenirs qui nous entourent simultanément . . .' (ibid., III, 889) is paralleled by Fromentin's definition of his own inner world as consisting of 'un . . . accord de sensations et de rêves' (*E*, 180).

Fromentin anticipates Proust by investigating the interdependence of climate and memory. The Goncourt Brothers had been quick to note Fromentin's memory as one which retained 'le souvenir du vent, du jour, du nuage'.[9] It is not surprising, then, that Dominique is captivated not so much by the hunt itself as by the impressions which lie on the periphery of attention and which are destined to return to him in later years with heightened acuity, the very substance of involuntary memory (*D*, 33).

Deliberately, and prompted by an urge akin to the animal's instinct to hibernate, Dominique will amass in retrospect a store of sense impressions in order, by recollection, to prolong into the dead season of the year his period of intense activity. He enlists memory, especially the memory of the senses, as his ally throughout the delicate process involved: the term, 'monde ailé, subtil, de visions et d'odeurs', is at once Baudelairean and Proustian; the deliberate recourse to memory, however, relates Fromentin to the poet rather than to the novelist[10]:

> Le recueillement qui descendait alors sur les Trembles était inexprimable; pendant quatre mois d'hiver, j'amassais dans ce lieu où je vous parle, je condensais, je concentrais, je forçais à ne plus jamais s'échapper, *ce monde ailé, subtil, de visions et d'odeurs*, de bruit et d'images qui m'avait fait vivre pendant les huit autres mois de l'année, d'une vie si active et qui ressemblait si bien à des rêves.
>
> (*D*, 39)

Dominique will equally deliberately store the impressions gleaned during his stay at Les Trembles in the company of Madeleine. The conscious enlistment of memory is interesting, as also the use of the idiom of painting:

> Je passai les derniers moments qui nous restaient à rassembler, à mettre en ordre pour l'avenir toutes les émotions si confusément amassées dans ma mémoire. Ce fut comme un tableau que je composai avec ce qu'elles contenaient de meilleur et de moins périssable.
>
> (ibid., 124)

Here, Fromentin goes beyond the 'resigned acceptance of time's passing' and attempts to build his own original defence-system against mortality without joining Proust in the recourse to a system of metaphysics to conquer time.[11]

Habit, the repetition of sounds associated with the seasons, these give Fromentin a degree of reassurance, affording him an extra dimension in time, enabling him to renew himself and to re-discover his essence. The rustic tradition is important to Fromentin, if only because its continuity ensures the survival of man's *Seelenjahr*, a theme evident in the *Nouvelle Héloïse* of Rousseau and the rustic novels of George Sand. The prolongation of sound within memory itself, 'retentissements de vibrations internes', the inner resonance of 'certains bruits', these are Proustian features and make one think of the bell which announced Swann's arrival and had never ceased to sound within the narrator's inner consciousness, thereby yielding proof of his continued identity. What is particularly Proustian about the pleasure which Dominique takes in his impressions is the concentration on fine detail and a preoccupation with their continued existence in his own mind:

> ... le seul témoignage un peu vif qui me soit resté de ces continuelles embuscades c'est la vision très nette de certains lieux, la note exacte de l'heure et de la saison, et jusqu'à la perception de *certains bruits qui n'ont pas cessé depuis de se faire entendre*
> (D, 33)

When Dominique attempts to reform his ways, he will list chief amongst his weaknesses his enslavement to sense impressions and his surrender to the determinism of climate or 'agents occultes' (A, 100); he will endeavour to renounce what is perhaps the most authentic part of his personality: his diehard of a 'baromètre',[12] to use Fromentin's term, or 'capucin', to use Proust's image:

> ... le malaise ou le bien-être produit par un rayon de soleil, ou par une goutte de pluie, les aigreurs qui me venaient d'un air trop vif et les bonnes pensées qui m'étaient inspirées par un écart du vent, toutes ces mollesses du cœur, cet asservissement de l'esprit, cette petite raison, ces sensations exorbitantes ...
> (D, 177)

Ironically, however, it is by marginal impressions rather than by central facts that Dominique realises and records his own personal tragedy: his renunciation of Madeleine is reflected in the mood of the elements. It is entirely fitting that the hero should record his awareness of this central issue in terms of sense impressions and at the same time imply that his extreme susceptibility to these is responsible for his tragedy. Such a technique seems to me to renew dramatically the 'tragic use of landscape':

> Je ne fis pas autre chose, dans le morne bercement de ce long murmure de vent et de pluie, que de penser au tumulte que le vent devait produire autour de la chambre et du sommeil de Madeleine, si Madeleine dormait. Ma force de réfléchir n'allait pas au delà de cette sensation puérile et toute physique.
> (D, 198)

By the way in which he attributes to nature the power not only to reflect but to determine the protagonist's mood, actions and destiny, Fromentin seems to me to anticipate Proust: changes in the weather hint at changes in Marcel's life and – so Proust implies – initiate a whole course of human action.[13]

> Puis un jour, je me décidai à faire dire à Albertine que je la recevrais prochainement. C'est qu'un matin de grande chaleur prématurée, les mille cris des enfants qui jouaient, des baigneurs plaisantant, des marchands de journaux, m'avaient décrit en traits de feu, en flammèches entrelacées, la plage ardente que les petites vagues venaient une à une arroser de leur fraîcheur.
> (RTP, II, 780)

In this last quotation, however, and generally, Proust goes further than Fromentin in analysing the connection between climate and memory: atmosphere has a profound effect on memory (ibid., II, 143); cold weather can release an unconscious memory in Marcel; seasons retrace before the narrator the outward journey of his former liaison with Albertine and he cannot lay the ghost of this love-affair in face of the resistance offered by climate (*RTP*, III, 484, 487); hot days are fully appreciated by an act of retrospection rather than at the moment of their occurrence, as Marcel discovers, when he succeeds in recalling one particular day without experiencing pain: '. . . comme on se rappelle certains jours d'été qu'on a trouvés trop chauds quand on les a vécus, et dont, après coup seulement on extrait le titre sans alliage d'or fixe et d'indestructible azur' (*RTP*, III, 486–7). Sunlight is an essential part of Marcel's memory of a certain drawing-room (*RTP*, II, 741).

As the indispensable condition of memory and artistic creation, absence forms a theme of major importance in the work of both writers. When Fromentin personifies 'l'absence', describing it as 'cette mystérieuse ouvrière', he anticipates strikingly the Proustian conception of this force; concerning the narrator's period of absence from Dominique, he writes as follows: 'Ce long intervalle de douze mois, grand espace de vie et d'oubli, n'a pas contenu un seul jour inutile . . .' (*D*, 13). Oblivion has ensured an unconscious growth of friendship between the two men, and a defeat of time by involuntary forces – a process of a Proustian nature. There is also a strongly Proustian sense of irony in the observation that voluntary and conscious friendships ,like the corresponding acts of memory, seem destined to yield nothing: '. . . elle [l'absence] accumule des mondes d'indifférence sur des promesses de souvenirs éternels' (ibid.). Fromentin develops his own variation on the theme of the *intermittences*, when he affirms that only involuntary friendships effectively renew and perpetuate the past. Like involuntary memory, friendship as conceived by Fromentin is compounded of an exact proportion of remembering and forgetting. Markedly Proustian in the passage describing the effects of absence are such features as the imagery: 'fils' and 'trame';[14] the elements of negation working towards a positive end: 'germe imperceptible'; 'lien inaperçu'; 'insaisissable rayon'; 'à notre insu'; the triumphant personification of 'l'ingénieuse absence' already mentioned; regret diagnosed as the 'tension' of the 'fils invisibles'; the writer's delight in vindicating the apparently trivial; and finally the spirit, style and syntax of the entire passage:

Et puis, d'un germe *imperceptible*, d'un lien *inaperçu*, d'un *adieu, monsieur*, qui ne devait pas avoir de lendemain, elle [l'absence] compose, avec des *riens*, en les tissant je ne sais comment, une de ces *trames vigoureuses* sur lesquelles deux amitiés viriles peuvent très-bien se reposer pour le reste de leur vie, car ces attaches-là sont de toute durée. Les chaînes composées de la sorte *à notre insu*, avec la substance la plus pure et la plus vivace de nos sentiments, par *cette mystérieuse ouvrière*, sont comme *un insaisissable rayon* qui va de l'un à l'autre, et ne craignent plus rien, ni des distances ni du temps ... Le regret n'est, en pareil cas, que le mouvement un peu plus rude de *ces fils invisibles* attachés dans les profondeurs du cœur et de l'esprit, et dont l'extrême tension fait souffrir.[15]

Only when Dominique fears that he is about to lose Madeleine, does he realise how deeply he loves her (*D*, 81). There is in the hero's response to the unattainable a Proustian gratuitousness, a love of the fleeting because it is fleeting. A predilection for beauty in proportion as it reveals its vulnerability to time pervades Proust's work. A similar nostalgia and sense of *lacrimae rerum mortalium* dominate the part of the narrative where Fromentin broaches the theme of *La Prisonnière* and *La Fugitive*: 'A ces êtres-là, à ces êtres de fuite, leur nature, notre inquiétude attachent des ailes' (*RTP*, III, 93). Accordingly, when Madeleine attempts to loosen gently the threads which bind her to Dominique:

Une appréhension, un regret peut-être, quelque chose dont l'effet seul était visible venait de s'introduire entre nous comme un premier avis de désunion. Rien de net, mais un ensemble de désaccords, d'inégalités, de différences, qui la transfiguraient en quelque sorte en une personne absente et déjà lui donnaient le charme particulier des choses que le temps ou la raison nous dispute, et qui s'en vont ... [16]

(*D*, 79–80)

Earlier, when Dominique visits Madeleine's room during her absence, he discovers that 'l'absence' is 'une présence réelle'. Here, Fromentin anticipates Proust's analysis both of Marcel's reactions to Albertine's disappearance and his experience of *les intermittences du cœur*:

La maison était vide ... toutes choses étaient remises en place. Ce n'était pas l'abandon, c'était l'absence ... Madeleine était partout ... une odeur exotique[17] qu'elle aimait ... le bleu qui la parait si bien ... tout cela revivait avec une lucidité surprenante, mais en me causant une autre émotion que sa présence, comme un regret, agréable à caresser, des choses aimables qui n'étaient plus là ...

(*D*, 63–4)

Madeleine herself recognises the scope afforded to the imagination and to metamorphosis by absence, when, on her return, she admits to Dominique: '... je vous voyais autrement quand j'étais loin' (*D*, 71). Fromentin sees absence as equally indispensable to memory and the artistic creation which this faculty prefigures. From the *Lettres de Jeunesse* we learn that he has only to be subjected to a change of weather in Blidah for Paris to be restored to him, and conversely:

Comme tout paraît extraordinaire à distance, et comme l'inconnu, quand on l'habite, est simple; ... Eh bien! Voilà, il pleut, il fait presque aussi froid qu'à Paris ... C'est au point que j'ai besoin de me transporter hors de ce pays-ci, à Paris, par exemple, pour lui restituer son prestige. Et ce qu'il y a de plus drôle c'est que ces détails si simples et si bien d'accord pourtant avec le pays lui-même, me deviendront délicieux en souvenirs. Voilà l'esprit. Je fais tous les jours des méditations profondes sur la mémoire. (Blidah, 29 novembre 1847.)

(LJ, 263)

In addition, Fromentin's memory seems to have functioned as obliquely as that of Proust:

> ... ses livres du *Sahara* et du *Sahel* avaient été écrits dans la réapparition de choses qu'il croyait ne pas avoir vues ... c'est de la vérité sans aucune exactitude ...
>
> (E. et J. de Goncourt, Journal, II, 167 [le 25 mai, 1865])

Fromentin himself is reported to have declared that details which he had thought lost beyond recall would return to him two or three years after the event (ibid., II, 1051).

Both Fromentin and Proust have the poet's faculty to 'be affected more than other men by absent things, as if they were present'. In Fromentin no less than in his successor, a prerequisite of enjoyment is the exercise of the imagination. For such natures, involuntary memory, *a fortiori* artistic creation, alone fuse the real and the ideal to perfection. Proust seems to speak for Fromentin and himself when he analyses the fascination of recollection as opposed to direct experience of the present, where all scope is denied the imagination (*RTP*, III, 872–3).

While Marcel's cult of memory is justified by his vocation as an artist, Fromentin feels ethically bound to defend the compromise adopted by Dominique between absolute renunciation and an intermittent nostalgia for the past; absolute sincerity seems to his creator to be an ideal incapable of practice in all its intransigence:

> L'absolu détachement des choses n'admettrait-il aucun regard jeté de loin sur les choses qu'on désavoue? Et quel est le cœur assez sûr de lui pour répondre qu'il ne se glissera jamais un regret entre la résignation, qui dépend de nous, et l'oubli, qui ne peut nous venir que du temps?
>
> (D, 2)

The inscriptions on the walls of Dominique's study bear witness to his search for an inner continuity. Like his successor in this quest, Proust's narrator, Fromentin's hero seems to have been haunted by a belief that personality is fleeting and that it is composed of a never-ending succession of *moi*. Fromentin's narrator leaves it to the reader to deduce Dominique's attitude to the evanescence of personality, by giving a choice of hypotheses in Proustian style:

> ... il y avait certaines maximes courtes et beaucoup de vers, tous à peu près contemporains de ce travail de réflexion sur l'identité humaine dans le progrès. La plupart étaient écrits au crayon, soit que le poète eût craint, soit qu'il eût dédaigné de leur donner trop de permanence en les gravant à perpétuité dans la muraille.
>
> (ibid., 21–2)

The narrator reiterates his doubts about the finality of Dominique's break with the past, when he ponders the latter's reasons for frequenting the room. The suggestion that there is apparently an indestructible continuity in the essence of memory is Proustian in spirit, imagery and in the very style: 'un certain écho des rumeurs anciennes':

> L'âme de trente annéesd' existence palpitait encore émue dans cette chambre étroite, et quand Dominique était là, devant moi, penché vers la fenêtre, un peu distrait et peut-être encore poursuivi par un certain écho des rumeurs anciennes, c'était une question de savoir s'il venait là pour évoquer ce qu'il appelait l'ombre de lui-même ou pour l'oublier.
>
> (ibid., 22–3)

Fromentin's hero experiences, as do Proust and Flaubert, a sense of being completely re-identified with the past, to the extent that the intervening years seem to fall away; for Dominique, it is the unchanged nature of the setting and, above all, of customs to which this effect is to be attributed: 'Les choses étant demeurées les mêmes, je vis de même . . .' (D, 35). This experience is strikingly Proustian in its overwhelming sense of a renewal of personality, in the conviction that, by a suppression of time, one can recover a former self intact. Habit and memory are strong mutual allies in the process. Fromentin observes this fact when he realises the power of a custom – such as 'cueillir du raisin' – to renew for his mother and himself the moods and personalities which were theirs in former days. These *trivia* of rustic life to which Fromentin is so closely attached: 'la séduction des faits qui se répètent', are as rhythmic in their recurrence as the seasons they reflect. They are perhaps grounded in a race-memory, their atavistic element explaining at least in part their pervasive quality:

> J'attache à ces petites occupations, si puériles qu'elles soient, un grand intérêt de souvenir. Je ne m'explique pas moi-même ce que je trouve d'émotion à *cueillir du raisin* avec ma mère; mais apparemment que tout cela tient à mon attachement à tous les détails de la vie champêtre.
>
> (LJ, 53 – author's italics)

As Barbara Wright has remarked, however, Proust differs from Fromentin in attaching more importance to an interruption of habit than to its continuation. Proust conceives of repetition as an anaesthetic and attributes only to a change of routine the power to renew the world. The two men stand apart from each other here, in proportion as Fromentin favours a belief in unity as the essence of personality and Proust the notion that disintegration is the natural state, failing the arbitrary, fortuitous grace of memory. Fromentin believes in man's natural power to help himself, to strew his life with signs, later to be deciphered *à la Petit Poucet*:

> . . . sans habitudes, un jour ne tiendrait plus à l'autre, et les souvenirs n'auraient plus d'attache, pas plus qu'un chapelet qui n'a pas de fil . . . adorons les habitudes; ce

n'est pas autre chose que la conscience de notre être déployée derrière nous dans le sens de l'espace et de la durée ... C'est le moyen de nous retrouver partout et de ne pas perdre en chemin le plus utile et le plus précieux du bagage; je veux parler du sentiment de ce que nous sommes.

(A, 58–9)

Fromentin and Proust meet on common ground, however, when they acknowledge the power of emotion to render memory firstly receptive, and secondly capable of reviving all the relevant, interwoven issues with the result that man is in a position to dominate time, 'toutes les époques de sa vie'. The following passage anticipates and contains Proust not only in its stress upon the interwoven threads of memory but in its affirmation that man can know absolute self-mastery by dominating and transcending time:

Une passion vraie, quoique superficielle en apparence, quand elle date de loin, a par cela même des racines profondes et des liaisons insaisissables avec tous les faits survenus depuis son origine ... elle est le lien de nos souvenirs, elle embrasse, résume et reproduit, dans ses proportions variables, toutes nos existences contemporaines. Elle en est la formule, la trame ...

L'événement qui la détermine, celui qui la déclare, celui qui la conclut ... en nous concentrant tout entier sur un point, en y attachant tout: passé, présent, avenir, nous donnent pour un instant la plénitude, la possession et la jouissance de nous-mêmes ...

... on est contemporain de toutes les époques de sa vie – on *est* dans la plus haute acception du mot.[18]

(LJ, 125–6)

The affinity between Fromentin's prose style and that of Proust has been observed by Jacques Vier and others.[19] The former's sentence is essentially synthetic in the sense that there is often a sustained build-up of subordinate clauses, and a tendency to indulge in parenthesis, but both features are never allowed to stray beyond control. As after a reading of Proust, one is left with the impression that, in the first place, the writer must have allowed his thought-processes and his sentence-structure to evolve as though his medium were an inflected language. For this reason Proust, and at times his precursor Fromentin, would undoubtedly have found German or Russian a more malleable instrument of expression, a medium more amenable to their designs and movement of thought. French, in its uninflected form, resists their efforts to use it as virtual Latin. A case-system would be required to make the following 'period' from Fromentin *immediately* intelligible:

Très-peu sensible aux choses qui nous entouraient, tandis que son élève en était à ce point absorbé, assez indifférent au cours des saisons pour se tromper de mois comme il se serait trompé d'heure, invulnérable à tant de sensations dont j'étais traversé, délicieusement blessé dans tout mon être, froid, méthodique, correct et régulier d'humeur autant que je l'étais peu, Augustin vivait à mes côtés sans prendre garde à ce qui se passait en moi, ni le soupçonner.

(D, 39)

156

Parenthesis is an integral part of the Fromentinian style and, closely related, the device of enumeration which is a technique reminiscent of painting, almost a *transposition d'art* in terms of syntax. It invests Fromentin's prose with a certain quality of 'still-life'. Generally, however, as in the following example, the writer's strong sense of clause-structure empowers the verbs to impart a saving dynamism:

> Je vous montrerais tel coin du parc, tel escalier de la terrasse, tel endroit des champs, du village, de la falaise, où l'âme des choses insensibles a si bien gardé le souvenir de Madeleine et le mien, que si je l'y cherchais encore, et Dieu m'en garde, je l'y retrouverais aussi reconnaissable qu'au lendemain de notre départ.
>
> (ibid., 117)

In respect of style, another passage is distinctly remarkable. I refer to the part of the lighthouse scene in *Dominique*, where the author's use of the imperfect as 'une source inépuisable de mystérieuses tristesses' (*CSB*, 170) is strikingly Proustian: 'Madeleine marchait légèrement dans les chemins détrempés . . .' (*D*, 126). In spirit and syntax, it might well be compared with the passage in *Du côté de chez Swann*, where Proust describes the narrator's function, as 'mémorialiste de la nature', to 'faire traverser tant d'années successives à ce parfum d'aubépine . . . à un bruit de pas . . . à une bulle formée contre une plante aquatique . . .' (*RTP*, I, 184).

The full measure of the influence exerted by Fromentin's *Dominique* has yet to be assessed. While it continues and subtly recalls a whole lineage of such novels as *Adolphe* and *Volupté*, couched in the tradition of psychological analysis, or others in the more avowedly Romantic vein, such as Balzac's *Le Lys dans la Vallée*, or George Sand's *Indiana*, *Valentine* and *Mauprat*, and perpetuates the nostalgia for the past of the latter novelist's *romans champêtres*, *Dominique* does more than abound in echoes; it anticipates, by its mood and enrichment of technique, the twentieth century. Its curious blend of Romanticism and Classicism, of idealism and disillusionment, appealed strongly to Alain-Fournier, whose *Le Grand Meaulnes* bears many traces of the *filiation*. The heightening of visual effect by a painter's technique and by an artist's preoccupation with optics and modulations of light, points forward in time to an application of Impressionism to the substance and form of literature, notably in Proust's novel. Yet Fromentin's principal claim to rank as precursor of Proust lies more probably in his intense awareness of the bonds between memory and sensations – the latter to be interpreted in the sense of the minutest reactions to climate and setting – in fact, in his weather-vane propensity.

While it is impossible to prove that Fromentin influenced Proust, there is undoubtedly a strong affinity between the two writers. One wonders whether Proust ever lighted upon a certain letter addressed by Fromentin to his mother, 18 June 1845 (*LJ*, 146–7), and whether, had he done so, he might have discerned there a facet of his own work, for his predecessor believed that man's emotional development reflects, repeats and perhaps even obeys rhythmically the cycle of the seasons. What matters here is not so much the question of scientific validity as the immense source of riches which such a theory brings to the artist:

> Nous avons dans l'esprit des évolutions périodiques analogues à celles des saisons. Je ne parle pas seulement des souvenirs que ramène naturellement le retour des mêmes époques, mais je parle aussi des dispositions d'humeur, des affections, etc., qui semblent revenir d'elles-mêmes, et comme éclore annuellement sous les mêmes soleils. A me retrouver aujourd'hui tel que j'étais l'année dernière à la même époque, je m'imaginerais n'avoir pas vieilli . . . et pourtant! . . .[20]
>
> (*LJ*, 146–7)

Fromentin certainly prepares the way for Proust, if only by virtue of the importance which he attaches to sense impressions as a means of recovering lost time – 'retrouver ma jeunesse à mesure que je m'en éloigne' (*Correspondance et Fragments inédits*, 139). Jean Santeuil's 'impressions retrouvées' represent an intermediate stage, before Proust gives to the interdependence of memory and sensation the depth of orchestration which such a theme challenges him to create in response. It remains for the Proust of *A la recherche du temps perdu* to vindicate the early awakenings of a kindred impulse in Fromentin, and epitomise the essence of 'passionate memory' in the triumphant yet poignant rediscovery of 'l'air oublié':

> Par le bruit de la pluie m'était rendue l'odeur des lilas de Combray; par la mobilité du soleil sur le balcon, les pigeons des Champs-Elysées; par l'assourdissement des bruits dans la chaleur de la matinée, la fraîcheur des cerises; le désir de la Bretagne ou de Venise par le bruit du vent et le retour de Pâques . . . je me détournais violemment, sous la décharge douloureuse d'un des mille souvenirs invisibles qui à tout moment éclataient autour de moi dans l'ombre . . .
>
> (*RTP*, III, 478–9)

Notes

[1] *CG*, III, 123. See A. R. Evans, Jr: *The Literary Art of Eugène Fromentin: A Study in Style and Motif*, Hopkins Press 1964, pp. 33 ff. A. R. Evans asserts that 'Fromentin does mention Vermeer's name in the *Maîtres* three times (pp. 191, 209, 241)', as also in the *Carnets de Voyage* of 1911.

[2] *LAURIS*, p. 53. It is possible that *Une Année dans le Sahel* impressed Proust more than *Les Maîtres*, since the former work belongs to the tradition of personal recollections; moreover, it abounds in exemplifications of Amiel's 'Un paysage est un état d'âme'. See Evans: op. cit., p. 18. For further allusions by Proust to Fromentin's work, see *RTP*, II, 327; III, 809; also *CG*, III, 125, 123; III, 106.

[3] 'En revenant avec lui, il nous parle de l'ennui que lui causa la peinture . . . et, en même temps du goût qu'il a à écrire, de la petite fièvre à laquelle il se reconnaît apte à écrire . . .'. E. & J. de Goncourt, *Journal* (4 vols), Flammarion & Fasquelle, Monaco 1956, I, 1266 (29 avril, 1863).

[4] E. Fromentin, *Correspondance et Fragments inédits*, Biographie et notes par Pierre Bianchon, Plon, Paris 1912, p. 151.

[5] J. M. Cocking: *Proust*, Bowes & Bowes, London 1956, p. 27: 'Dominique, with gifts and problems of temperament not unlike Marcel's, takes what Proust, in his moral incapacity, must have felt to be an abysmally philistine course, rejecting the riches of his sensibility for the well-ordered but morose and half-frustrated life of a gentleman farmer'. Professor Cocking finds in *Jean Santeuil* passages which 'directly recall *Dominique*': 'Both boys . . . read their own emotions into the historical situations they are writing about . . . Dominique, like Jean and Marcel, is emotionally dependent on sense impressions . . .' (ibid., p. 28).

[6] See also *D*, 19–20 and 125

[7] Cf. Proust: '. . . mes rêves de voyage et d'amour n'étaient que des moments . . . dans un même et infléchissable jaillissement de toutes les forces de ma vie' (*RTP*, I, 87). (See also Ch. IX of the present work.)

[8] Goncourt: op. cit., II, 1051 (mardi, 9 mars, 1875).

[9] Ibid., cf. *D*, 33.

[10] See Barbara Wright: *D*, Introduction, p. xlvi.

[11] See ibid., p. xlvii.

[12] '. . . servir de miroir aux choses extérieures, mais volontairement, et sans leur être assujetti . . .', *A*, 192 (Entry for August 1853). Cf., ibid., 100. Augustin is Dominique's foil in this, as in so many other respects. See *D*, 41.

[13] Equally, unique moments are due to a change in the weather (*RTP*, III, 25).

[14] Cf., the narrator's reflections on his justification for associating retrospectively Saint-Loup with Albertine. The imagery is strikingly similar: '. . . les navettes agiles des années tissent des fils entre ceux de nos souvenirs qui semblaient d'abord les plus indépendants . . .' (*RTP*, III, 848).

[15] '. . . d'un *adieu, monsieur*': here, the italics are the author's.

[16] J. Vier (*Pour l'étude du 'Dominique' de Fromentin*, Archives des Lettres Modernes No. 16–17, Oct./Nov. 1958, p. 55 n. 13) finds this last sentence, 'Rien de net . . .' strongly Proustian.

[17] Like Proust, Fromentin stresses the power of scent to recall the past: 'Une odeur dit tout' (*M. d'A*, 256), quoted by B. Wright *D*, xl.

[18] Fromentin exemplifies this theory that emotion releases the mechanism of memory when, in *Dominique*, the curlew's cry and certain conditions of atmosphere combine to revive before the hero's 'inward eye' Villeneuve and 'tout ce qui avait charmé sa première enfance' (*D*, 89). The italics are the author's own.

[19] 'Outre la démarche initiale (dès le début du roman, Dominique est dans la situation de Proust à la fin de son œuvre . . .) il faudrait citer quelques curieux échantillons de style proustien.' Vier: loc. cit.

[20] Cf., *A*, 99–100.

Notes for further reading

In the introduction to her 1965 edition of *Dominique* (Blackwell), Barbara Wright draws attention to 'certain analogies' between Fromentin and Proust (pp. xxiii–xxv and xliv–xlvii), while referring for further discussion of the topic to the following:

Camille Reynaud   *La Genèse de 'Dominique'*, Arthaud, Grenoble 1937, pp. 172–3.

Jean-Pierre Richard   *Littérature et Sensation*, Paris 1954, pp. 227, 249–50.

E. Czoniczer   *Quelques Antécédents de 'A la recherche du temps perdu'*, Droz, Geneva 1957, pp. 99–102.

J. Vier   *Pour l'étude du 'Dominique' de Fromentin*, Archives des Lettres Modernes, No. 16–17, Oct.–Nov. 1958, pp. 37–8.

J. Monge   'Un précurseur de Proust: Fromentin et la Mémoire affective', *Revue d'Histoire littéraire de la France*, Oct.–Dec. 1961, pp. 564–88.

In addition, it is of vital interest to mention the following important work:

A. R. Evans, Jr   *The Literary Art of Eugène Fromentin: A Study in Style and Motif*, Hopkins Press, 1964, pp. ix, 63, 72, 122.

Chapter IX

Flaubert

On avait séché l'écriture avec les cendres du foyer, car un peu de poussière grise glissa de la lettre sur sa robe, et elle crut presque apercevoir son père se courbant vers l'âtre pour saisir les pincettes. Comme il y avait longtemps qu'elle n'était plus auprès de lui, sur l'escabeau dans la cheminée, quand elle faisait brûler le bout d'un bâton à la grande flamme des joncs marins qui pétillaient! . . . . Elle se rappela les soirs d'été tout pleins de soleil. Les poulains hennissaient quand on passait, et galopaient, galopaient . . .
(*Madame Bovary, FLAU*, I, 448–9)

. . . donc cet imparfait, si nouveau dans la littérature, change entièrement l'aspect des choses et des êtres, comme font une lampe qu'on a déplacée, l'arrivée dans une maison nouvelle, l'ancienne si elle est presque vide et qu'on est en plein déménagement. C'est ce genre de tristesse fait de la rupture des habitudes et de l'irréalité du décor, que donne le style de Flaubert, ce style si nouveau quand ce ne serait que par là.
('A propos du "style" de Flaubert', *CSB*, 590)

One wonders why, in *Le Temps Retrouvé* (*RTP*, III, 919–20), Flaubert should have been omitted from the 'noble filiation' of writers whose 'sensation transposée' and 'ressouvenirs inconscients' inspired Proust in his turn to defy time and to build his masterpiece on a similar foundation. In the essay 'A propos du "style" de Flaubert', however, he admires unreservedly Flaubert's

161

ability to make music of the tenses: 'Le premier, il les met [les changements de temps] en musique',[1] and he acknowledges him as his precursor in respect of his power to give 'l'impression du Temps', citing as illustrations passages where Flaubert conveys the flow of time in a highly individual manner. It seems to Proust as though, by leaving lacunae, by interposing a veritable architecture of space and so of time between the bare verbs, the novelist had achieved a new and arresting effect. In *L'Éducation Sentimentale* we read:

> Et Frédéric béant reconnut Sénécal.

> Il voyagea. Il connut la mélancolie des paquebots, les froids réveils sous la tente etc. Il revint.[2]

If Proust had ever lighted upon the first version of *Madame Bovary*,[3] he would have felt more than a passing affinity with the author; he might almost have been tempted to believe that he and Flaubert shared the same spiritual landscape[4] as far as the conception of time is concerned. Certainly both writers cultivate the imperfect tense, Proust for its intense affective power,[5] both men for its fluidity, for the permanence which, in common with metaphor, it confers upon style.

Albert Thibaudet[6] had already called posterity's attention to the Proustian character of a certain passage of *Madame Bovary*: during a visit to the 'Comices Agricoles', Emma, held in thrall by a present sensation – the scent of Rodolphe's hair – lives now in the present, now in various vistas of the past. There is a gentle intimation of reverie: 'Il se tenait les bras croisés sur ses genoux . . .', before tenses and times blend in rhythmic dance. The transposition of sensation, here released by the scent of hair oil, enables Emma and the reader to transcend time. The vanilla and lemon exhaled by Rodolphe's hair recalls the Vicomte de la Vaubyessard, because the latter's beard was impregnated with the same scent. Next sight intervenes; after half closing her eyes in an effort to concentrate on the scent and draw from it all its power, Emma arches her neck,[7] and in so doing she catches a glimpse of the yellow coach, *L'Hirondelle*, intimately associated with Léon's frequent journeys to join her, as also with his final departure. As she imagines that she feels Léon's hand in hers,[8] the part of her past evoked by the scent struggles again to recover ascendancy, does in fact return; she feels that she is again moving to the rhythm of the waltz,[9] but it never ousts Léon's image or Emma's sense of his imminence. In the primitive version the counsellor's droning tone of delivery recalls her to present reality, in contrast with the final version where, more subtly, it is Rodolphe's head, and by implication the scent ,which finds its way back into the immediate context, and so brings to a close the very dream it had initiated.[10] Whereas the primitive version left the reader free to interpret, as he wished, the emotion released in Emma by the scent, the final version clearly indicates that this sensation underlies and subtly revives a compound of past longing.

Confronted with the original version, Thibaudet might have been tempted to apply the term 'Proustian' to a host of other passages. One cannot help pondering the fact that so much of this material concerns incidents of involuntary memory and the dislocation of time. The passages in question almost threaten to prevent the plot from evolving chronologically, and present in essence the same danger to syntax and the novel's structural evolution as did Proust's interpolations and disrespect for outer time.

Certain experiences can grow so much a part of ourselves, of our 'inner duration', that, dormant within us, they remain totally impervious to the flow of outer time. When, yielding to Rouault's persuasion, Charles returns to the Bertaux after his first wife's death, he finds everything apparently unchanged; only the natural season reflects mobility and a sense of flux. This experience leads him to believe that within his mind there has been no interruption. Whatever the change in the outer season, inwardly the unity remains inviolate. The whole of this incident falls into two parts: the first, where the present appears to be identical with the past, exemplifies unity; the second, where the differences and consequently the interval of elapsed time become sharply apparent, exemplifies division within time. Thus Flaubert, anticipating Proust, demonstrates unity and disintegration within time, and vividly illustrates his own generalisation in the *Correspondance*.[11]

> On se dit: 'Il y a dix ans j'étais là', et on est là, et on pense les mêmes choses, et tout l'intervalle est oublié. Puis il vous apparaît, cet intervalle, comme un immense précipice où le néant tournoie.

On the return to the Bertaux the main stimulus to ponder time, and above all inner time, is afforded by the external scene, with perhaps something of a visionary light shed on the external objects from within, a kind of union between subject and object.[12] The identity of scene is all the more surprising since, despite the interval of five months, even the fire seems unchanged. Only from one who had returned to life as a result of resurrection might be expected such intensity of vision as we find in the first part of the early *Madame Bovary*. An air of expectancy prevails:

> La longue crémaillère de la cheminée avait toujours, à son dernier crochet d'en bas, la même grosse marmite de fonte, se noircissant au fumignon de la bûche, qui semblait presque la même ou n'avoir pas brûlé sous ses cendres.
>
> (*NV*, 162)

Such an experience as this was to make Verlaine in the poem 'Kaléidoscope' exclaim at the supernatural clarity and apparently reinforced identity of things. Any experience of this kind would seem to refute the Leibnizian theory of 'Les Indiscernables', or the traditional claim that the static is impossible, that flux must always triumph.

In the incident in question, the clock forms the immediate sensation, establishing a link with the past, and eventually enabling the present to be displaced by the past; thus unity bridges any apparent gulf between the present and days long past:

> Le grand balancier de l'horloge aussi battait toujours dans la cuisine heurtant de droite et de gauche, à temps égaux contre les parois de sa boîte sonore – et les aiguilles marquant les mêmes heures . . . ramenèrent la pensée de Charles à des jours qu'il avait passés. Comme si depuis eux rien autre chose dans son existence n'avait eu lieu, il ne se rappela qu'eux seuls.

> (*NV*, 162–3)

This sense of continuity is bound, by its creative element, to be in conflict with conventional time. A memory can, we know, be recalled so suddenly and so vividly as to seem an integral part of ourselves and to be closer to our core of identity than all that has happened in the interval. Proust explains this striking immediacy of the forgotten and now resurrected past by claiming that its very detachment in oblivion has alone enabled it to preserve our reactions and spontaneous selves completely intact, shielded from the ravages of habitual use, or voluntary memory. There is here a foretaste of Gide's belief that only the essence of spontaneity, 'l'acte gratuit', in fact, can embody and reveal the true personality, the 'moi profond'.

All moments intermingle and are in reality indivisible. Only one's intelligence establishes artificial distinctions, or divisions. As Proust writes of the subsequent intervention of intelligence:

> . . . Mes rêves de voyage et d'amour n'étaient que des moments – que je sépare artificiellement aujourd'hui, comme si je pratiquais des sections à des hauteurs différentes d'un jet d'eau irisé et en apparence immobile – dans un même et infléchissable jaillissement de toutes les forces de ma vie.

> (*RTP*, I, 87)

Only at the end of this moment, in *Madame Bovary*, when reproduction of the past within the present threatens to overwhelm the novelist, does Flaubert's sense of disunity within time begin to reassert itself. This is the supreme moment of unity as long as it endures, past and present merging indissolubly as they did for the narrator when the bell at Combray prolonged its ringing over the years, and only superficially knew interruption from forgetfulness. Here, indeed, one might imagine for a moment that one was hearing the authentic voice of Proust:

> Un instant interrompue par cet intervalle oublié, sa sensation lointaine continuait, le passé se trouvant être maintenant le présent et son souvenir une émotion renouvelée.

> (*NV*, 163)

The vision splendid is already beginning to fade from the moment Charles awakens to a realisation of the seasons and recognises the law of flux and change, when in fact he emerges from his world of timelessness. Withheld from sight as long as man remained engulfed in the stream of inner consciousness, the differences between past and present now begin to stand out clearly. The division within time which the last part of this incident reveals so distinctly, is exemplified in almost Proustian terms in *L'Education Sentimentale*, 1845 version. While *dédoublement*, if not disintegration of the personality, amazed and confounded Flaubert to the point of making him assume an earlier existence, 'une vie antérieure', we are reminded that such fragmentation in life was to take Proust further and make him doubt whether unity of personality survives beyond death. Flaubert's glance is still retrospective, but his mention of the part played by the scene in reviving an experience surely foreshadows the rôle of setting, and analogous sensation in Proustian incidents:

> Effrayé de la fidélité de ses souvenirs, rendus plus vivaces encore par la présence de ces lieux où ils avaient été des faits et des sentiments, il se demandait si tous appartenaient au même homme, si une seule vie avait pu y suffire, et il cherchait à les rattacher à quelque autre existence perdue, tant son passé était loin de lui![13]

Unity and disintegration seem to be subtly related. Indeed, unity paradoxically expresses itself in and through its opposite. Flaubert believes strongly in the unity of spiritual life, and he finely observes that a change in routine, anything which breaks the continuity and introduces silence, alone enables us to recognise most clearly the strength of a previous experience. The force of the prolonged vibration, he asserts, can best be measured by the silence which ensues; just as we become aware of sounds more powerfully through silence,[14] so inner life makes itself perhaps most powerfully felt through an interruption.

The terms which Flaubert uses vividly foreshadow Proust's 'sonorité identique'. The notation of sound by silence, of sensation in negative terms, derives in Proust's case from an innate tendency to syncopate with external time, to enjoy reality always at a remove, never directly but always through a medium. Such a temperament finds full scope and vindication in memory and in metaphor. His natural endowment and perhaps illness propelled Proust in this direction, transforming him into an artistic equivalent of the Noah of legend, cut off from direct enjoyment of reality by the flood. In the *dédicace* of *Les Plaisirs et les Jours* (*JS*, 6–7), he confesses that illness really enabled him to understand Noah's depth of spiritual vision. From a strange combination of nature and necessity, Proust seems to exemplify a form of inversion in his innermost essence as well as in technique. In a letter written to Princesse Marthe Bibesco, 1 May 1912, he reveals the obliqueness both of his quest and of the approach: 'Rien ne m'est plus étranger que de chercher dans la sensation immédiate, à plus forte raison dans la réalisation matérielle, la présence du bonheur' (*CG*, V, 141–2).

For Proust the cooing of pigeons partakes of silence but most subtly, before reaching him, it has to pass through colour and the image of 'une première jacinthe déchirant doucement son cœur nourricier pour qu'en jaillît, mauve et satinée, sa fleur sonore'. At Combray, scents are 'la fine fleur d'un silence . . . nourricier . . .'. The stress on the elusive essence as opposed to the directly accessible reality, 'trop en mon pouvoir' (according to Proust in the above-mentioned letter), is everywhere apparent in this writer, lying at the root of his conception of metaphor, and relating him closely to Mallarmé and the Symbolists. Flaubert already here experiences the essence of unity at a remove and through its apparent negation. He thus anticipates what I would call the artist's Platonic condition, so exalted by Proust, namely his enjoyment of reality in a spiritualised form, never in the present but always in the past or the future, and even by a sheer *raffinement* between the past and the present, therefore in some sense outside time. Proust prefers to experience reality at a remove: through memory, through dreams, and above all through art; Marcel revels in discovering the world through Bergotte's writing or through another's 'optique'. The world is transformed by the interplay of analogy. Without being to anything like the same extent as Swann an artist who has failed, Emma Bovary is in many respects consubstantial with her creator, and her *delectatio morosa* is charged with the artist's dilemma in general and with that of Flaubert and Proust in particular: it is the problem of the disproportion between reality and the dream, although for Emma admittedly the drama remains on the purely emotional plane; 'Emma palpitait au bruit de ses pas; puis, en sa présence, l'émotion tombait' (*NV*, 297).

When Léon has left Yonville for Rouen and thereby plunged Emma into despair, Flaubert analyses and extends this reaction until it assumes universal significance. Since the experience owes its birth to the fact that an external event has interrupted habit, it is an intensely human situation and leads to the correspondingly human *lacrimae rerum mortalium*, the nostalgia for 'ce qui ne se retrouve jamais':

> C'était cette tristesse qui suit l'accomplissement de tout ce qui ne reviendra plus, cette fatigue sans fond, que tout fait laisse derrière soi, cette douleur enfin qu'apportent au corps ou à l'âme toute action résolue, les séparations, les morts, les départs, les arrivées quelquefois, *les habitudes brisées*, les plaisirs accomplis, l'interruption de tout mouvement accoutumé, la cessation brusque de toute vibration prolongée. Le silence qui lui succède devient ainsi la mesure même de sa sonorité et l'on s'aperçoit de sa durée à l'étourdissement qui vous saisit.[15]

Does not Flaubert stress here the need to lose an experience at least in time and in terms of external, material reality, before one can realise its true depth and value? For Proust a further logical consequence of this syncopation between events and their realisation will be the artist's need to withdraw from the world in order to create (*RTP*, I, 645).

Involuntary memory inspires Flaubert generally with a sense of void, a feeling that the past has somehow become detached, belongs to another 'moi' and now leads an independent existence. Proust shares with Flaubert this 'sensation du gouffre' and its accompanying vertigo. Although he uses the same term, Baudelaire's act of recoil before the infinite is more Pascalian, more purely metaphysical. In a letter to Louis Bouilhet, 23 August 1853 (*Corr.* (Conard) III, p. 317), Flaubert records his impressions on revisiting Trouville after a lapse of eleven years. 'Il semble, à certains moments, que l'univers s'est immobilisé, que tout est devenu statue et que nous seuls vivons.' This state of mind is the very opposite of the mood mentioned earlier (above, p. 163) as demonstrating unity, the opposite, too, of the Baudelairean sense of inner petrification as opposed to outer flux evident in:

> Paris change! mais rien dans ma mélancolie
> N'a bougé!

Flaubert's terms are Proustian as he contemplates the inner fragmentation, a veritable form of death before its time.[16]

Nothing in external nature would seem able to match our own speed of inner flux, of infinite mobility. This is truly time in disintegration:

> Et est-ce insolent la nature! . . . On se torture l'esprit à vouloir comprendre l'abîme qui nous sépare d'elle. Mais quelque chose de plus farce encore, c'est l'abîme qui nous sépare de nous-mêmes. Quand je songe qu'ici, à cette place, en regardant ce mur blanc à rechampi vert, j'avais des battements de cœur et qu'alors j'étais plein de 'Pohésie', je m'ébahis, je m'y perds, j'en ai le vertige, comme si je découvrais tout à coup un mur à pic, de deux mille pieds, au-dessous de moi.
>
> (*Corr.* (Conard) III, pp. 317–18)

We are reminded of Proust, baffled by the extent to which desire over-reaches itself and parts of the human personality syncopate with events. At the end of *Le Temps Retrouvé*, he experiences the same sense of vertigo on beholding the space of time which he contains: 'J'éprouvais un sentiment de fatigue et d'effroi à sentir que tout ce temps si long . . . était moi-même . . . qu'il me supportait, moi, juché à son sommet vertigineux, que je ne pouvais me mouvoir sans le déplacer' (*RTP*, III, 1047).

Both Flaubert and Proust conceive of the past either as a potential burden, ever ready to assert its claims and oust the present if it can, or when dwindling, as likely to indulge in elegiac lament and plead for rebirth, but hardly ever achieving balance with the present and future. Action alone as opposed to reverie would seem capable of redressing the balance, but Emma notably belongs to a world where, as for Baudelaire, action bears little relation to the dream.

The awareness of successive selves (*NV*, 319), of detached moments of existence owning no unity other perhaps than that a person called Emma Bovary has experienced them, gradually becomes on occasion obsessive. It is like a variation of Lamartine's question, but applied already to this life and not to the hereafter: 'Où le temps a cessé, tout n'est-il pas présent?' It is possible that the sense of division within oneself springs from the fact that one has artificially expressed time in terms of space, separating into component parts a continuous and indivisible experience: achieving, to use Bergson's image, nothing more than 'des instantanés pris artificiellement sur la transition'.[17] Proust, for all his belief in successive selves, had, I believe, a stronger conviction that unity is the reality within the mind, before the latter attempts to analyse and express itself.[18]

So Flaubert causes Emma to ponder the mystery surrounding this division or fragmentation to which the human mind and even experience, by their very nature, seem to subject time. Emma is surprised to see the garden again on her return from La Vaubyessard, for the ball so fully occupies her memory still, that the present space around her seems another and alien world; the ball, now demoted to the 'climat intérieur', joins her dream-world, belonging as it does to a previous self. She realises as acutely as ever the relativity of time. Similarly, Proust will wonder why Guermantes and Méséglise seem so distinct from each other, almost hermetically sealed. Flaubert analyses the same mystery:

> Comme le bal déjà lui semblait loin! Comme il s'étendait emplissant tout son souvenir! Qu'est-ce qui écartait ainsi l'un de l'autre à distance si longue le matin d'avant-hier et le soir d'aujourd'hui, si bien que maintenant c'était comme deux existences différentes rapprochées bout à bout?
>
> (*NV*, 221)

Flaubert and Proust share the faculty for what the former names 'une perception double et simultanée'. By virtue of analogy, the present sensation serves as a point of departure for a train of reverie: it solicits some imagined or previously experienced kindred sensation, which almost imperceptibly supersedes the original and ever-present reality. This culminates in the process of enjoying one thing through the medium of another and at a remove – the basis of metaphor.[19] All the fragments of imagination illuminate and transfigure present reality, but still artfully use the texture of the present to convey the substance of a dream. In *Madame Bovary* we find what I consider to be a key passage: Emma deliberately imagines a life shared with Léon and this she contrives to introduce into the framework of the present:

> C'était le soir. Elle était couchée, dans son lit, comme maintenant et elle en sentait même sous son corps la chaleur élastique; car, par une *perception double et simultanée* ce qu'elle pensait avec ce qui l'environnait se confondant, ses rideaux de damas de laine étaient en damas de soie, les flambeaux de la cheminée des candélabres de

168

vermeil et des bougies roses y brûlaient. A la place de la chaise, une robe de chambre à revers bleus pendait même d'un sopha sur une peau de tigre étendue... Il était là ... quelque part et allait venir. Mais tout s'écroula soudain.

(NV, 288)

We are here close to the creation of metaphor, an alliance of words outside the contingencies of time, and it is on metaphor in the sense of reality being reinforced, if not displaced, by imagination that Proust compliments Flaubert (see the essay 'A propos du "style" de Flaubert'). Complete and effectual metaphor would entail actual displacement of the present reality by the imagined experience. Flaubert blends reality and the dream subtly the one with the other and has an extraordinary capacity to dilate reality with imagination, to embody the dream in the context of the present.

After stating that 'la métaphore seule peut donner une sorte d'éternité au style', Proust proceeds in the same breath and sentence to deny the existence of 'une seule belle métaphore' in the entire range of Flaubert's work, modifying this judgement only by 'peut-être'. Yet he gives Flaubert credit for a technique which I believe to be the metaphor *en puissance* – that is, the juxtaposition of imagined experience and actual reality, the one enjoyed through the medium of the other, and the line of demarcation at times disappearing utterly, even while both worlds remain present. Proust carries this method further, his mind almost working by a process of metaphor proper. After aligning a kindred sensation with the present one, he so generalises the experience as to release and enjoy the essence or identity of character of the two sensations, possessed as he always is by 'le bonhomme de l'analogie'.

Proust goes so far as to claim that such an indirect technique is his sole means of perception. Flaubert indulges in this method of approach constantly, not explicitly by the orthodox channel of metaphor proper, that is not by actually substituting imagined for experienced reality, but rather, implicitly, by his use of the Imperfect, contriving to enjoy both worlds simultaneously. The 'style indirect libre' enables him to pass freely between the two realms of imagination and of external reality, without the shade of a transition being evident: 'donc cet éternel imparfait, composé en partie des paroles des personnages que Flaubert rapporte habituellement en style indirect pour qu'elles se confondent avec le reste (*CSB*, 590; cf., epigraph to the present chapter).

While a dynamic form of involuntary memory stemming from chance analogy holds good in general for Proust's moment of exaltation, there are instances, especially in 'Vacances de Pâques' (*CHRON.* (GALL), 110; *RTP*, I, 393), where the substitution assumes a more deliberate and voluntary character, and recalls the Flaubertian 'perception double et simultanée'.

As soon as Proust crosses the line separating what he has before him from what he hopes to recover, he tends to stress the dream to the exclusion of a present reality. Whereas Flaubert continues to juxtapose, Proust achieves a more complete suspension of disbelief than his precursor, in the involuntary as well as in the consciously willed moments of exaltation. We find an instance of the latter type in 'Vacances de Pâques': the chestnuts, undaunted harbingers of warmth, are Proust's sole inducement to dream that by the wayside winter has changed to spring, or that Florence is a present reality. Here is the 'perception double et simultanée' such as Flaubert knew, but the stress has shifted from present reality to the object desired. Whereas Flaubert thrives on the simultaneity of imagined experience and present sensation, after the manner of Baudelaire in 'La Chevelure', Proust here presents a contrast. Always inclined to cultivate a feat in direct proportion to the difficulty involved, Proust moves, so it seems to him, miraculously from the present setting to the imagined essence; Flaubert ranges still between desire and reality.[20] Proust is content only when he has replaced the present by the substance of a dream and, like Baudelaire, made of his 'pensers brûlants' 'une tiède atmosphère'. This is the logical, deliberately contrived conclusion of a movement which begins in Flaubert's fluctuation. Proust writes:

> ... ce que j'avais cru jusque-là impossible, je me sentis vraiment pénétrer dans ce nom de Florence; par une gymnastique suprême et au-dessus de mes forces me dévêtant comme d'une carapace sans objet, de l'air de ma chambre actuelle *qui n'était déjà plus ma chambre*, je le remplaçai par des parties égales d'air florentin, de cette atmosphère indicible et particulière, comme celle qu'on respire dans les rêves et que j'avais enfermée dans le nom de Florence; je sentis s'opérer en moi une miraculeuse désincarnation.
>
> (*CHRON.* (GALL), 111–12; cf., *RTP*, I, 393)

Proust dwells on the metaphysical quality of time and shares Bergson's belief that the present can be dilated:

> Le temps ... est élastique; les passions que nous ressentons le dilatent, celles que nous inspirons le rétrécissent.
>
> (*RTP*, I, 612)

Flaubert equally has an acute sense of the relativity[21] of time, and perhaps nowhere does he succeed in conveying it more vividly than when Emma feels inspired by a glimpse of the convent walls to recall her past. She is startled to hear the convent bell:

> Quatre heures! seulement, et il lui semblait qu'elle était là depuis l'éternité, car elle venait, en effet, d'y revivre tous ses jours; un infini de passions peut être condensé dans une minute, comme une multitude dans un petit lieu.
>
> (*NV*, 559)

Again, Emma will find it impossible to re-discover[22] the niche for these moments in chronological time or to replace them in their exact context; they are elusive as only haunting memories can be, and they assail mind and senses.

For Flaubert and Proust, time remembered involuntarily is qualitative, of no particular epoch, because it represents time within the soul; outside the jurisdiction of measured time, this is indeed 'le temps souverain':

> Ce n'était pas la première fois qu'elle se trouvait errant ainsi le matin, la tête toute pleine de tapage, de couleurs et de tristesse. Mais il lui était impossible de se rappeler le lieu, la cause ni *l'époque*. En cherchant ainsi dans ses sensations perdues, elle rencontra de nouveau le bal qu'elle venait de quitter tout à l'heure.
>
> (*NV*, 570)

Proust often records such experience, even using the same imagery as Flaubert. He mentions the rapid succession of 'couleurs remuées' which characterises an incident of involuntary memory. This is particularly evident when he describes his attempts to locate the memory of the madeleine incident (*RTP*, I, 45–6) or generalises upon the rôle of chance in bringing into play only certain threads of communication (*RTP*, III, 1030).

Flaubert had used the phrase 'cylindre qui tourne' (*NV*, 259), also 'spirale' (*Corr*. (Conard) II, p. 371), and the former image foreshadows Proust's 'insaisissable tourbillon'. Both writers have in common this effort to re-incarnate the soul of memory in the portion of the past to which it belongs. By his own exploration in depth, Flaubert has prepared the way for Proust, and both stand indomitable in their search to renew time:

> A peine si je perçois le reflet neutre où se confond l'insaisissable tourbillon des couleurs remuées; mais je ne puis distinguer la forme . . . lui demander de m'apprendre de quelle circonstance particulière, de quelle époque du passé il s'agit . . .
>
> Et tout d'un coup le souvenir m'est apparu. Ce goût, c'était celui du petit morceau de madeleine.
>
> (*RTP*, I, 46)

It is almost impossible to examine Flaubert's dislocation of time except in relation to the incidents of involuntary memory from which such a technique naturally flows. There are in Flaubert's work many examples of the way in which ordinary time-laws are reversed, as when his characters fall under the spell of a sensation or are simply benumbed by sleep. Proust we know to have been so fascinated by the havoc wrought upon time by dreams that he sought to bathe his novel in an atmosphere of half-sleep;[23] characteristically, he goes as far as he can in analysing sleep with his mind without the intervention leading to his awakening.

Although lacking Proust's subtle sense of tension between intuition and reason, between obscurity and clarity, Flaubert delights in analysing 'le demi-sommeil'. As Charles Bovary mounts his horse to go in answer to a summons from Bertaux, his brain has not yet introduced order into the chaos of intuitive elemental forces:

> A travers son demi-sommeil, il voyait passer des fémurs ressoudés, des attelles, des tours de bande. Puis . . . il retombait dans une tiède somnolence où la sensation la

plus récente revenait, et il se voyait *en même temps*, à la fois marié et étudiant, couché dans son lit près de sa femme, comme il l'était tout à l'heure, et marchant affairé dans une salle d'opérés . . .

(*NV*, 152)

This confusion of two periods of time – Charles's married life and his student-days – has a physical point of departure, a fact which is essentially Proustian. One cannot help thinking of the opening chapters of Combray where, in one dream, the author lay beside a woman 'qui naissait pendant mon sommeil d'une fausse position de ma cuisse'. Memory and dreams often take a physical point of departure; memory does this notably in the opening of George Eliot's *The Mill on the Floss*, a novel which we know to have fascinated Proust deeply (cf., Ch. VII, p. 130). We do not know, however, whether Flaubert read George Eliot, but the elbow is again the key to the *déclenchement*:

Il avait à la fois la sensation d'une table d'amphithéâtre sur son coude et celle de son oreiller.

(*NV*, 152)

Synaesthesia works its magic. Confusion of touch leads swiftly and easily along the scale to confusion of scent. It is again the 'perception double et simultanée' but whereas in the incident previously quoted (above, p. 168), past and present merge for Madame Bovary, as she lies in bed, here two elements of the past come together, the comparatively remote past of Charles's days as a medical student and the immediate memory of the feel of the pillow. The analogy of the impending situation, the need to operate, has revived the memories of Charles's student-days. The most recent segment of his past, complete with its attendant sensations, principally the scent of his wife's hair, vies with the newly resurrected past, taking, if anything, second place, but the degree to which they merge is remarkable. We observe, as in Proustian incidents, that, although the scent of the hair and the thought of the future operation recall to life a part of the past, the essence has difficulty in rising to the surface, never achieving complete rebirth:

Et le tout se mêlant, ne faisant qu'un, au fond cherchant quelque chose d'un désir inquiet, qui ne pouvait ouvrir ses ailes surmontées de plomb, tandis que le souvenir confus tournait en place, en dessous.[24]

(*NV*, 152)

Proust speaking of his attempts to re-discover the 'moi inconnu' or 'souvenir ancien' for which the taste of the madeleine spelt felicity, uses similar imagery with the difference that he portrays a successful quest on this occasion; a subterranean world reveals itself to both men:

Je remets en face de lui [mon esprit] la saveur encore récente de cette première gorgée et je sens tressaillir en moi . . . quelque chose qu'on aurait *désancré* à une grande

172

profondeur; je ne sais ce que c'est, mais cela monte lentement; j'éprouve la résistance et j'entends la rumeur des distances traversées.

(RTP, I, 46)

Flaubert, however, does not pursue the memory in the intellectually avid manner which we associate with Proust. Complex obscurity pervades Charles's sensation, yet Flaubert never attempts, like Proust, to introduce clarity, much less conceive of a tension between sensation and intelligence. At least, he never so consciously and deliberately assumes the rôle which Proust assigns to himself, of 'l'Ange des ténèbres' (*JS*, 393), to introduce light into darkness, without destroying the nature and essence of obscure sensations.

External nature interrupts the process for Flaubert's character at this crucial point: 'Le vent s'éleva, il faisait froid' (*NV*, 152).

Later, at Yonville, after a meal, Emma goes to bed, and just before she falls asleep, occurs that moment which we all must surely experience even if, in contrast to Proust or Joyce, we lack the courage or creative urge to transform such a *chiaroscuro* of waking and sleeping into the substance of art.

Flaubert here reminds us of Proust's belief that periods of time express themselves most readily in terms of space. ('Chambres' [*CSB* (FALL) and *RTP*, I, 6–9]) The fact that Emma has changed her abode seems to make her confuse time in her memory. The only difference between Flaubert and Proust here is that the former is doing naturally what the latter will transform into a technique of time transposed. Proust believes that to change from one place to another often gives one the illusion that one is gaining time, and he seems to have been peculiarly sensitive to movement, especially in trains and coaches. Emma feels that all must surely be different now that she has entered a new house, mistakenly trying to apply to time and action a change which she operates only in space;[25] previous disappointment will, she feels, turn to happiness. As she thinks ahead to possible halcyon days, the memories of the past of which she can never effectively divest herself move before her in terms of places. Sometimes their accompanying apparently irrelevant images on the very periphery of sensation re-appear too, much as we find in Proust's incidents of involuntary memory, but in Proust usually the trivial and peripheral has become central in the act of remembering. Proustian vision, which F. Gregh qualified as 'polygonal' when applied to sensation, remains so when applied to memory (cf., Ch. IV, p. 74). Flaubert's act of remembering discloses a hint of this, in that images on the fringe of the central experience return strikingly on so many occasions, seeming in some way inseparable from the rest. They do not, however, move from the edge to the centre as for Proust but file past detached like 'tableaux' in one sense, yet, as Flaubert admits, colouring each other.

> Alors les vieux souvenirs défilèrent: la cour des Bertaux, la classe de son couvent, ses noces, le vicomte qui valsait sous un lustre (*elle revit même appuyée contre un lambris,*

173

une tête de musicien soufflant de la flûte), et puis Tostes là-bas, la diligence d'Yonville, le dîner de tout à l'heure, la pauvre Djali qu'elle avait perdue.

(NV, 259)

The time sequence of the last two incidents has been reversed, probably under the impact of emotion, but otherwise chronological order reigns, for Emma is still awake. Then as reason retreats and sleep approaches, all becomes a whirling confusion; spatialisation causes the memories from different epochs of her life to stand together in defiance of chronology (ibid.). In the cylindrical movement already mentioned, these images 'lui semblaient se tenir au même plan à des éloignements pareils de l'heure présente' (ibid., 259).

Transported virtually outside time, Emma is abruptly recalled to reality, as at the 'Comices' by Rodolphe's presence at her side, so here by Charles's breath on her cheek. 'C'était Charles qui dormait; elle fut étonnée de le voir là, elle n'y pensait plus, tant sa conscience était absente de la réalité du moment.' (ibid., 260)

Here the spiritual, subjective reality has triumphed to the point of excluding the outer world, no longer even juxtaposed. Ironically it is to the accompaniment of orthodox time, 'une heure', that Emma finally falls asleep, but Flaubert, who often uses 'râle' to convey a sense of time's fatality, cannot resist transferring the image of human sleep and death to this symbol of time external and alien to the inner, qualitative time so recently alive in Emma:

> L'horloge de l'église tout à côté battait derrière le mur et elle s'assoupit elle-même, peu à peu, à ce tic-tac cadencé, qui râlait doucement dans les ténèbres, comme une poitrine rauque endormie.

(NV, 260)

From Emma's impassioned regret, 'car Dieu lui-même ne pouvait faire que le passé revînt' (*NV*, 578), it is a short step to Proust's affirmation: 'Car les vrais paradis sont les paradis qu'on a perdus' (*RTP*, III, 870).

When Léon leaves Yonville for Paris, forsaking Emma, the latter experiences despair to the point she had done on returning from the Vaubyessard. A trick of memory causes Léon's image to pursue and haunt her, 'souvenir si proche et si lointain'. This image and her sadness form a focal point around which the past reassembles in a confused revival of sensation, giving a perfect demonstration of the *correspondances*.[26] In this part of the novel dealing with the period subsequent to Léon's desertion, Flaubert's reflections on memory and the rôle of oblivion seem intensely Proustian, and any commentary on them inevitably expresses Proust's thought. Days unnoticed at the date of their chronological appearance, therefore just the ones into which the deepest concentration of feeling may well have flowed, now clamour for rebirth, rising from the depths of oblivion. The only difference is that Proust's trees lament his failure to recognise and so release their memory from limbo, whereas Flaubert's 'days' lament the fact that they were never used on the date of their appearance in time. To Proust goes the credit for having turned such loss into ultimate, corresponding gain, although it is true that some past impressions 'siègent dans la mémoire', in a nether world from which they are destined never to rise again, for want of an analogous sensation to recall them to life. So for Flaubert:

> Il y avait des jours, inaperçus jadis, couchés maintenant dans l'oubli et qui se relevaient tout entiers, accourant autour d'elle, pâles et longs comme des fantômes de vierges qui sont mortes d'amour et qui lui disaient: 'C'est nous! C'est nous! il fallait nous prendre quand nous vivions!
>
> (*NV*, 320; cf., *RTP*, III, 867)

Flaubert displays here the traditional nineteenth-century attitude towards time, since he resorts to evocation, but fails actually to recapture 'un peu de temps à l'état pur'. Proust alone really accomplishes this feat.

Memory for Flaubert as for Proust[27] can so easily become obsessive and block action and normal time. After the affair with Rodolphe, Emma almost becomes imprisoned in the past moment: 'Emma restait ainsi perdue dans ce souvenir comme dans la réalité même' (*NV*, 381). It savours at once of Baudelaire and Proust to believe that part of our personality becomes embedded in the past and that our inner essence will be restored through involuntary memory subsequently.

By analysing the blankness which often attends the return of previously powerful stimuli, Flaubert anticipates Proust's 'intermittences du cœur',[28] or, more specifically, the way in which one reacts to an event *after* its occurrence in chronological time. Accordingly, when the passage of time has removed or at least softened Charles's memory of paternal brutality (*NV*, 508), he is amazed at the affection which he still finds within himself for a man who had hitherto left him completely indifferent. Still pursuing this retrospective direction, he characteristically, almost by chance, encounters a memory of Mme Dubrie, his first wife, and 'il la regretta'. An interval of repose in oblivion, although Flaubert does not expressly say so, increases the power which an incident can exert over us, to the extent that we are astonished at our depth of feeling so long after the event.

Flaubert sounds a more resonantly Proustian note when Charles's emotions become personified and his tenderness wanders distractedly seeking an object, until quickly the thought of Emma reasserts its claim on his affection and restores the balance. While explaining that all the intensity expended in Charles's previous relationships (father, first wife)[29] now focuses on Emma, Flaubert accounts for the momentary diversion and resurrection of the past intact. The closing sentence reverses time-laws and so syncopates emotions in an arresting manner, causing each to be reinforced by the other:

Il la chérissait de tous les amours qu'il n'avait plus, de même que son affliction nouvelle provoquait les tristesses oubliées.

(*NV*, 509; cf., *FLAU*, I, 425)

What is Flaubert's final judgement on the cult of the past? *Madame Bovary* he seems to have identified with some such cult, and, in relation to this novel, he reacts strongly in favour of the present against the past. In the letter to Louis Bouilhet already mentioned (p. 167 above) he goes on to say most significantly that 'avec la *Bovary* finie, c'est l'âge de raison qui commence'. Probably the same kind of reaction in favour of a more virile treatment of time prompted him to eliminate from the original draft so much of the material concerning involuntary memory. Did he fear that, allowed to grow wild, time renewed, or 'une émotion renouvelée', might engulf not only Emma principally amongst the characters but the novel and perhaps in turn the author himself? However that may be, his conclusion seems in advance to be in harmony with Bergson's and Péguy's frontal attack on time, rather than with the oblique syncopation of Proust's retrospective glance. To Flaubert Proust might well have appeared a man consumed not only by the act of creation as he did to Mauriac, but by the past which gave him the essence of his work, and Flaubert discerns all the implications for practical life:

Et puis à quoi bon s'encombrer de tant de souvenirs? Le passé nous mange trop. Nous ne sommes jamais au présent qui seul est important dans la vie.

Of the invisible phantoms or memories which clamour for re-incarnation within the dream, Bergson writes: 'Être vivant et agissant, j'ai autre chose à faire que de m'occuper d'eux'.[30]

In art, however, as opposed to life, it is necessarily on the past that the creative writer will draw for a spiritualised form of experience, for material already transformed into his own substance, often at a subconscious level and merely awaiting a call to new life in the unique medium of his utterance. In art, the past can never be said to have consumed an artist to no purpose, if we acknowledge that memory transforms the substance of experience, anticipating by its technique and alchemy the final act of creation.

Notes

[1] 'Flaubert le premier, les débarrasse du parasitisme des anecdotes et des scories de l'histoire.' (*CSB*, 595)

[2] *Ibid.*, 595. Of Flaubert's 'mérites' Proust writes: 'L'un de ceux qui me touchent le plus parce que j'y retrouve l'aboutissement des modestes recherches que j'ai faites, est qu'il sait donner avec maîtrise l'impression du Temps. A mon avis, la chose la plus belle de *L'Education sentimentale*, ce

n'est pas une phrase, mais un blanc... "Et Frédéric, béant, reconnut Sénécal!" Ici un "blanc", un énorme "blanc" et, sans l'ombre d'une transition, soudain la mesure du temps devenant au lieu de quarts d'heure, des années, des décades (je reprends les derniers mots que j'ai cités pour montrer cet extraordinaire changement de vitesse, sans préparation):
"Et Frédéric, béant, reconnut Sénécal.

Il voyagea. Il connut la mélancolie des paquebots, les froids réveils sous la tente etc. Il revint.
Il fréquenta le monde, etc.
Vers la fin de l'année 1867, etc." '
The lacuna here between 'Et Frédéric, béant, reconnut Sénécal' and 'Il voyagea' marks the transition from Chapter V to Chapter VI. Fascinated as he was by Flaubert's technique, Proust has taken an unfair advantage but, with rare perception, he surely singles out here Flaubert's tendency to compose by 'tableaux', a procedure which probably derives in the first place from a habit of involuntary memory: 'Des tableaux de leur amour lui passaient devant les yeux, nets, précis, distincts les uns des autres et emportés dans un tourbillon.'

³ *Madame Bovary* was begun at Croisset, Friday 19 September 1851, and completed perhaps at Paris, April 1856. The period of composition falls roughly into three main divisions: the first part of the novel was probably written from September 1851 to July 1852, the second from September 1852 to the end of 1854 or later, and the third from the beginning of 1855 to April 1856. The primitive version was reconstructed from the manuscripts by the labours of J. Pommier and G. Leleu. Their edition is described as 'Nouvelle Version' and I therefore refer to it as '*NV*', although in fact it is the edition which is new, the text it gives being the 'primitive version'. The definitive version is that of the Pléiade edition: Flaubert: *Œuvres*, vol. I.

⁴ 'Chaque artiste semble ainsi comme le citoyen d'une patrie inconnue, oubliée de lui-même, différente de celle d'où viendra appareillant pour la terre, un autre grand artiste.' (*RTP*, III, 257)

⁵ 'J'avoue que certain emploi de l'imparfait de l'indicatif – de ce temps cruel qui nous présente la vie comme quelque chose d'éphémère à la fois et de passif, qui, au moment même où il retrace nos actions, les frappe d'illusion, les anéantit dans le passé sans nous laisser comme le parfait, la consolation de l'activité – est resté pour moi, une source inépuisable de mystérieuses tristesses.' (*CSB*, 170)

⁶ A. Thibaudet: *Gustave Flaubert*, Plon, Paris 1922, p. 336: 'Lisez cette page de *Madame Bovary*, et voyez à quel point elle contient (avec son style tout opposé) les tours, détours et retours du temps perdu, à la manière de Marcel Proust'.

⁷ '. . . en se cambrant le cou', *NV*, 360; 'en se cabrant sur sa chaise', *FLAU*, I, 425.

⁸ 'Elle crut l'entendre qui parlait et sentir dans sa main le frémissement de la sienne; tout se confondit un moment . . .'. (*NV*, 360) From the definitive version, the auditive and tactile are omitted, to be replaced by a purely visual impression, balancing the earlier form: 'Elle crut le voir en face, à sa fenêtre . . .'.

⁹ 'Il lui sembla qu'elle tournait encore dans la valse, défaillante, sous le feu des lustres, au son des flûtes . . .' (*NV*, 360). In the definitive version, however, the vicomte is mentioned, inseparable as he is from Emma's memory of the waltz: '. . . il lui sembla qu'elle tournait encore, dans la valse, sous le feu des lustres, au bras du vicomte . . .' (*FLAU*, I, 425).

¹⁰ 'Et toute la tendresse des anciens jours flottait confusément au milieu de l'envahissement de cette senteur, qui se répandait sur toute son âme et qui l'engourdissait.' (*NV*, 360) Definitive version: 'La douceur de cette sensation pénétrait ainsi ses désirs d'autrefois . . .' (*FLAU*, I, 425).

¹¹ Flaubert: *Corr.* (Conard), Vol. III, pp. 331–2. See also G. Poulet: *Etudes sur le temps humain* Plon, Paris 1950, Ch. XV, p. 320.

¹² The union of subject and object preoccupied Baudelaire in 'L'Art philosophique': 'une magie suggestive contenant à la fois l'objet et le sujet, le monde extérieur à l'artiste et l'artiste lui-même' (*BAU*, 1099). A quotation which G. Poulet selects (*Etudes*, p. 310), from Flaubert's *Tentation* of 1849 (Conard, p. 417), suggests an interpenetration of subject and object verging on pantheism: 'Un degré de plus et tu devenais nature, ou bien la nature devenait toi.' Flaubert conceives of the way in which one groups and arranges sensation as supremely important: 'Il n'y a de vrai que les "rapports", c'est-à-dire la façon dont nous percevons les objets' (*Corr.* (Conard), Vol. VIII, p. 135); cf., Proust 'Ce que nous appelons la réalité est un certain rapport entre ces sensations et ces souvenirs qui nous entourent simultanément' (*RTP*, III, 889).

¹³ Flaubert: *L'Education sentimentale*, Version de 1845, Conard: *Œuvres complètes* 1902, Vol. III, p. 242. This passage is quoted by G. Poulet: *Etudes*, p. 320.
The 1845 version of *L'Education sentimentale* is quite distinct from that published in 1869. It is Flaubert's first novel. It was begun in February 1843, resumed in September and October of the same year, and completed between May 1844 and January 1845. Fragments were published by the *Revue de Paris* from 15 November 1910 to 15 January 1911.

¹⁴ So the narrator will say that the sobs which he repressed in his father's presence, but to which he gave vent before his mother, have never really ceased; only the fact that silence surrounds him causes them to sound clearly now, 'comme ces cloches de couvents que couvrent si bien les bruits de la

ville pendant le jour qu'on les croirait arrêtées, mais qui se remettent à sonner dans le silence du soir' (*RTP*, I, 37).

¹⁵ *NV*, 319. Without having read Flaubert's original draft, Proust seizes upon the sadness born of 'la rupture des habitudes' as the veritable keynote of his precursor's style ('A propos du "style" de Flaubert', *CSB*, 590), an act of shrewd literary perception which perhaps his own close affinity with Flaubert helped to inspire: 'C'est ce genre de tristesse, fait de *la rupture des habitudes* et de l'irréalité du décor, que donne le style de Flaubert, ce style si nouveau quand ce ne serait que par là.'

¹⁶ More recently, Julien Green dwells at great length on the death of a part of the individual occasioned by the physical extinction of a person with whom he is intimately associated. Like memory itself, man in turn becomes dependent on the chance incursion of past into present for revival of a part of himself (J. Green: *Journal*, Plon, Paris 1935, Vol. VIII (1950–54) p. 161). The author has just learnt of his friend's death in a part of the world familiar to both of them. Mention of memory significantly precedes his reflections on a form of death before its time:

> J'ai appris la nouvelle par téléphone. J'ai raccroché et j'ai continué à faire ce que j'étais en train de faire, mais je n'étais plus la même personne. Quelque chose en moi me quittait à jamais. Entre Jim et moi, il y avait la complicité des années que nous avions vécues à l'Université . . .
> C'était mon plus vieil ami. Avec lui toute une partie de ma première jeunesse descend au tombeau. Nous mourons avec chacun de nos amis.

¹⁷ Bergson: *Durée et Simultanéité*, Alcan, Paris 1926, p. 54.

¹⁸ Compare the quotation from Proust about the artificial separation into moments of an 'infléchissable jaillissement'.

¹⁹ 'La nature ... n'était-elle pas commencement d'art elle-même, elle qui ne m'avait permis de connaître souvent la beauté d'une chose que dans une autre, midi à Combray que dans le bruit de ses cloches, les matinées de Doncières que dans les hoquets de notre calorifère à eau?'(*RTP*, III, 889–90)

²⁰ 'Ce que nous désirons' and 'ce que nous voyons effectivement'.

²¹ Léon experiences a strong desire to advance time when he awaits the moment of departure from Yonville. The infinity of desire makes him reluctant to accept the limited span of human life, and, impatient, like so many of Flaubert's characters, to have relief from 'la condition humaine', 'd'en avoir fini':

> '. . . la longue aiguille qui semblait ne pas tourner. Combien de jours dans sa vie avait comptés cette horloge, qui battrait encore quand il ne serait plus là? Les heures l'une après l'autre, sonnaient dans l'air avec un râle enroué. Autrefois aussi, il les trouvait lentes à se pousser, mais aujourd'hui il les trouvait plus lentes encore, il

eût voulu les retenir, ou les précipiter toutes à la fois, tant il avait hâte d'en finir'.
(*NV*, 313–14)

[22] This difficulty in locating a memory seems to be universal: 'Je ne peux distinguer la forme, lui demander de m'apprendre de quelle circonstance particulière, de quelle époque du passé il s'agit' (*RTP*, I, 46).

[23] *RTP*, opening and III, 912: 'Et c'était peut-être aussi par le jeu formidable qu'il fait avec le Temps que le Rêve m'avait fasciné'.

[24] Hair casts its spell by the media of scent and touch; as for Baudelaire, so for Flaubert, its sensuous power is indisputable and to be pondered: 'Il éprouvait dans les mains une multitude de commotions sourdes à tenir ces innombrables fils minces qui se rattachaient quelque part, invisiblement à toutes les racines de son être.' (*NV*, 529) Proust has observed the fetish which Baudelaire makes of hair (*CSB*, 629), but has failed to detect it in Flaubert.

[25] Proust goes a stage further when he openly states the change wrought on space by inner time: '. . . et les maisons, les routes, les avenues, sont fugitives, hélas! comme les années' (*RTP*, I, 427). Cf., Ch. II, p. 42 of the present work.

[26] There returned with the memory of Léon a confused version of the past: 'Des causeries d'autrefois, des regards surpris lui revinrent à la mémoire par bouffées, plus mélodieuses et plus chantantes que des bouffées d'harmonie . . .' (*NV*, 320).

[27] 'Les romanciers sont des sots qui comptent par jours et par années.' (*CHRON*. (GALL), 'Vacances de Pâques', p. 106).

[28] *L'Education sentimentale*, 1845 version, p. 242. Jules discovers that he no longer responds as in the past to the self-same surroundings and virtually expounds *avant la lettre* Proust's theory of 'Intermittences': 'On s'étonne qu'un squelette ait eu la vie, que ces yeux creux aient regardé avec amour; mais on s'étonne aussi parfois que notre cœur ait possédé ce qu'il n'a plus et qu'il ait tressailli en vibrations mélodieuses sous des pressions qui ne lui font plus rendre d'écho.' Here again, we draw close to the nostalgia for 'ce qui ne se retrouve jamais' and to the sadness which charges 'la cessation brusque de toute vibration prolongée', a Proustian syncopation indeed.

The culmination occurs when Jules experiences a sensation in its purity in some sense outside time and in the process recovers lost time (ibid., 243): 'Voilà d'où venait son étonnement en retrouvant dans le bruit des feuilles mortes qu'il écartait avec ses pieds les restes de trésors qu'il croyait n'avoir jamais possédés.'

[29] Proust stresses the state of mind as more important than external reality, especially in love.

[30] Bergson: *Le Rêve, Conférence faite à l'institut général psychologique*, 26 March 1901, Skira, Geneva, pp. 94 ff.

180

Notes for further reading

This chapter forms a development of the theme which I broach in my book: *Proust's Challenge to Time* M.U.P. 1962, pp. 26–36. Proust's literary relationship to Flaubert has not been treated at length except by Douglas W. Alden: 'Proust and the Flaubert Controversy', *Romanic Review*, no. 28, Oct. 1937, pp. 230-40.

Epilogue

'Soyez franc, mon cher ami, vous-même m'aviez fait une théorie sur les choses qui n'existent que grâce à une création perpétuellement recommencée. La création du monde n'a pas eu lieu une fois pour toutes, me disiez-vous, elle a nécessairement lieu tous les jours.'

(*RTP*, III, 796)

After observing that, in *Le Temps perdu*, are to be found the traces and filiations of nearly all the great novels of the nineteenth century, Ramon Fernandez qualified this judgement as follows: 'Si ces traces ne sont pas toujours reconnaissables (sauf pour quelques initiés), c'est que l'intelligence et la sensibilité proustiennes (l'imagination proustienne aussi) ont fait subir à ces traces, à ces éléments, des pressions plus fortes, comme ces températures, ces agents chimiques qui déforment certains métaux. Il faut toujours avoir en vue ces grands thèmes romanesques, et l'on constate alors ce qu'ils *pouvaient* devenir dans certaines conditions psychologiques déterminées'.[1] (The italics are the author's own.) In Proust, the 'specific psychological conditions' are his dichotomy now of the imagination, now of the heart, and the intellect, a conflict which he dramatically projects in his novel in the form of a protracted debate between the claims of art and life. Paradoxically, his only hope of reconciling and synthesising the rival forces of feeling and thought lies in art. He knows only too well that the very nature of human experience precludes the realisation of his ideal in all its purity: a work of art composed solely of truths apprehended by intuition; and, in a mood of compromise, he sets out to achieve a delicate balance in which the complementary forces of heart and mind will enhance each other (*RTP*, III, 898).

183

What, then, are the major themes of the nineteenth-century novel and how does Proust set about transposing them? How far did the authors whom he cultivated develop in him that power of self-understanding which he endlessly craved, and conform to his conception of authentic artists by making him 'lecteur de lui-même'? To what extent did they meet his twofold requirement: that they should enable him to establish his irreducible individuality and, at the same time, give him a reassuring sense of affinity? Social ambition, love, dreams and, more rarely, the artistic vocation are amongst the most important themes favoured by nineteenth-century novelists. In the first three activities, Proust thought he detected an unconscious and unassuaged yearning for the fourth; or, to modify Baudelaire's terms slightly, 'un goût de l'art qui se trompe de route'. It is a French tradition, dating back possibly to Medieval times but vividly apparent in Marivaux, Stendhal and Balzac, for social ambition and love to be closely associated. Proust makes a bold innovation by subordinating both these potential rivals of art to his narrator's artistic vocation, as also by suggesting that love prefigures art.

While Balzac's sympathies seem so often to lie with his young *arrivistes*, Proust, for all his cult of the aristocracy, passion for genealogical tables, and social snobbery, strongly satirises social ambition as a delusion and an attempted substitute for art. Paradoxically, social attitudes and the vanity of social aspirations continue to fascinate him, especially in so far as they have repercussions on the potential artists: Swann, Charlus and Marcel; or on another who has already embarked and fulfils a mirror-function within the novel: the memorialist, Mme de Villeparisis. Proust finds a kind of poetic justice in the apparent law that vulgarity should be a prerequisite of genius as in Balzac's personal case; he ensures that Swann and Charlus pay dearly for their social graces. Probably the feature which distinguishes Balzac most sharply from Proust is the former's attempt to equate life and art. Ironically it is precisely this foible which Proust attributes to his own *artistes manqués*: Swann and Charlus. If both the latter characters read Balzac with relish, it is chiefly because, as 'idolâtres esthétiques', they revel in his easy, almost imperceptible transitions between life and art which spare them any qualms of conscience about the need for intense creative endeavour.

At the same time there was much in Balzac to give Proust the impression of a kindred spirit. He found inspiration in Balzac's markedly implicit treatment of homosexuality; it is typical of Proust's strong urge to compose by a process of synthesis that, consciously or unconsciously, he should seem to fuse characteristics of both Vautrin and the Baron Hulot (particularly the latter's decadence), in the Baron de Charlus. He was quick to appreciate the sense of continuity conveyed by Balzac's 'retour des personnages' and attempted to achieve a similar effect within the exceptionally wide compass of his own novel. He admired also the retrospective unity of La Comédie humaine, a feature perhaps more true of Proust's than of Balzac's work. It is possible that we have here an example of Proust's tendency to project his own ideals and methods into the novels he was studying, a process not unlike the Stendhalian 'cristallisation' but applied to literary criticism as opposed to love.

In Flaubert, differences from Proust seem to be out-numbered by affinities. While Flaubert's characters share with those of Proust a passion for travel or dreams of travel in time and space – a desire to be elsewhere in both dimensions is, after all, the essence of *bovarysme* – Flaubert preserves in Emma, Frédéric and others a more even tension than Proust between memories of the past and dreams of the future, and finally seems to accord his qualified approval to the latter as the lesser of two potential evils; at the same time, he sees life as inevitably entailing the profanation of ideals, and his attitude is, like that of Proust towards memories and dreams, essentially ambivalent. For both men, a re-creation of external reality whether or not to the point where it becomes art, must necessarily be an improvement upon life in the raw. A fundamental difference between the two authors, and closely associated with their respective attitudes towards time, lies in the concentrated, strongly disciplined quality of Flaubert's style and output, on one hand, and in the intensely synthetic, almost indefinitely expansive nature of Proust's creative impetus, on the other.

Amongst the affinities which relate Flaubert to Proust must rank foremost the condemnation by each of attempts to equate life and art, whether the protagonist be Emma Bovary or Proust's narrator. However, while Marcel is able to achieve his salvation in art, Emma fails to the last to distinguish between her dreams and reality in matters concerning social ambition and romantic love. Denied the outlet of artistic creation, she pays the price for attempting to equate life and the dream – the latter mostly in the form of Romantic literature – and seems to exemplify in advance Proust's youthful tenet with its suggestion of Symbolist overtones: 'Il vaut mieux rêver sa vie que la vivre, encore que la vivre ce soit encore la rêver . . .' (*JS*, 111). (Cf., Ch. III, p. 49 of the present work.) A further strong affinity between the two novelists lies in what Flaubert terms: 'la sensualité mystique'. For Emma and for Marcel, sensuousness frequently gives rise to a visionary experience and transcendence; in fact, in both Flaubert and Proust the mysticism seems to be a measure of the sensuality and vice versa. There is an interesting parallel to be drawn between Emma's reactions at the time of her taking communion (*FLAU*, I, 486–7) and Marcel's response to hawthorn blossom with its religious and erotic overtones.

If Proust deplored Balzac's failure to transpose external reality adequately, Flaubert must have seemed to him to afford the perfect antidote in this respect, reflecting in subject-matter and in style a unique quality of vision. Again, Flaubert's predilection for showing characters as they are seen through the eyes of others rather than from an allegedly objective viewpoint, relates him to Proust as opposed to Balzac. Moreover, Flaubert presents his characters in a state of flux; if not in the throes of disintegration (Frédéric Moreau), then evolving dynamically (as for instance Homais). Such a method anticipates Proust's technique, thereby marking an advance upon Balzac's much more static presentation. For innovations in modes of expression alone, especially for the range of perspectives opened out by a bold experimentation with tenses, Proust recognises his indebtedness to one of his most important sources of inspiration. It is to be noted that his concern is almost exclusively with Flaubert's style:

> J'ai été stupéfait, je l'avoue, de voir traiter de peu doué pour écrire, un homme qui, par l'usage entièrement nouveau et personnel qu'il a fait du passé défini, du passé indéfini, du participe présent, de certains pronoms et de certaines prépositions, a renouvelé presque autant notre vision des choses que Kant, avec ses Catégories, les théories de la connaissance et de la réalité du monde extérieur.
>
> (*CSB*, 586)

As might be expected, Flaubert's power to convey by 'cet éternel imparfait' 'ce genre de tristesse, fait de la rupture des habitudes et de l'irréalité du décor' and to render a haunting sense of human transience, strikes Proust as perhaps the most impressive innovation of all (*CSB*, 590). (See Ch. IX, p. 166)

Although Proust must have found much to attract him in Fromentin's disillusionment with romantic love and in Dominique's withdrawal from the social sphere, he may have joined George Sand in questioning the motives and purpose of such a renunciation of love; especially in view of the fact that the sacrifice remains sterile, amounts to self-mortification on the part of a man of Dominique's sensibility and benefits no tangible cause, much less artistic creation, in striking contrast to Marcel's decision to subordinate everything to his artistic vocation. On the other hand, Dominique's rare sensibility and power first to register and then to re-live sensory experiences, re-creating them in memory, would be of supreme interest to Proust. The rich perception of nature and the subtle analysis of the laws of memory make *Dominique* resemble a foretaste of Proust to an uncanny degree. It remains tantalising that Proust should appear to have confined his interest almost exclusively to Fromentin the art critic (*CSB*, 188, 189, 518, 580, 639). As a transposition of Romantic themes – notably the *mystique* attaching to the life and customs of a small community (close to nature in the Rousseau tradition) and constant indulgence in the delights of sense-perception and memory, of emotion recollected and analysed in tranquillity – Fromentin's novel must have made its impact on Proust but it is most strikingly Proustian by virtue of Fromentin's constant preoccupation with sensory experience extended and intensified by re-enactment in the extra dimension of memory. In his own highly individual manner, Fromentin (no less than Flaubert) seems to me to renew Romantic

186

themes, and perhaps by this very feat, he may have made his contribution to setting on the way towards artistic creation that master of transposition, Proust himself.

While George Eliot ranks for many as the most important of the English influences brought to bear on Proust, and affinities seem to abound between the two authors, there is at least one significant difference: her strong didactic urge. Paradoxically Proust combines amorality with a capacity for a sense of guilt. Homosexuality he regards now as a biological phenomenon over which man has little or no control, given the caprices and intermissions of heredity, now as a sin provoking a deep sense of shame and meriting nemesis; here we are inevitably reminded of the attitude and tones of the Old Testament. Perhaps it is precisely this ambivalence which prevents Proust from being repelled by a certain Puritanical strain evident in George Eliot's outlook, divided as she is between conservatism and rebellion. However that may be, her dichotomy of heart and intellect relates her very closely to Proust and there seems to be a vivid parallel between Maggie Tulliver and Marcel in at least one major respect: both feel the pull of instinctive, strongly emotional family loyalties and yet are intellectually aware how narrow and restrictive is the closely spun social web of their childhood associations, in itself a microcosm of the successive clans to which they may or may not be admitted in the world at large. George Eliot's belief that childhood patterns of behaviour persist into maturity or, in Wordsworthian terms, that 'The Child is Father of the man' and that childhood impressions are the 'mother tongue of the imagination' may well have led Proust to self-awareness and helped him to elucidate his own philosophy. Certainly memory plays a supremely important rôle in the works of both writers, serving above all as the binding thread (or 'fibre', to use George Eliot's image) which ensures and protects the unity of personality against the forces of change. Proust's techniques in the treatment of time are obviously far more sophisticated than those of George Eliot and his syntax infinitely more convoluted. However, George Eliot's use of the flash-back in *Mr Gilfil's Love-story* seems in some respects to anticipate *Un Amour de Swann* and reflects a Proustian awareness that a man can still contain an aspect of his emotional life for which the justification has died. Further, she shares with Proust the view that love causes man to project an inner image upon the person he beholds, and both authors may owe to Stendhal this theory which so closely approximates to that of 'cristallisation'. Finally, one wonders whether Proust discerned in George Eliot traces of Ruskin's influence, as for instance in her cult of poetic realism.

Ramon Fernandez might justifiably have extended his remark about Proust's literary antecedents to include poets, writers of memoirs and moralists, for these also Proust knew well. As already stated, Proust openly acknowledges that Chateaubriand, Nerval and Baudelaire anticipated him in the use of involuntary memory as a method of transition from one level of time to another. In Chateaubriand, he deplored the occasional subordination of literature to the interests of a political career and, comparing him in this respect to Barrès, he expressed a strong dislike of the 'Chateaubriand rien qu'éloquent', adding that 'En règle générale, tout ce qui dans Chateaubriand continue ou présage l'éloquence politique du XVIIIe et du XIXe siècle n'est pas du vrai Chateaubriand' (*CSB*, 598). As one might expect, he distinguishes Chateaubriand's Voltairian aspect from his true essence. Proust evidently preferred Chateaubriand's notes of lyricism to his bursts of rhetoric, even finding a special term, 'le chant de la chouette', to characterise this lyrical vein, ironically inspired by a sense of human transience but testifying to the eternity of art (*CSB*, 651). This antithesis of the ephemeral and the transcendent which, for Proust, forms the essence of Chateaubriand's lyricism, is in itself Proustian, particularly the elegiac strain. In the 'Notes sur Chateaubriand', there is a curious harmony of tone, whether Proust is writing on his own account or quoting direct from Chateaubriand. The latter's elegiac vein is as appropriate as that of Proust to treatment of the memorialist's theme *par excellence*: 'Tout ce qui nous semble impérissable tend à la destruction' (*RTP*, III, 669*; cf., ibid., 1019).

Nerval, by the quality of his Romanticism, reflects Proust's inner tension between reason and intuition, as well as his constant fascination with the irrational (*CSB*, 239). According to Proust, even Nerval fails to achieve such a necessarily fine balance to perfection, and intellectual honesty compels Proust, in his rôle as critic, to qualify his otherwise ready praise: '. . . Gérard a trouvé le moyen de ne faire que peindre et de donner à son tableau les couleurs de son rêve. Peut-être y a-t-il encore un peu trop d'intelligence dans sa nouvelle'. Proust may have hoped to strike a more delicate balance between the irrational and his powers of analysis and he probably considered that only this difference of degree separated him from Nerval. In addition, Proust's classicism causes him to deplore Nerval's (and Baudelaire's) hesitation between various modes of expression (*CSB*, 235). Both writers are concerned with life and the dream, the analysis of art and love, the transposition of sensations and, above all, the *intermittences*, Proust with those of the heart principally and Nerval with those of dreams. Of overriding importance in the work of both is the alternation of dreamer and analyst. It is difficult to understand why Proust never mentions *Aurélia*, parts of which (for instance Chapters V, VI, and VIII) are of special interest to the student of comparative literature, since they bear a strong resemblance to *Heinrich von Ofterdingen*; in addition, *Les Mémorables* has affinities with Novalis's *Hymnen an die Nacht* (see Notes for further reading, Ch. III, p. 63).

There can be little doubt that a particularly strong affinity exists between Proust and Baudelaire. Proust detects a major difference in the element of will-power which characterises Baudelaire's process of memory (*RTP*, III, 920). It remains significant that, while both writers deplore their lack of will-power, Baudelaire cultivates in art the quality of which he felt himself to be devoid in life; Proust, on the other hand, stakes all on the element of chance in the context of memory and the narrator's artistic vocation. It is possible that Proust here projects in his novel a measure of the sense of inadequacy which he experienced personally in his life. As already suggested, one of the most striking differences between Proust and Baudelaire arises from the former's relative lack of religious terms of reference; Baudelaire's intensity of remorse gives his poetry a resonance unknown in Proust's novel. Otherwise the affinities are numerous and remarkable. With Baudelaire as with Proust, time is an obsession. Baudelaire's analysis of homosexuality may have led Proust to a deeper understanding of his own problems; the portrayal of physical love which he found in *Les Fleurs du Mal* was closely related to some of his own literary aspirations. However, in my opinion, Baudelaire ranks as Proust's precursor chiefly by virtue of his masterly art of evocation, his power to suggest the essence of an experience by weaving an infinitely subtle web of associations, his ability to 'peindre non la chose mais l'effet qu'elle produit'. He brilliantly anticipates Proust's theory of extended metaphor whereby one sensation is contained within another, almost *ad infinitum,* as well as his method of oblique presentation; therefore it is not surprising that Proust's manifesto about the multiple, interlarded nature of the most trivial human actions should have distinctly Baudelairean overtones. What follows seems to me to savour, in equal proportions, of Baudelaire and Proust, and of each at his most characteristic:

> ... la moindre parole que nous avons dite à une époque de notre vie, le geste le plus insignifiant que nous avons fait, était entouré, portait sur lui le reflet de choses qui logiquement ne tenaient pas à lui, en ont été séparées par l'intelligence qui n'avait rien à faire d'elles, mais au milieu desquelles ... le geste, l'acte le plus simple reste enfermé comme dans mille vases clos dont chacun serait rempli de choses d'une couleur, d'une odeur, d'une température absolument différentes ...
>
> (*RTP*, III, 870)

A study of Proust's affinities with Novalis further enhances our appreciation of the former's Symbolist vein and, as already suggested, Proust may have assimilated much of Novalis's thought through the intermediary of Nerval. It could be claimed that Proust resembles Novalis whenever they meet on the common ground of Symbolism, and that, since Proust reveals many features which one would associate with Classicism, as for instance a love of clarity, a belief in the existence of one ideal mode of expression, there are important points of divergence. At the same time Proust often seems to expand and illuminate an aphorism of Novalis, notably: 'Jeder geliebte Gegenstand ist der Mittelpunkt eines Paradieses' (*NOV*, II, 23; Ch. V, p. 96). Both are equally

189

concerned with the way in which art, or poetry, removes the barriers between subject and object and transcends time-laws. In common with the Symbolists, both use images to convey the artist's inner world, seek an original essence of the self and conceive of art as the ideal means of communicating this irreducible individuality.

In a *moraliste* such as La Bruyère, Proust could find much the same combination of sensibility and cruelty as he noted in Stendhal and Baudelaire and no doubt observed, also, in himself. However, amongst the *moralistes*, it seems to me to be first and foremost with Pascal that Proust has a truly deep affinity; in fact, very often one tends to discover what is Pascalian in Proust rather than what is Proustian in Pascal. There appears to be a deliberate attempt, on Proust's part, to make of art a religion where memory serves as veritable grace. Both writers assign similar rôles, in their hierarchy, to *le cœur* and *la raison*, and both are equally ruthless in exposing the fallibility of human perception, always allowing for the difference that Pascal's motive is that of the religious apologist, while Proust seeks to found on memory a system of metaphysics. One wonders to what extent Proust was conscious of his impregnation in Pascal's thought. Was the affinity so deep that, like the pulse or rhythm which he believed art alone capable of recording, the pervasiveness of the Pascalian element in his work remained imperceptible to him to the last? It is probably significant that, in contrast to Valéry, Proust never actually parodies Pascal at any length. (There is a single interesting example of such an approach in Saint-Loup's reaction to the narrator's request for the privilege of *tutoiement*: see Ch. I, n. 8, p. 31.)

Proust was fascinated by the way in which one artist can have affinities with other artists and, at the same time, retain his irreducible individuality, 'sa note à lui' (*CSB*, 306). His own case presents the same paradox but magnified to an incredible extent. Proust's precursors will no doubt appear to some readers to be legion and yet paradoxically the originality, that unmistakably Proustian note, remains exclusively his own. H. de Régnier's affinities with Anatole France absorb Proust's attention in much the same way as Proust's affinities with the precursors discussed in the foregoing pages have aroused and retained mine; perhaps Proust here ponders a mystery which ultimately defies analysis. His reflections on the baffling fusion of the general and the particular in any great artist provide a fitting epigraph to the discussion of what constitutes his own essential originality in the midst of so many literary echoes, for does he not contain and transcend the artists whom he resembles?

> Il est si personnel, si unique, le principe qui agit en nous quand nous écrivons et crée au fur et à mesure notre œuvre, que dans la même génération les esprits de même sorte, de même famille, de même culture, de même inspiration, de même milieu, de même condition, prennent la plume pour écrire presque de la même manière la même chose et ajoutent chacun la broderie particulière qui n'est qu'à lui, et qui fait

190

de la même chose une chose toute nouvelle, où toutes les proportions des qualités des autres sont déplacées. Et ainsi la gamme des écrivains originaux se poursuit, chacun faisant entendre une note aussi belle qui cependant, par un intervalle imperceptible, est irréductiblement différente de celle qui la précède et de celle qui la suit.

(CSB, 306)

Proust's division between the general and the particular is dramatically reflected in his fluctuation between transcendental idealism and intellectual classicism, and, as already stated, this dichotomy is echoed in Swann's reaction to the Vinteuil sonata, on one hand, and Marcel's reception of the Vinteuil septet, on the other. One cannot help wondering how far Proust was conscious of this self-contradiction and, if so, whether he intended to imply that his final position is that of Marcel, as the latter stresses the importance of each individual's irreducible originality.

Proust saw one form of art as predestined to extinction and replacement by another; in fact, he conceived of destruction and creation as inseparable, the former a condition of the latter in a phoenix-like process of renewal.[2] He regarded schools of criticism as subjected to the same laws of succession and he delighted in the ironical reversals to which judgements fall prone as a result of the shifting perspectives of time. He revelled in the paradox that the truly great 'innovateurs' are 'ces classiques non encore reconnus'.[3] Thus Proust triumphantly reconciles innovation and classicism in a synthesis which he largely attributes to time: 'Je crois que tout art véritable est classique, mais les lois de l'esprit permettent rarement qu'il soit à son apparition, reconnu pour tel'.[4] Proust believes that, paradoxically, subsequent generations alone will enjoy the degree of *recul* necessary for appreciation, in seventeenth-century masterpieces, of 'des beautés qui s'y trouvent réellement et que le xviie siècle n'a guère aperçues'.[5] Ingres and Manet would have 'rubbed shoulders' much earlier in the sense of artistic recognition, if only their audiences had been able to relate the particular to the general: Proust seems to imply his own strong approval of the art critic's search for the eternal 'essences' of truths beneath the fluctuating appearance of temporal art forms (*RTP*, II, 420). He considered it the duty and prerogative of artist and critic alike to form new groupings of elements in nature and art, to be at once creator and catalyst (*RTP*, I, 861). Always he stresses as supremely creative in the operation of artist, critic and reader the rôle of analogy, the discovery of 'coïncidences' (*CG*, I, 220), of 'anticipations de pensée'. Indeed, as already stated in the Prologue, Proust personally seems to open the way for a study of his precursors, provided that, in common with all art and criticism, such an enterprise is conceived like this book, as part of a wider search for truth and interpreted as a beginning and not an end (*CSB*, 182). Proust is in his element disentangling the threads of personal or literary relationships, and his

191

comment on the web of associations which life spins between inner and outer worlds applies equally to a study of his own position in relation to other authors: here also, 'tout est fécond', for this time in the actual sphere of literary criticism '. . . un riche réseau de souvenirs ne laisse que le choix des communications' (*RTP*, III, 1030).

Notes

[1] Ramon Fernandez: *Proust*, Edition de la Nouvelle Revue critique, Paris 1943, p. 106.

[2] The idea that destruction is as intrinsic to creation as oblivion to memory, recurs like a leitmotif in Proust's work. (See the present author's article: 'Le général et le particulier dans l'œuvre de Proust', *BMP*, 1970.) (See also Ch. I, n. 12 and 13, and Ch. III, n. 9 of the present work.) Proust extends this theory to apply to friendship (*RTP*, I, 671). Charlus's parody of this favourite notion of the narrator is quoted as epigraph to the epilogue of the present book (p. 183). Proust remains forever fascinated by the discovery that the law of succession itself contains the principle of creation.

[3] Marcel Proust: *Textes retrouvés*, p. 229, 'Enquête sur le romantisme et le classicisme' (1921).

[4] Ibid.

[5] Ibid., p. 230.

Index